The Knitting Book

The Knitting Book

JO COMPTON

A&C BLACK · LONDON

Dedication
to Tom and Daisy Neville

Drawings by the author, Hilary Evans
and Susan Hughes, and photographs by Rob Cox.

British Library Cataloguing in Publication Data

Compton, Jo
The knitting book.
1. Knitting – Manuals
I. Title
746.43′2

ISBN 0–7136–2953–3

First published 1990
A & C Black (Publishers) Limited
35 Bedford Row, London WC1R 4JH

ISBN 0-7136-2953-3

Typeset by Latimer Trend & Company Ltd, Plymouth
Printed in Singapore by Tien Wah Press Ltd.

Contents

Colour plates

Introduction

This book is about ways of creating something unique. Using knitting to make a personal statement is a very satisfying and rewarding experience, whether you are making something for yourself or for someone else.

It is not difficult to design and write knitting patterns and you will find lots of suggestions and ideas to help encourage you to try. There are many good reasons for making up your own patterns. Perhaps you find it difficult to buy the 'right' pattern for a yarn you like or you have a lovely pattern but cannot find a yarn you like that is suitable. Perhaps you have found the yarn and pattern but some detail is wrong – such as the collar or neck opening. You may want to re-vitalise garments that you already have – or you may be reluctant to throw out unloved or out-grown knitting. All these 'problems' are solved in the text and some more, too.

We start with a chapter on choosing the right yarn, stitch and style combination – the basic ingredients for any design. This chapter contains information and advice about which combinations work well and ways of evaluating your choice. There are illustrations to show the variety possible through altering any one of the three basic ingredients. The stretchiness of most knitted fabrics can cause problems: there is advice about how to avoid these difficulties and how to use the stretchiness to your advantage.

Chapter 2 provides three basic patterns written so that you can experiment with variations of yarn and stitch as well as with details such as sleeve length, neckline or collar shape. The instructions cover sizes from toddler to large adult and make use of the most popular yarn types, double-knit and 'chunky'.

Basic pattern A presents a set-in-sleeve, suitable for slipover, body warmer, jumper or cardigan. It has a shaped sleevehead set into a shaped armhole.

Basic pattern B has a raglan sleeve, suitable for a jumper or a cardigan, with or without a yoke neck. The shaping is shared between body and sleeves.

Basic pattern C has a dropped shoulder, suitable for a jacket or coat. The body is extended over the shoulders and the sleeve shape is simple.

All these patterns are written for a given tension, i.e. number of rows and stitches over 10 cm (4 in.) It is important that you knit to this tension for otherwise your garment will not be the shape you want. A full explanation of how to check this is given in chapter 2. Chapter 5 offers many different stitch patterns you could choose from.

When you feel confident enough to try writing your own patterns, chapter 3 will give you lots of ideas about how to start. It shows you how to measure someone and how to use the measurements to draw up a paper pattern shape. It then explains how to convert your diagram into details of rows and stitches. The easiest way for you to begin designing is to adapt or develop an existing idea – the chapter gives a number of ways of doing this.

There is a simple one-piece garment pattern based on a dressmaker's pattern and an existing dress; a piece of classic pattern-writing for a raglan-style cardigan based on body measurements; a pattern developed from a large jacquard graph motif and one inspired by a stitch/yarn idea. With all these patterns are explanations of how they were written. This may help you draft your own ideas by following my example.

The remainder of the book is designed to be a resource.

Chapter 4 includes details of how to work out instructions for collars, pockets, bands and hoods; how to give your work a professional finish; and how to add Swiss darning and beadwork.

Chapter 5 is an illustrated library of stitch patterns, which gives detailed knitting instructions and also a rough guide to the tension to be achieved with the yarn and needle size quoted.

Chapter 6 gives advice on re-vamping or altering existing garments, and on re-cycling yarn by unravelling an existing garment and removing the wrinkles.

Finally, there are a list of abbreviations and an index.

1 Knitting design

Introduction: Solving the mystery of good knitwear design

In this chapter I want to throw some light on knitting design. The secret of successful knitwear design lies in the way that the yarn, the stitch and the shape of the garment relate to one another. The skills I shall describe will help you gain the experience and expertise to choose a convincing relationship.

When you set out to do some knitting you usually start with one of the three basic components: a favourite yarn, a particular stitch to try or a shape and style of garment you want to create. Whichever one you start with, the next step is to try and piece together the other two parts of the whole that will be your own unique design. Each of these starting points is covered in the following pages.

Starting with yarn

A good yarn is the basic ingredient of knitting. Every yarn has its own characteristics which will affect the type of fabric that is created from it. I have included in this first section a guide to the different yarns commonly available with details of their origin and suitability for different types of work. They have all been photographed to the same scale so that some comparison can be made between yarn thickness and the resulting tension for stocking stitch on given needle sizes. (This will also highlight the differences in so-called standard thicknesses between one brand and another – the only way to be sure what a yarn will be like is to knit a sample yourself!) Also given in this section is a detailed guide to knitting a sample of your chosen yarn and so assessing its characteristics and tension.

Starting with a stitch

Using a stitch is like mixing the ingredients in cooking. How you mix them is going to affect the final result – in this case your knitted fabric. A stitch may be chosen for its own attractiveness and so be the most distinctive part of the fabric. It may also be exploited to change or enhance a yarn's natural characteristics. The type of stitch you choose will control the nature of the fabric and this section gives descriptions of what effects stitches are likely to produce. Using this information will give you some idea of what your chosen stitch and chosen yarn may produce, but the key to a successful combination of yarn and stitch is trying it out. This is not a waste of time - it really pays off. Once you have such a 'sample' you can see what it's like – how it behaves; whether it works as a combination; if it is really what you wanted. The sample is not only a way of evaluating your ideas but it is also the first step in writing a knitting pattern – all the calculations for the numbers of rows and stitches are based on your sample.

Starting with a garment idea

The styling of a garment is the presentation of the prepared ingredients – it is what turns them into a unified design idea that is right for the occasion. If you are starting with a garment shape you will need to understand what type of fabric (yarn and stitch combination) will suit your idea. You may be starting with an idea for a jacket like illustration 1.1 which calls for a fairly chunky fabric – but not too stretchy or the 'off the shoulder' sleeve may become an 'on the elbow' look. You may have created a fabric with a very stable and somewhat stiff texture that just would not suit the soft styling of the garment in illustration 1.2.

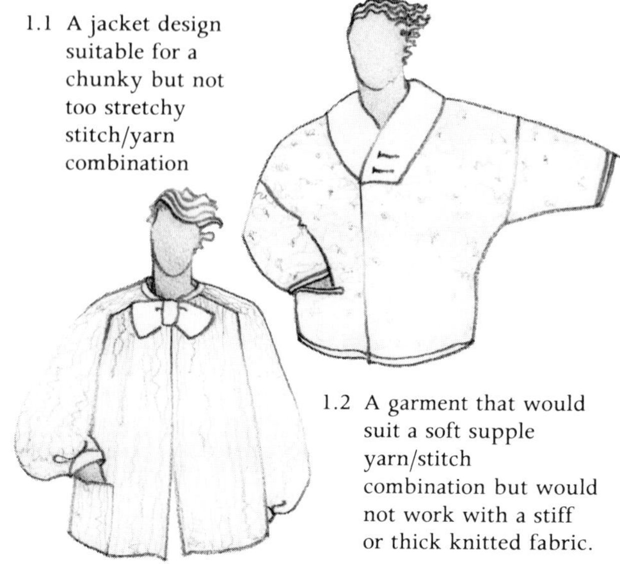

1.1 A jacket design suitable for a chunky but not too stretchy stitch/yarn combination

1.2 A garment that would suit a soft supple yarn/stitch combination but would not work with a stiff or thick knitted fabric.

The way of being sure that your garment shape will truly marry with your fabric is to use the technique of sampling recommended throughout. When you start designing it is best to knit a large sample so that you can get a good sense of how it works as a fabric and whether it may be too heavy, too stiff, too stretchy or too transparent, etc., for the style of garment you have in mind. This section of the chapter gives lots of help in avoiding problems caused by the behaviour of knitted fabric and ways of turning them round so that they work to your advantage rather than against you.

As a beginner you may well feel that all these variables are too complicated for you. I would advise that you start experimenting with yarn and stitch combinations and stick to the classic styles of the basic patterns given in Chapter 2. A few successful results using this formula will give you the confidence to start trying garment styling ideas using one or other of the techniques suggested in Chapter 3.

Choosing the right yarn

GENERAL ADVICE

To make a choice about yarn type you either need a good idea of what yarns are like and how their various characteristics affect their knitted behaviour or else leave deciding what to do with the yarn until you have found this out. You may decide to buy a yarn because the colour is just right or because it feels wonderful or perhaps you like the texture or a combination of these qualities. But it is wise to leave deciding what to do with the yarn until you know more about what the yarn is like. The best way to do this is to knit some up using stocking stitch. To get an appropriate needle size use the information on the ball band or label or else get advice from the yarn supplier.

Work at least:

20 st by 25 rows for chunky yarn on 5-7mm (no. 6-2) needles

or 25 st by 35 rows for double-knit equivalents on $3\frac{1}{4}$-$4\frac{1}{2}$mm (no. 10-7) needles

or 30 st by 40 rows for 3-4ply types on $2\frac{1}{2}$-$3\frac{1}{4}$mm (no. 12-10) needles

This will ensure that your sample is at least 10cm (4in.) square.

When it is knitted up you need to look at it critically and decide what it is like – both before you steam it and after. It is important to take account of steaming as it may alter a great deal, not only characteristics but tension as well. As you get more experience with this process it will be easier to identify a yarn's characteristics.

It is a good idea to keep your samples and build up a library. Label each with a swing ticket giving information about the yarn, needle size and resulting tension. In this way you will be able to compare and contrast yarns with one another.

Questions to ask about the yarn sample:

What does it feel like?

- Is it hard like a rug?
- Is it springy?
- Is it floppy?

How does it behave?

- How much does it stretch across the width of the row?
- How much does it stretch vertically?
- How quickly does it return to its original size when it is stretched?
- How interesting is it?

When you have answers to these questions the next section gives some guidance.

Stiff and inelastic

If these are the predominant characteristics of the sample it is probably knitted on too small a needle. Try again using a larger size.

Limp and slow to return to its original shape

The problem with yarns like these is that the garment you knit from them will possess these qualities. It will easily become distorted and misshapen quite early in its life – particularly if it is washed carelessly. This is most likely to happen with pure synthetic yarns. You may have chosen a brushed acrylic, for example, because of the price, that looks attractive and fluffy on the ball. But when it is knitted and washed it loses all its life.

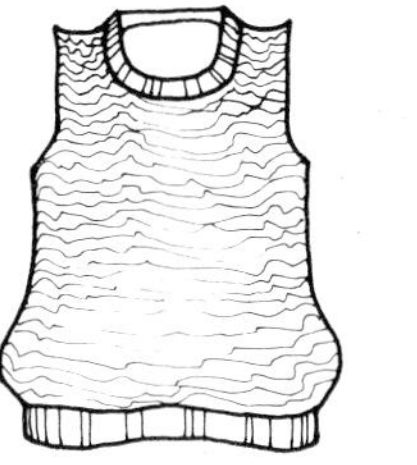
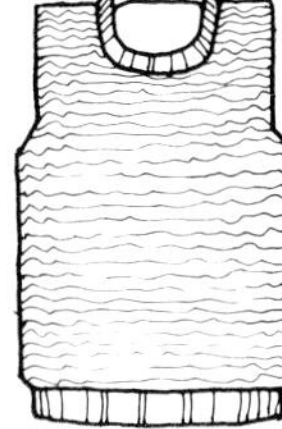

1.3 The left-hand drawing shows the bulbous shape caused by knitting a heavy yarn in too loose a stitch. (This can be produced by poor washing and ironing.)

Cotton yarns may also be problematic when knitted up – their weight is the problem. The garment stretches from the shoulder over the upper section but not the lower, producing an ugly bulbous shape. This may be caused by careless washing/drying.

> ALL KNITWEAR SHOULD BE DRIED FLAT AND NEVER TUMBLE DRIED.

Springy and elastic
Yarns of this type are the most versatile and can be used in the widest number of situations and stitch patterns.

Full of interest
Yarns that are very interesting in texture or appearance when knitted up in stocking stitch need to be treated carefully. There is so much interest in the fabric that other detail can be easily lost. So avoid small stitch patterns and shaping that is too complicated.

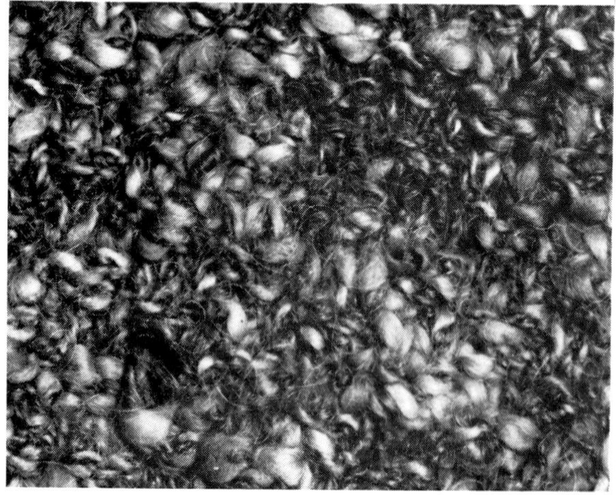

MIXTURES OF FIBRES

I prefer to work with natural fibres when possible. I will choose a mixture when the addition of a synthetic yarn enhances the properties of a natural yarn or increases its viability.

Wool and acrylic
The addition of acrylic fibres to wool in small quantities produces a harder wearing and cheaper alternative to pure wool. It also increases the washability of the mixture and is particularly suitable for children's things.

Cotton and synthetic mixtures
Adding acrylic or other fibres to cotton produces a lighter yarn – so reducing the problem of stretch and dropping often associated with pure cotton. The synthetic mixture is easier to wash than the pure fibre.

Mohair and synthetic mixtures
The synthetic fibre is used in brushed yarns as the binding thread that holds the brushed fibres secure and produces a consistent thickness and strength that makes the yarn possible to work with. The binding thread may be made of cotton. The synthetic fibre may also be used as a bulking agent – to increase the volume of the yarn while keeping costs low.

Hair yarns and synthetics (angora, alpaca, cashmere)
The addition of man-made fibres is common with hair yarns to reduce the cost, and also because some hair yarns may have a short 'staple'–that is, the individual hairs or staples are so short that the spun yarn tends to snap easily. As synthetics can be produced in a continuous filament of infinite length, they do not have this problem. So a judicious mixture of hair and filament results in a workable alternative.

Both the examples on the left are knitted in double moss stitch but the pattern is almost invisible in the top photo because the coloured flecks in the yarn stand out so much.

Wool is a warm-feeling fibre that will absorb excess moisture without feeling cold or clammy.

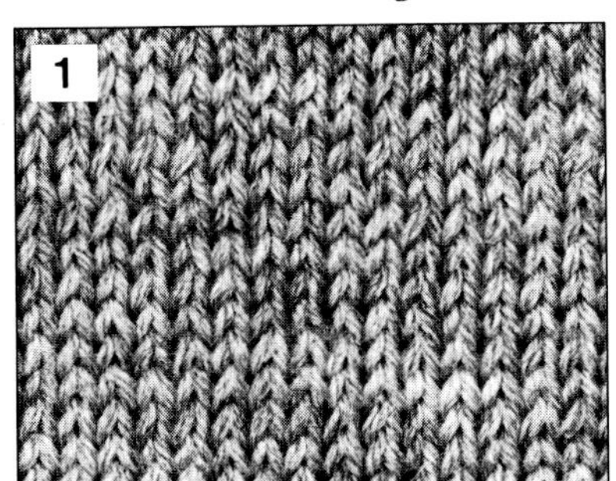

Fibre: **cross-bred wool, superwash**
Thickness: double-knit
Origin and properties: the most commonly available wool is spun from cross-bred sheep. This quality is treated so that it can be machine washed – see ball band or label for details.

Use: smooth texture; any type of stitch pattern; good for texture and elasticity.

Patons 'Clansman';
4mm needles
10cm square = 23 st × 26 rows

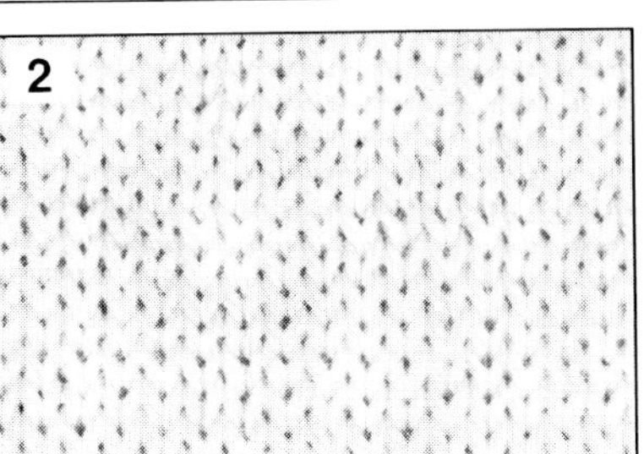

Fibre: **Shetland wool**
Thickness: 2-ply but knits as 4-ply
Origin and properties: a light-weight yarn with a slight fluff, originally from the Shetland breed of sheep, but may be an imitation.
Use: smooth texture; good for Fair Isle or jacquard.

Pingouin 'Type Shetland';
4mm needles
10cm square = 24 st × 27 rows

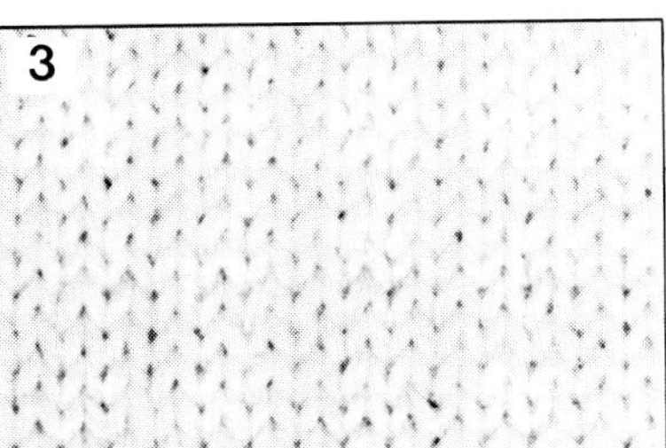

Fibre: **Aran wool**
Thickness: 4-ply, sometimes called 'triple knitting'
Origin and properties: a hard-wearing yarn originally left undyed and used by traditional knitters in the Irish islands.

Use: smooth; good for Aran-style patterns and thicker garments.

T. Forsell 'Slalom aran knitting' (oiled); $4\frac{1}{2}$mm needles
10cm square = 21 st × 27 rows

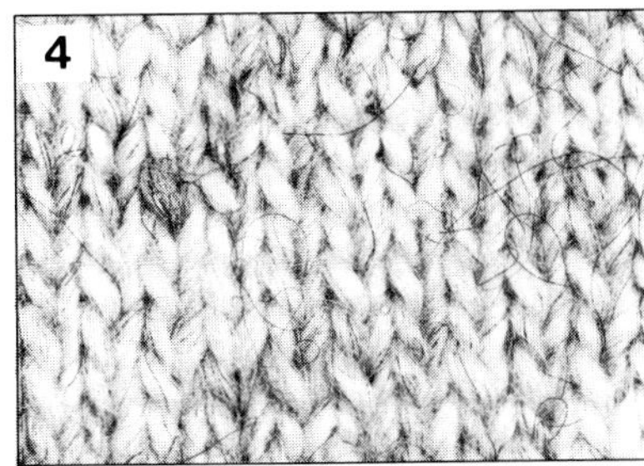

Fibre: **Lopi wool**
Thickness: a single plied yarn 'double double'
Origin and properties: a light thick wool used in traditional Icelandic knitting, rather weak because of the spinning method.

Use: smooth; good for warm outer garments.

Alafoss 'Lopi';
6mm needles
10cm square = 16 st × 18 rows

Fibre: **wool twist**
Thickness: double-knit
Origin and properties: a yarn spun from two plies of different colours.

Use: bold stitch patterns; good combined with a plain yarn that matches one of the constituent colours.

Emu 'Harlech';
4mm needles
10cm square = 22 st × 27 rows

Fibre: **wool tweed**
Thickness: double-knit
Origin and properties: a thick lumpy yarn, sometimes coarse with speckles of different colours.

Use: bold stitch patterns; good for outer garments.

Kilcarra 'Donegal tweed';
4mm needles
10cm square = 22 st × 27 rows

Fibre: **wool mixture or heather mix**
Thickness: double-knit
Origin and properties: a yarn made by spinning together fibres of different colours.

Use: smooth as for plain wool.

Wendy 'Shetland';
4mm needles
10cm square = 23 st × 30 rows

Fibre: **pure new wool**
Thickness: 4-ply
Origin and properties: a good-quality yarn that conforms to the Woolmark specifications for composition and colour fastness; requires careful washing.

Use: very versatile smooth yarn.

Pingouin 'Pingolaine';
$3\frac{1}{4}$mm needles
10cm square = 28 st × 31 rows

Fibre: **pure new wool**
Thickness: 3-ply
Origin and properties: a good-quality yarn that conforms to the Woolmark specifications for composition and colour fastness; requires careful washing.

Use: fine lace patterns and complex stitch patterns, traditionally used by Scottish island knitters.

Sunbeam '3-ply';
3mm needles
10cm square = 32 st × 38 rows

5 6 7 8 9

Fibre: **angora 70%, wool 30%**
Thickness: as 4-ply
Origin and properties: angora comes from the hairs of the Angora rabbit and is mixed with wool to make spinning easier. Soft and warm though the hairs may drop and irritate.

Use: not suitable for babies (who may choke on the hairs); use bold stitch patterns.

Jaeger 'Angora spun';
$3\frac{3}{4}$mm needles
10cm square = 27 st × 33 rows

Fibre: **alpaca**
Thickness: double-knit
Origin and properties: comes from the long hairs of the alpaca and llama, both members of the camel family from South America. In short supply because of conservation. It is a warm, slightly lustrous yarn, less hard-wearing than mohair. Expensive and not often available.

Use: smooth fibre, most attractive in natural shades of white, grey, fawn, brown and black, worked in coloured stitch patterns.

Emu 'Alpaca';
4mm needles
10cm square = 23 st × 28 rows

Fibre: **cashmere**
Thickness: as 4-ply
Origin and properties: the short hairs that form the under coat of the Cashmere goat are used for this fibre that is produced in Northern India and other parts of Asia. It is extremely soft, smooth and light. Blends well with wool to make it harder-wearing and less expensive.

Use: smooth fibre. Price a factor in larger items.

Vidna 'Cashmere-wool';
3mm needles
10cm square = 31 st × 39 rows

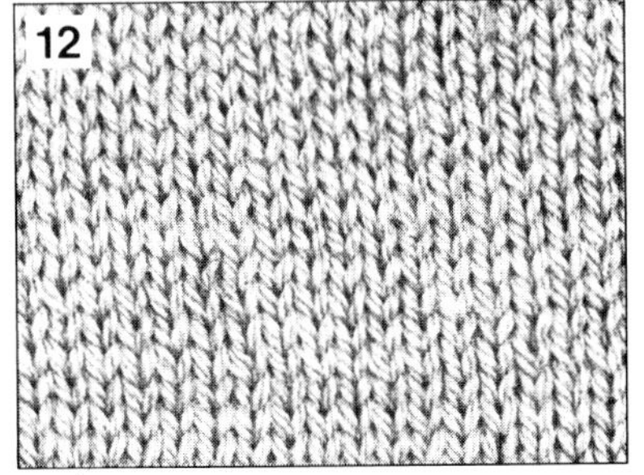

Fibre: **mohair 52%, acrylic 40%, nylon 4%, polyester 4%**
Thickness: chunky
Origin and properties: mohair comes from the white long hairs of the Angora goat, mainly produced in Turkey. It is a lustrous, smooth and strong fibre but difficult to spin, so it is usually mixed with other fibres when conventionally spun or made into a brushed or loop yarn. Takes dye well.

Use: fluffy yarn best for coloured patterns or very bold stitch patterns.

Hayfield 'Lugano';
6mm needles
10cm square = 18 st × 17 rows

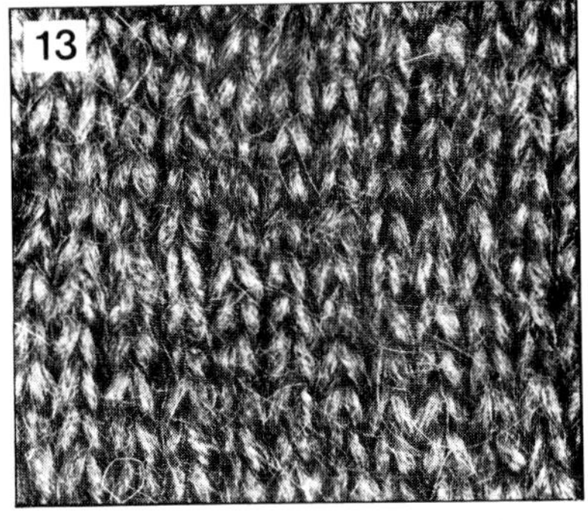

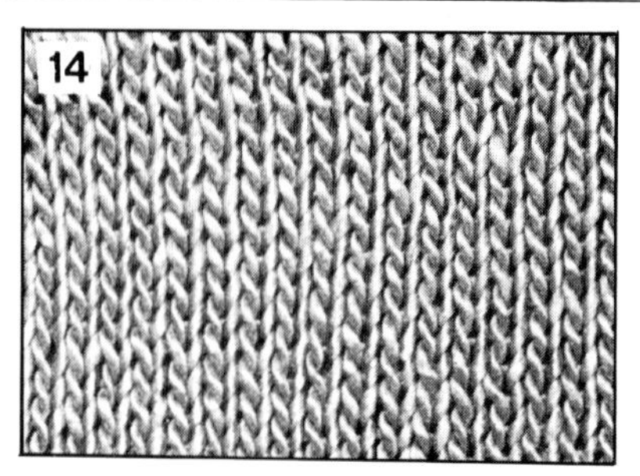

Fibre: **silk (spun)**
Thickness: as 4-ply
Origin and properties: the only natural filament, it is spun by the silkworm to make its cocoon. Silk fibres are warm, lustrous, fine and strong. The best quality filaments are extremely expensive. Most silk comes from China and Japan. (Tussore silk comes from India; it is obtained from wild silkworms and is naturally brown and uneven.)
Use: depends on type – price a factor in larger items.

Hjerte 'seta';
$3\frac{1}{4}$mm needles
10cm square = 30 st × 36 rows

VEGETABLE

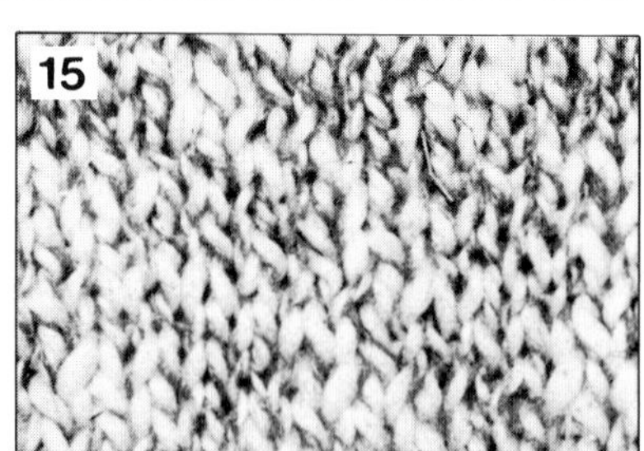

Fibre: **linen 52%, cotton 48%**
Thickness: double-knit
Origin and properties: linen is a long fibre, fawn in colour that is obtained from the stem of the flax plant. Usually mixed with cotton. It has two qualities – the best is called 'line'; the poorer form 'tow'. It is cool, lustrous, strong and very hard wearing.
Use: as cotton.

Kilcarra 'Linencraft';
4mm needles
10cm square = 24 st × 26 rows

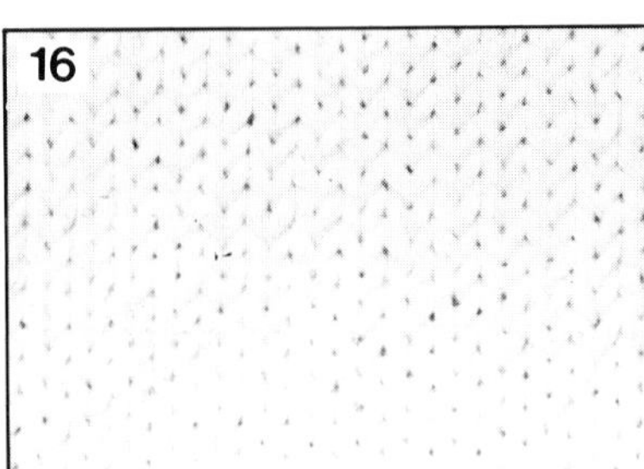

Fibre: **cotton**
Thickness: as double-knit
Origin and properties: comes from the seeds of the cotton plant in white fibres. The better the quality the longer the fibre and the stronger and softer the feel. Origin in order of quality: Egypt, America, India. Takes dye well.
Use: smooth, fairly versatile – problem with weight.

Pingouin 'Coton naturel 8 fils';
4mm needles
10cm square = 20 st × 27 rows

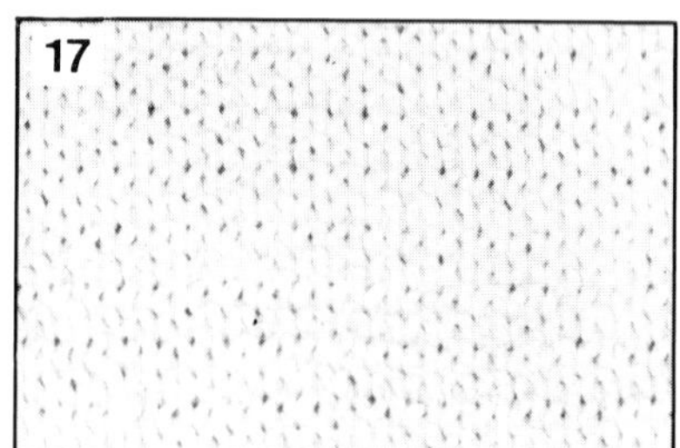

Fibre: **mercerised cotton**
Thickness: as 4-ply
Origin and properties: as above but treated by the mercerising process which gives a permanent lustrous finish.
Use: use as above.

Twilleys 'Perléspun';
$3\frac{1}{4}$mm needles
10cm square = 28 st × 33 rows

15

16

17

18

19

SYNTHETIC OR MAN-MADE

The first two yarns listed are rarely spun on their own, they are usually mixed either together or with wool to form more acceptable yarns.

The example illustrated below is the mixture called 'Courtelle' which contains 70% acrylic, 15% nylon, 15% wool and knits as double-knit.

Fibre: **acrylic**
Origin and properties: spun in a continuous filament from acrylonitrile. Can be made to resemble wool and is warmer feeling than other man-made fibres. Acrylic absorbs little moisture, is a poor insulator, forms pulls and is subject to static electricity. Great care must be taken with washing and use of the iron, to avoid distortion and a shiny surface. (Modacrylic is a modified form that gives flame resistance.)
Use: as for wool.

Fibre: **nylon**
Origin and properties: a polyamide spun in a continuous filament from acid chloride and an amine. Similar to acrylic in properties but the fibres shine and take dye badly – so available in only a limited colour range. Often blended with wool to increase wear.
Use: as for wool.

Patons '200';
4mm needles
10cm square = 22 st × 29 rows

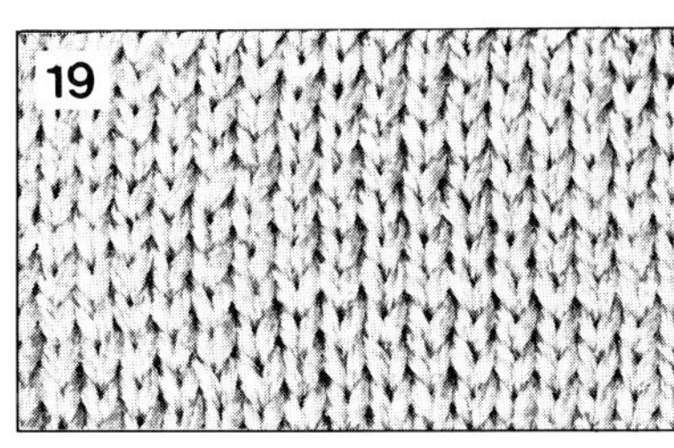

Fibre: **viscose rayon**
Thickness: as double-knit
Origin and properties: a natural polymer fibre formed from cellulose extracted from wood pulp. When dry the yarn is strong and elastic but it is very absorbent and when wet becomes much less strong and easily distorts. It feels cool and limp and is usually chosen for its shiny appearance.
Use: as for wool.
Pingouin 'Viscosa';
4mm needles
10cm square = 24 st × 25 rows

FANCY SPINNINGS – common types

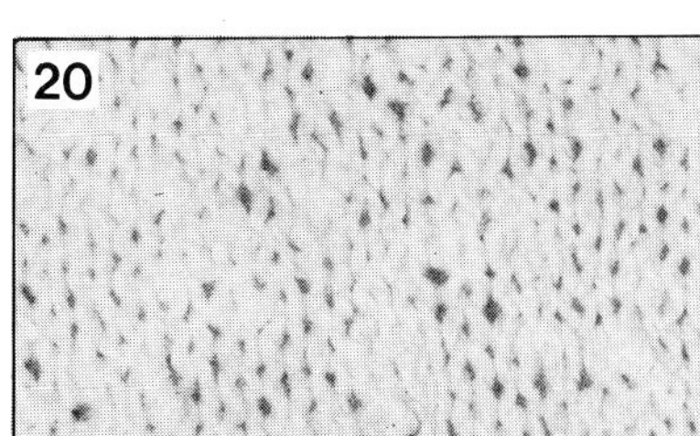

Type: **bouclé**
Fibre availability: mixtures
Example: Hayfield 'Hawaii', 50% nylon, 50% acrylic
Thickness: as double-knit

Definition: formed by one twisted strand being twisted unevenly between two binding strands to form knobs or 'bouclés' at irregular intervals.

Hayfields 'Hawaii';
4mm needles
10cm square = 24 st × 24 rows

Type: **chenille**
Fibre availability: cotton, synthetics
Example: Rowan 'Designer Collection Fine Cotton Chenille'
Thickness: approx. 3-ply

Definition: formed from short-cut hairs held by central strands, like velvet. Should not be twisted as it is knitted.

Rowan 'Designer Fine Cotton Chenille'; $3\frac{1}{4}$mm needles
10cm square = 25 st × 31 rows

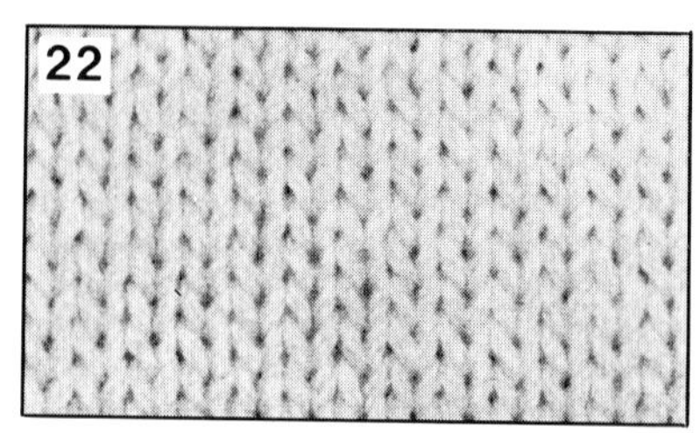

Type: **crepe**
Fibre availability: mixtures
Example: Sirdar 'Wash'n'wear double crepe', 55% nylon, 45% acrylic
Thickness: double-knit
Definition: two plied strands are twisted together producing a crinkled appearance.
Use: stitch patterns and garments for hard wear.

Sirdar 'Wash 'n wear double crepe'; 4mm needles
10cm square = 24 st × 29 rows

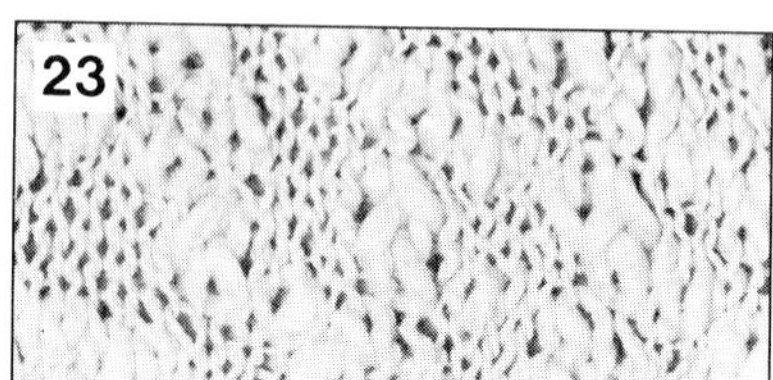

Type: **slub**
Fibre availability: cotton/variety
Example: Twilley's 'Bubbly'
100% cotton
Thickness: 4-ply
Definition: spun to give fine and lumpy sections. Knit on surprisingly large needles.
Twilleys, 'Bubbly';
$3\frac{3}{4}$mm needles
10cm square = 27 st × 30 rows

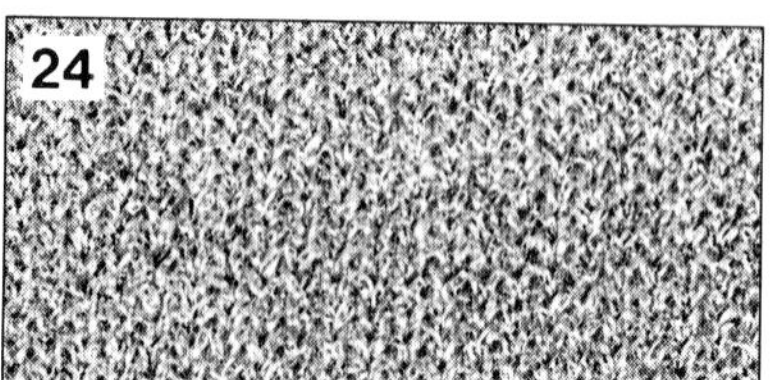

Type: **glitter or metallic yarns**
Fibre availability: synthetic
Example: Schürer
Thickness: approx. 2-ply
Definition: formed by laminating aluminium foil and plastic film with coloured adhesives. Formed into a yarn usually with other fibres.
Twilleys 'Goldfingering';
$3\frac{1}{4}$mm needles
10cm square = 31 st × 38 rows

Type: **spiral**
Fibre availability: wool/variety
Example: Patons 'Twirl' 56% acrylic, 17% wool, 17% nylon, 10% cotton
Thickness: chunky
Definition: an untwisted strand wound round a fine binding strand.
Patons' 'Twirl';
6mm needles
10cm square = 16 st × 17 rows

Choosing the right stitch

GENERAL ADVICE

The choice of stitch you make will affect both the behaviour and the appearance of the fabric you will create. In order to make a choice you need some idea of the probable effect your chosen stitch will produce. Some stitch patterns affect the elasticity or lack of it, in one or other direction, a property that can be exploited or avoided. Other stitch patterns may be chosen for their textural or visual qualities.

Different types of stitch pattern are categorised according to the techniques used to produce them. Some general descriptions of the possibilities, the type of yarn suitable to them and the probable nature of the fabric produced are given below. Examples and detailed instructions are given in the stitch dictionary (see p. 78)

Jacquard cardigan

Yarn: Patons 'Diploma' double-knit
Basic pattern B, Chapter 2

Yoke-neck sweater

Yarn: Wendy 'Shetland' double-knit
and 3 colours miscellaneous double-knit
Basic pattern B, Chapter 2

Detail of Fair Isle garment

Cable stitch pattern

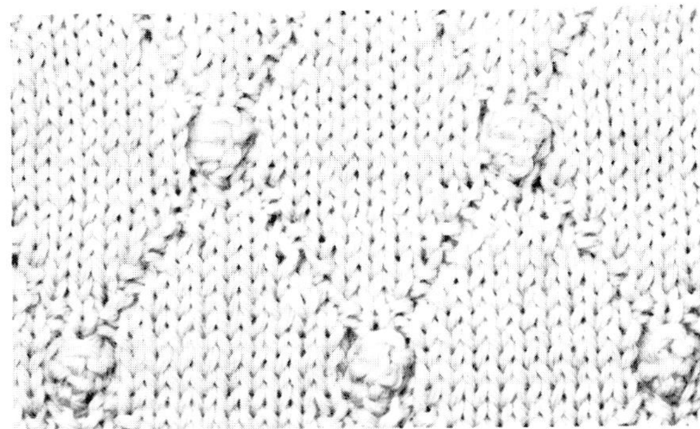
Bobble pattern

Slipped tuck stitch patterns

Jacquard or Fair Isle coloured patterns
Yarn: any
Properties: little widthwise stretch due to yarn loops behind.
Description: these are knitted in stocking stitch using coloured yarns for different stitches. The yarn not being knitted is looped behind the work. The term Fair Isle comes from a tradition of knitting in Fair Isle to the north of Scotland in which symbolic designs are worked in several colours on a neutral ground.

Cable or transferred stitch patterns
Yarn: elastic yarns, preferably wool or wool mixes
Properties: fairly stable if worked with a slightly tight tension which produces the maximum raised effect.
Description: these are knitted in a combination of stocking stitch and either reverse stocking stitch or moss stitch. The right-side stitches are transferred in front or behind the work on short 'cable' needles. Cable patterns are used extensively in 'Aran' work traditional in the Aran islands and parts of Ireland.

Bobble patterns
Yarn: any, though difficult to work in fancy yarns
Properties: bobbles may be positioned on any part of a background stitch, whose qualities will affect the fabric. Often worked with a cable pattern. Interesting when worked in a contrast colour or yarn.
Description: bobbles are made by increasing a number of stitches in the chosen place for the bobble, then casting them off (to give a larger bobble the stitches may be knitted several times before being cast off).

Slipped tuck stitch patterns
Yarn: any
Properties: gives little vertical stretch to fabric and requires more rows to the cm (in.).
Description: these are worked to give texture and create coloured patterns when a number of different yarns are used. They are worked by holding one or several stitches, without knitting, for a number of rows. In a slipped-stitch pattern the yarn is passed behind the slipped stitch which produces a raised effect on the front of the work. For tucked-stitch patterns the yarn is carried over the needle and slipped stitch each row; the more rows worked in this way, the more the fabric will pucker.

Reverse stocking-stitch patterns
Yarn: smooth yarns
Properties: similar to stocking stitch.
Description: these patterns are worked by using the

'pips' of the purl or 'wrong' side of stocking stitch to form motifs on a background of 'right-side' stocking stitch. Patterns of this sort are traditionally used in the fisherman's guernsey or gansey sweater of oiled wool. The combination of a close-knit stitch pattern and an oiled wool makes the sweaters both warm and waterproof.

Close textured patterns
Yarn: smoother types
Properties: may produce stretch across the width.
Descriptions: these are usually worked with a combination of plain and purl stitches, alternating frequently, with the addition of slipped or twisted stitches.

Lace patterns
Yarn: any – complex pattern best in fine wool
Properties: gives a loose open fabric with elasticity (this is dependent on yarn type).
Description: these patterns are worked by increasing stitches (by putting the yarn over the needle which creates a hole) – and later by decreasing them, to maintain the number of stitches worked. The positioning of the increases relative to the decreases can cause the knitted stitches to slope and change direction creating intricate effects.

Coloured stitch patterns
Yarn: any – experiment and see
Properties: dependent on type of stitch pattern used - see other definitions.
Description: this refers to the use of changes of yarn and colour when combined with a stitch pattern to produce an interesting effect. There are many possibilities and permutations possible and a rich source of potential discovery.

EVALUATING YOUR CHOICE

Once you have an idea of the stitch, you will need a suitable yarn. (See previous section for discussion of yarn types.) Try out your combination by knitting a sample to test out your choice. Use the size of needles recommended for the yarn and work your sample with the same number of rows and stitches as the stocking stitch sample suggested in the yarn section (see p. 9). By doing this you get a very direct comparison of tension and characteristics with the yarn used for stocking stitch.

When it is completed ask yourself the same sort of questions as suggested on page 9. Remember to examine the sample before and after steaming it. You must be very critical of your choice at this stage – time spent now on knitting a number of samples may

Reverse stocking stitch

Close textured pattern

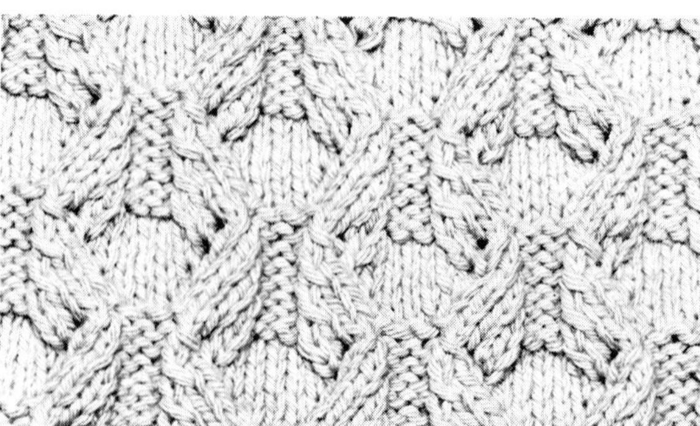

Lace pattern

Coloured stitch pattern

well save the hassle of working out the whole pattern only to find you have to start again from scratch. Do not be afraid to try the sample on at least two or three different sizes of needle to get the best possible tension. If you are not sure about the stitch pattern spend time trying out a number of possibilities before making a decision and embarking on the garment.

Choosing the garment shape

PROPERTIES OF KNITTED FABRICS

Most knitted garments are designed to fit fairly close to the body – something which is particularly suited to the elastic nature of knitted fabrics. Where the fabric is close to the body it is to some extent supported by the body and how the fabric behaves is not too important providing it is fairly stable, that is, not too stretchy and not too stiff. Difficulties may arise if the fabric is particularly stretchy or will not stretch in one or other direction.

Stretch and garment shape

Some of the problems caused by this can be overcome by anticipation, and using the great versatility of knitting, the ability to create exactly the right fabric for the situation.

In the diagram are indicated the directions which are most likely to cause stretch or 'drop', as it is called. Drop is caused by gravity – the weight of the fabric pulling down towards the earth. It follows that the heavier the yarn and the more stretchy the stitch used, the more the fabric will drop. If the chosen stitch has the ability to stretch in a particular direction it is best not to use the stitch in a place where it will be subject to most force.

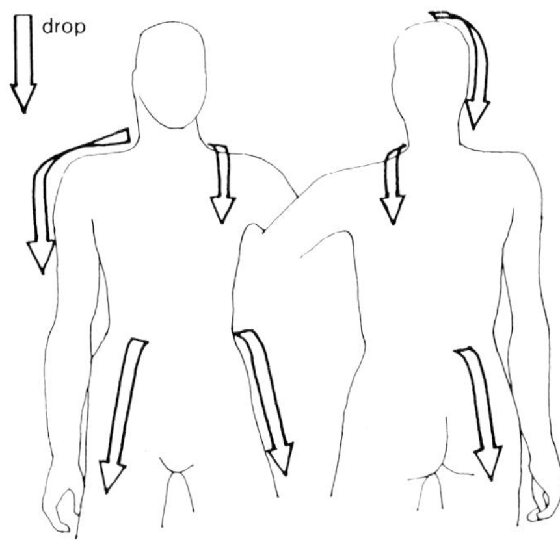

1.4 The arrows show the places where kitted fabric is most likely to stretch under its own weight—or drop.

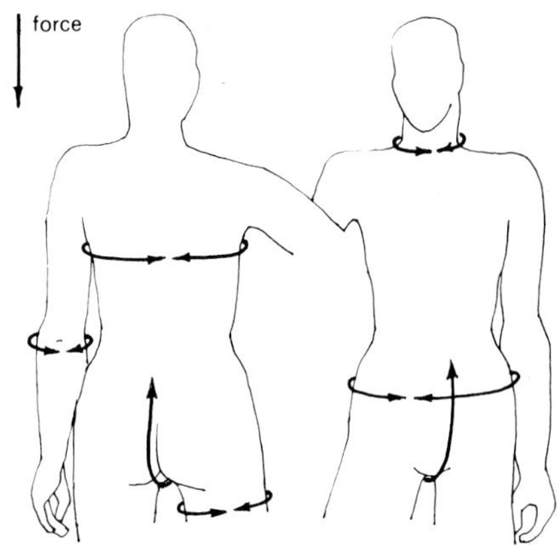

1.5 The arrows show the areas of the body which move most and this factor must be allowed for in the design.

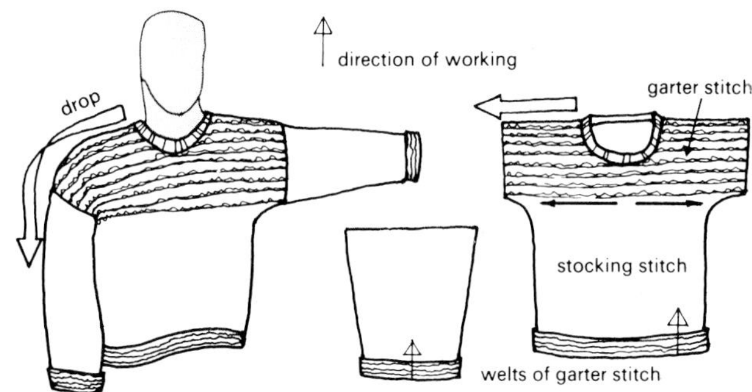

1.6 Problems from a stretchy stitch used in a place where drop will make it worse.

In this diagram are shown the parts of body that need to be able to move. The garment must allow for this either by stretching or by carefully positioned openings. Care should be taken when choosing a finish for the neck opening that the head will be able to pass through, or else a fastening will need to be allowed for.

Fig 1.7 shows a problem with a stretchy stitch on a garment with dropped shoulders and a garter-stitch yoke. Because garter stitch has a tendency to stretch widthwise the yoke will stretch a fair amount over the shoulders, which means the sleeve would become increasingly long.

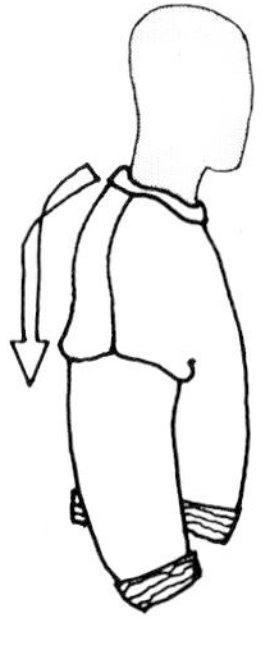

1.7 The shoulder drop causes a bulge at the top of the sleeve.

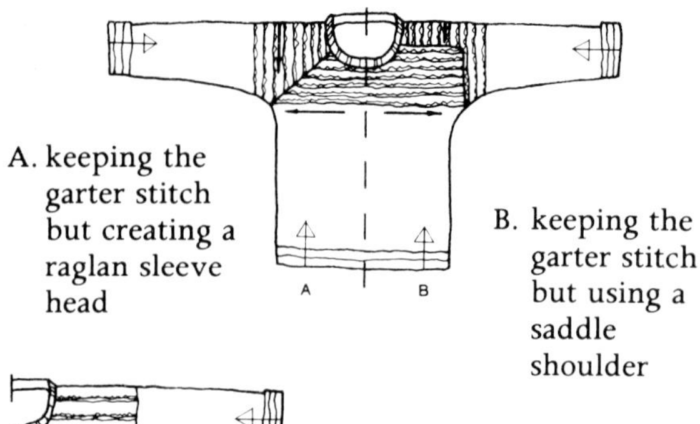

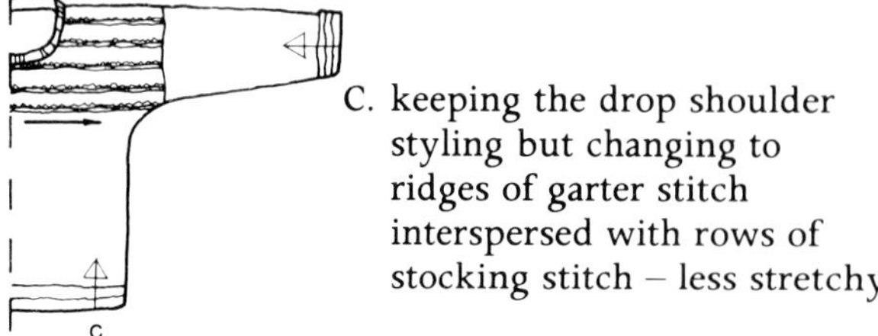

1.8 (A) and (B): Two ways of solving the problem by using the stitch in a different direction
(C): Changing the stitch to lessen the shoulder drop

Not only would the shoulder drop but it would also become narrow in relation to the original sleeve head, creating an ugly bunching at the join, as shown in Fig. 1.7. But provided you are aware that this may happen, by trying out your fabric with a knitted sample, it is possible to design round or to enhance the qualities of the knitted fabric. In the sweater with the garter-stitch yoke, for example, the design could have been changed in several ways had the problem been anticipated.

Larger knitted garments

For knitted garments that hang away from the body, particularly larger and heavier items, more care is needed. It may be worth knitting a whole section of the garment and monitoring how it behaves – to see whether it drops, twists or curls – and then decide how to work the edges to counteract any problems. Usually twisting and curling can be identified on the first small sample – before it is steamed it will nearly always curl – but if it persists after steaming you will need to take care.

Side edge curl

Stocking stitch curls both across its width and at either end. This could cause a problem in the example here of a tube top (Fig. 1.9) – seamed to the hips – then left to hang at front and back.

Because nothing has been done to stop this, the natural inclination of the stocking stitch causes the panel to curl under at the sides. The problem is more likely to happen with a tightish tension. To avoid or remedy the problem, work an edging strip. If this is anticipated it may be worked integrally by consistently knitting the edge stitches with a stitch pattern that will not curl, e.g. garter stitch, moss stitch, twisted rib, etc. If this is not possible, the edge may be picked up vertically and band knitted at right angles to the edge. See p. 68.

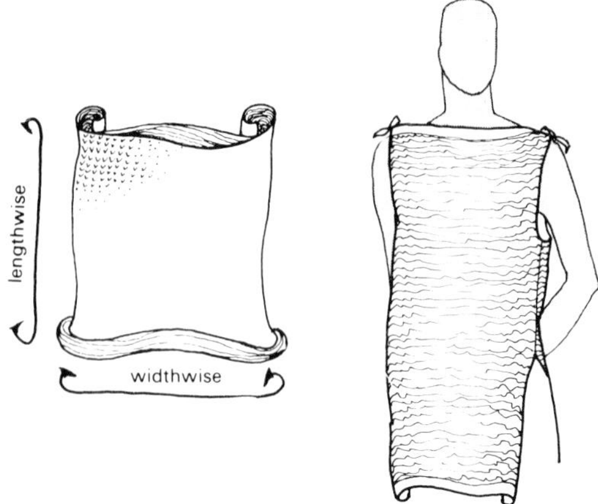

1.9 This sample square shows how ordinary stocking stitch curls at both sides and edges.

1.10 The design of this garment in stocking stitch illustrates a problem that can be avoided.

Problems with skirts

When knitting skirts it is advisable to use a stitch that stretches vertically over the hips. If the pattern is carefully drafted, this will ensure that the fabric fits closely. Doing this will prevent a bulky look developing, particularly if gathers are used.

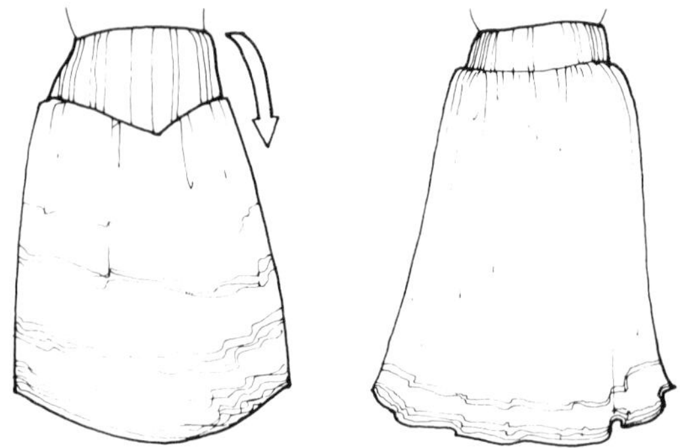

1.11 Left: Using a rib and the natural drop of the fabric to produce a neatly fitting yoke to a skirt.

1.12 Right: Working the skirt sideways to avoid hem problems or to give a flared or gored effect

Problems with hems

Curling may happen at the hem line if no edging rows are worked in a suitable stitch (rib, moss, garter,

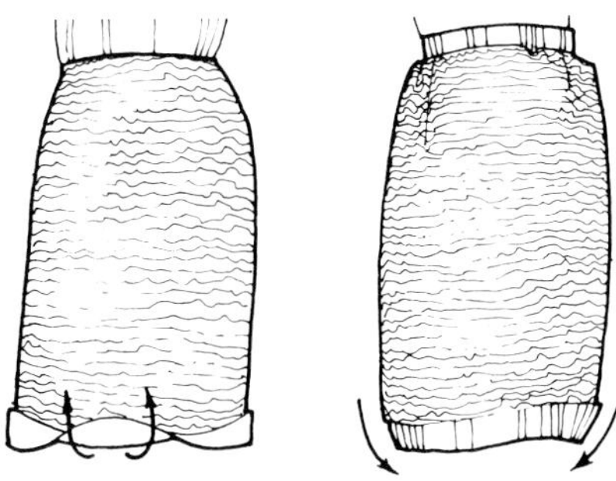

1.13 Left: A picked-up hem may curl up along the picked-up row

Right: A ribbed hem that is too tight produces a 'hobbled' look.

etc.). As little as four rows may be sufficient to avoid this. Curling may also occur when a picked-up hem has been worked.

To avoid a hem that does not lie flat, looks bulky and tends to bend up along the picked-up row, experiment on your tension sample. Knit the first rows on a smaller needle size and change to main-work needle size for the reverse stocking stitch row that will mark the fold. Then change to a larger needle size to work the row that knits together the lower edge. (Remember to change back.) If you work a ribbed welt or border, take care not to allow it to pull the hem inwards, unless this is an intentional design feature.

To avoid this problem try the rib out on your tension sample, sew up the sides to form a tube to see what will happen at the seams. Using different needle sizes, or altering the number of stitches of plain and purl that make up the rib, may work. (A k2, p2 rib is less elastic and therefore less likely to narrow than the standard k1, p1 rib.)

Another solution to both of these problems of curl and narrowing is to knit the fabric sideways – from seam edge to seam edge. Using this technique it is possible to knit a flared or gored skirt by working more rows near the hem edge.

GENERAL ADVICE ON EDGES

Always try picking up stitches for edge welts, etc., on your stitch or tension sample – that way you will be able to anticipate and probably avoid problems. The more trouble you take over these aspects of finishing detail the more professional your garment will look.

Twist or shear

This is not a very common problem, particularly if you stick to yarns that are intended for knitting. If you experiment with yarns that are designed for weaving you may come across this phenomenon. It happens with yarns that are a single strand or ply, a collection of fibres that are spun together in a single strand. If the spinning is quite tight then it can cause problems for the knitter when stocking stitch is worked. It may also happen with stitch patterns that are predominantly stocking stitch. When a garment is knitted up the shear causes the side seams to twist towards the front. A similar effect appears on the sleeve seams.

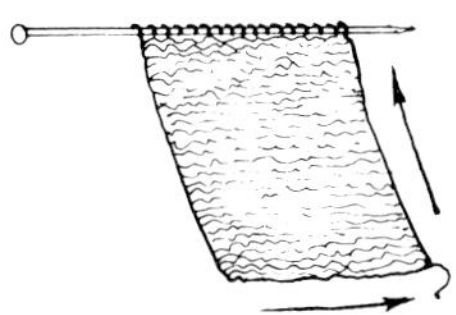

1.14 If the sample hangs to one side from the needle there will be problems with shear or twist.

This may be so slight that it may not trouble you. The way to avoid it altogether is to work in garter or moss stitch, then there will be no shear. (Other patterns that involve frequent changes of purl to plain from row to row may also work – experiment and see.)

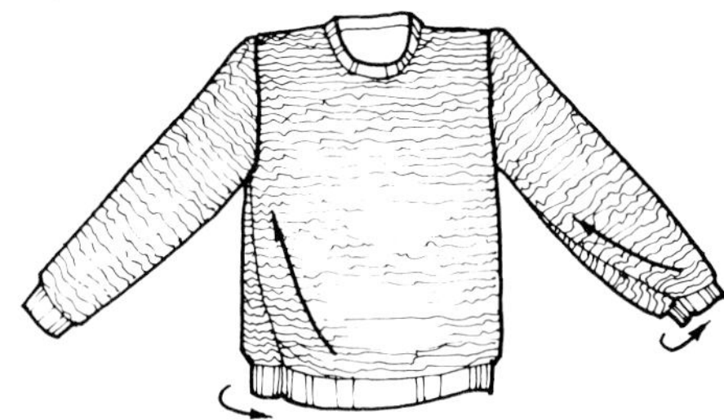

1.15 If a garment is knitted from a sheared stitch or yarn the seams will tend to twist round

CONCLUSION

Most of the problems dealt with in this section need not trouble you if you start your design work with conventional styles of knitted garments – the jumper, the slipover, the cardigan, the blouson or jacket, etc. They are the most common styles for use with knitted fabric – not by chance but by design. The solutions that work best for the vast majority of hand-knitting projects use the most popular yarns (4-ply to Aran weight) and the usual needle sizes 4 to 6mm (no. 8 to no. 4) needles. If you are starting out on knitwear design, it is best to stick to the classics until you feel confident enough to try a more elaborate and more adventurous shape.

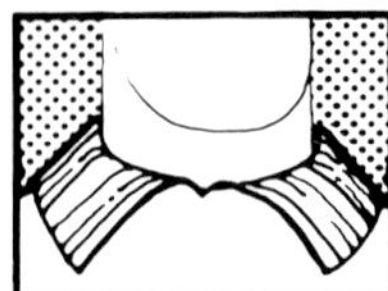

2
Basic patterns

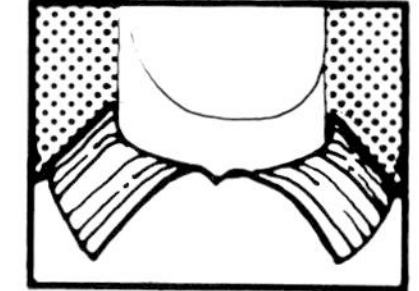

The aim of this chapter is to give you a basic vocabulary of classic styles of knitted garments in a large number of sizes. The patterns are presented so that they can be adapted in a wide variety of ways – giving any number of possible permutations. If you follow the instructions and check your tension you will be sure to get a successful garment. By developing your ideas through practice with the basic patterns I hope you will gain confidence and feel able to start designing from scratch.

Seven garments have been knitted to the basic patterns given in this chapter. These are in different yarns and stitch patterns and they have been photographed in colour. Details are given at the end of each set of basic pattern instructions (but before the size charts).

About the patterns – what's possible

(a) Set-in sleeve pattern This is written in fourteen sizes from 48cm(19in.) to 112cm(44in.) chest for double-knit yarn on a guide size of 4mm(no. 8) needles. It can be knitted either as a jumper or with a front opening to make a cardigan or waistcoat. It can be made with no sleeves (a slipover); with short sleeves or long sleeves; and with a number of front openings (round neck, V neck or shirt neck). Further variations are possible by following the instructions given in Chapter 4 for items such as pockets, hoods and additional bands.

(b) Raglan-sleeve pattern Like the set-in sleeve pattern above, it is written in fourteen sizes for double-knit yarn. It can also be knitted either as a jumper or with a front opening as a cardigan, blouson or waistcoat. It can have long or short sleeves and a number of different neck openings: round, V neck or shirt neck. It can also be knitted as a 'yoke neck' – as traditional Fair Isle or Icelandic sweaters are often worked – where all the stitches from body and sleeves are decreased to give a circular patterned yoke. Further variations are possible for which instructions are given in Chapter 4.

(c) Dropped shoulder jacket/cardigan/blouson pattern This is written in only six sizes for 53cm(21in.) to 112cm(44in.) but in six different stitch tensions for 'chunky' type yarns. It can be made with no sleeves as a bodywarmer; or longer to be a coat, long jacket or dressing gown. It can have different openings: round neck or V neck (deep or shallow). It can be made into a sweater or smock if the fronts are knitted as one (with the same number of stitches as given for the back). Other details can be added by reference to Chapter 4, for items such as pockets, hoods, bands, ties and tassels.

CHOICES

Choosing yarn, stitch and garment shape

Chapter 1 gives you lots of advice about choosing. For patterns A and B you are limited to a double-knit-type yarn – but the stitch pattern you select may well affect the resulting tension, so you must knit a tension square in the exact yarn and stitch pattern you want to use. Chapter 5 – the stitch dictionary – gives a number of stitch patterns that can be used for the basic patterns and detailed advice about checking tensions. Chapter 3 on pattern writing gives instructions for calculating stitch multiples (see page 43) to fit the pattern. The style you choose for the garment shape is bound to be a question of practical use or appropriateness for the wearer and the wardrobe.

What size and fit to choose

The patterns are given in standard sizes from baby to adult. They are presented according to chest measurements. Patterns A and B are an average medium fit; pattern C is quite a generous fit. This means that in every case the sizes quoted are not the actual width of the garment. Before starting it is good practice to measure the person the garment is for. Use the information in Chapter 3 to help you. To assess the fit of the basic patterns you will need to measure:

chest
neck to chosen back length
neck to wrist.

To compare the person's measurements with those of the pattern you will need to work consistently in either centimetres or inches. First compare the person's chest measurement with the sizes given at the top of the instructions. Choose the size nearest for an average fit. Then calculate the size of the knitting to double-check your choice. For example, my chest measures 82cm; the nearest size on pattern B is 81cm. The tension used to calculate the number of stitches is 24 stitches over 10cm or 1cm = 2.4 stitches. For the front and back the pattern uses 108 stitches, so 216 stitches in all. Dividing by the number of stitches to the centimetre: 216 ÷ 2.4 = 86.6cm. So the actual size of the knitting will be 86.6cm, or 5.6cm($2\frac{1}{4}$in.) of ease. If you feel this is insufficient or too generous you can always try the calculation for the next sizes and see whether this seems better.

If you have difficulty in visualising this 'ease' you can hold the tape measure at the size including ease round the chest of the person and see whether it appears to be all right. (Don't forget that knitting stretches but tape measures don't!) Or else get hold of a jumper that does fit and measure it, then compare the figures with those of the pattern.

Adjusting patterns

When you have sorted out the chest fit, length is a comparatively simple matter. The patterns are written so that their length can be adjusted below the armholes. The instructions control the armhole depth which should **not** be adjusted. First see whether your chosen back length matches the one given in the pattern, then adjust the length of your knitting at point (a) in the instructions by the difference between the quoted length and what you want.

For example, on the 81cm-size pattern the back length quoted is 55cm. I want to knit a longer jumper – measuring 62cm from the back neck point, 7cm longer than the quoted length. On the pattern the length to point (a) is 35cm (giving an armhole depth of 20cm). So when I knit it I will need to make my work 7cm longer at point (a), i.e. 42cm, which will increase the total back length by 7cm. And I do the same for the front.

The neck to wrist measurement is given to help you to adjust the sleeve length. Like the armhole depth, the instructions control the shoulder width and sleeve head – and so any adjustments should be made to the sleeve-seam length in the same way as described for overall length.

Using pattern instructions and size charts

The basic patterns are presented in the form of written instructions which refer to charts that give the figures for each size:

e.g. cast on the required number of stitches (see chart)
or knit to required length (a) (see chart).

Following the charts

When you have worked out what size to knit, use a pencil to identify the chart column you will be following. Read through all the instructions before you start and make any adjustments to the required length in pencil in the chart column. This should prevent your forgetting to adjust, for example, the length given for the neck opening if you have previously adjusted the length of the armholes to (a).

SYMBOLS USED IN PATTERN INSTRUCTIONS

★ or ★★★★, etc. stars, used to denote the beginning and end of a section which will be referred to or repeated.

⬅ ADJUST HERE arrow with the reminder to adjust the length consistently throughout the garment, i.e. to make the change in the first section and then take account of those changes in the later armhole or sleeve sections.

◧ HALVE FOR CARDY Patterns A and B are written in 'jumper' form with a front similar to the back. To make a front opening the number of stitches quoted for the front should be halved throughout and the shapings worked on opposite sides to create left and right fronts. The same process is followed for a waistcoat or blouson. Pattern C is written for a front opening which overlaps slightly but may conversely be worked without by following the totals given for the back and shaping both sides for armholes, etc.

▼ SLIPOVER follow these directions for a slip-over version.

(a) Set-in sleeve pattern instructions

In written instructions read sizes as follows:
all children's (81–97cm/32–38in.: 102–112cm/40–44in.)

FRONT

Welt

Using smaller needles $3\frac{1}{4}$mm(no. 10) cast on required no. of st from size chart. ◧
Work in chosen rib for at least 4cm($1\frac{1}{2}$in.) ⬅

Main pattern

Change to larger needles, 4mm(no. 8) and chosen st patt. Knit until work measures (a) from cast-on edge (see chart). ⬅

Armhole shaping
Maintain st patt – cast off 6(8:10) st from armhole edge(s).
Then dec 1 st at armhole edge(s) every row until required no. of st remain (see chart). ◧★★
Choose neck shaping and proceed accordingly:

Round neck – neck shaping
Knit until front measures (b) from cast-on edge. ⬅
Maintain st patt – work across row and slip central 18(24:26) st onto a stitch holder. ◧
★ Then dec 1 st at neck edge each row until required no. of st remain for shoulder (see chart).
Knit until front measures (c) from cast-on edge.
▼ for slipover, allow $2\frac{1}{2}$cm(1in.) extra length here.

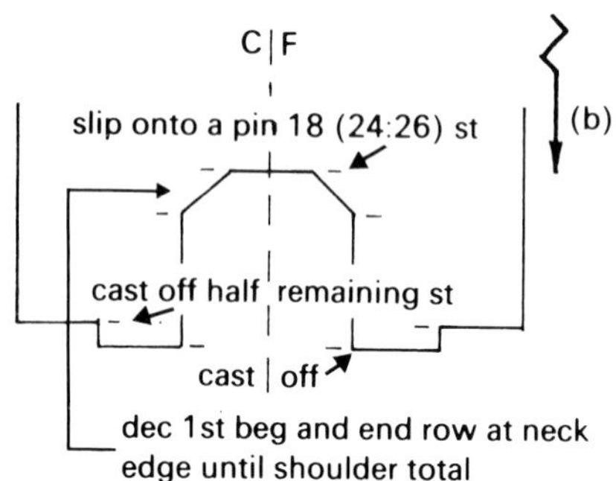

2.1 Pattern A: round neck detail (front)

Round neck – shoulder shaping
From side edge cast off half remaining st.
Finish row. Work 1 row.
Cast off remaining st.
Work opposite side to match.

V neck – neck shaping
Maintain st patt. Work across to centre. Turn work.
Dec 1 st at neck edge this and every alt row until shoulder total remains (see chart).

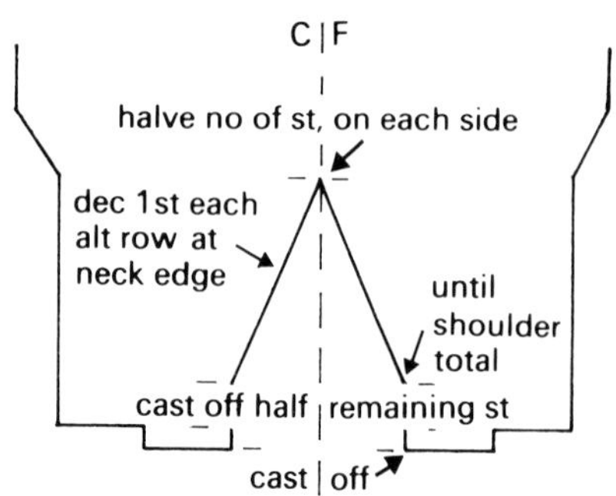

2.2 Pattern A: V neck detail (front)

Continue in patt until work measures (c) from cast-on edge.
▼ for slipover allow $2\frac{1}{2}$cm(1in.) extra length here

V neck – shoulder shaping
Work as for round neck.

Shirt neck
Maintain st patt. Work across row and slip central 6(8:8) st onto a safety pin.
On each side in turn continue in patt until work measures (b) from cast-on edge, finishing with a row ending at neck edge.
Slip 6(8:9) st from neck edge onto a safety pin.
Knit as for round neck from ★ to end.

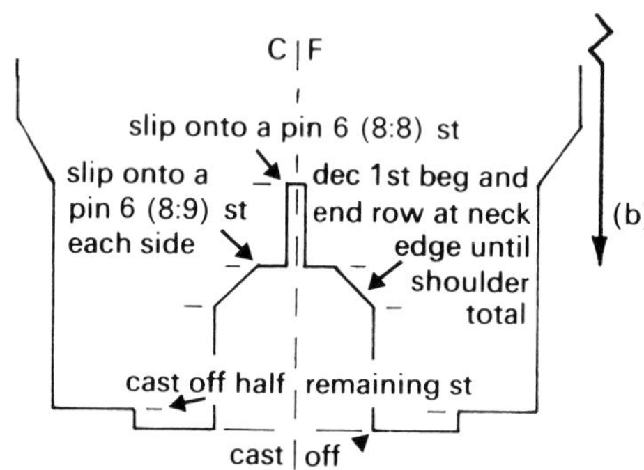

2.3 Pattern A: shirt neck detail (front)

BACK

Body
Knit as for front to ★★
Knit until back measures (c) from cast-on edge
⬅ **match front**

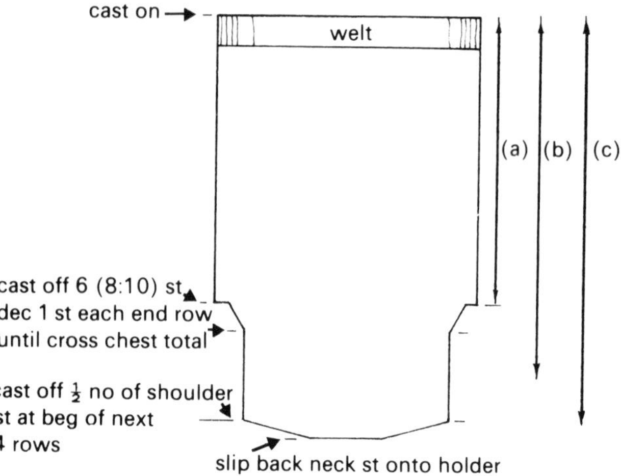

2.4 Pattern A: diagram for back

Broken cable sweater

Yarn: Sirdar 'Double crepe' double-knit
Basic pattern A, Chapter 2

Blue lace waistcoat

Yarn: Pingouin 'Corrida 4' double-knit
Basic pattern A, Chapter 2

Inset: back view of neckline

Fair Isle slipover

Yarn: Patons 'Diploma' double-knit
Basic pattern A, Chapter 2

These are examples of what can be knitted with basic pattern A. Variations of opening, length and details like hoods and fancy edge stitches can be tried. Guidance on all these is given in the book.

Shoulder shaping

Maintain st patt. Cast off half required no. of shoulder st (see chart) at beg of next 4 rows.

▼ slipover

Slip remaining st onto a stitch holder for neck.

LONG SLEEVES

Cuff welt (both alike)

Using smaller needles cast on required no. of st (see chart) and knit in chosen rib for at least 4cm($1\frac{1}{2}$in.). ⬅

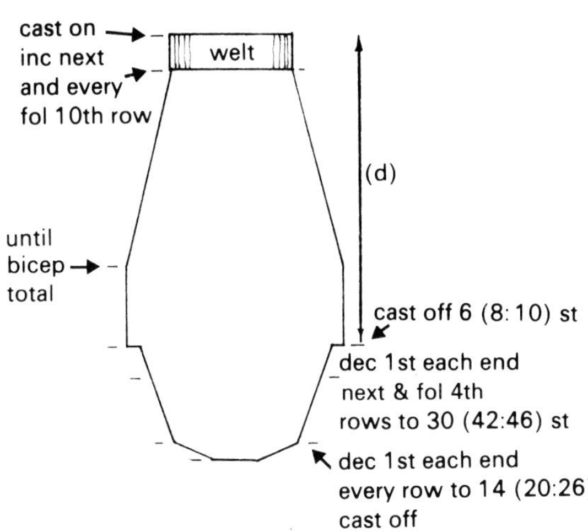

2.5 Pattern A: diagram for sleeve

Sleeve shaping

Change to larger needles and chosen st patt. Inc 1 st at each end of next and every foll 10th row until sleeve bicep total reached (see chart).
Continue until work measures required sleeve seam length (see chart). ⬅

Sleeve crown

Maintain patt. Cast off 6(8:10) st at beg of next 2 rows. Then dec 1 st each end of next and every foll 4th row until 40(52:52) st remain. Then dec 1 st each end of every row until 12(14:20) st remain. Cast off.

SHORT SLEEVES

Welt

Cast on 14(20:22) more st than for long sleeves (see chart). Work chosen rib.

Sleeve shaping

Change to larger needles and main st patt. Inc 1 st each end of next and foll 4th rows to required total. Continue in patt to desired length of sleeve seam.

Sleeve crown

Work as given for long sleeves.

BANDS

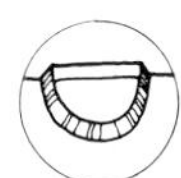

Round neck

After blocking work (see p. 75) sew up right shoulder seam with back st and press.
With RS facing, using smaller needles, pick up evenly and k required no. of st from left-side neck (see chart). k 18(24:26) st from front neck st holder. Pick up and k from right-side of neck to match left side; k st from back neck st holder. Check total with chart.
Work chosen rib for at least 3cm($1\frac{1}{4}$in.).
Cast off in rib using larger needle or suspended cast-off technique (see p. 65).

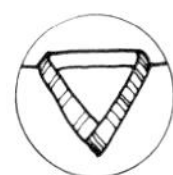

V neck

Prepare work as given for round neck.
These instructions involve no decreasing and produce an overlap at the apex of the V. To sew up, see instructions in section on overlapping V-bands (see p. 65).

Left-side band

With RS facing using smaller needles pick up evenly and k st required from left-side neck (see chart for V neck). Work in chosen rib for at least 2.5cm(1in.). Cast off in rib using larger needle or suspended method (see p. 65).

Right-side band

With RS facing using smaller needles pick up evenly and k the same no. of st as for left-side neck, then k st from back neck st holder. Check your total by adding V neck left-side to round neck back amount given on chart.
Work to match left-side band.

Sleeve or armhole band

Work chosen neckband first, then sew up together with left shoulder seam and press.
With RS facing and using smaller needles pick up evenly and k required no. of st (see chart) from front and back armholes. Work at least $2\frac{1}{2}$cm(1in.) rib. Cast off with larger needle or suspended method (see p. 65) to ensure stretch.

(a) Set-in sleeve: Adult size Chart

Chest sizes	in. 32	*cm 81*	in. 34	*cm 86*	in. 36	*cm 91*	in. 38	*cm 97*	in. 40	*cm 102*	in. 42	*cm 107*	in. 44	*cm 112*
FRONT														
Cast on – st	108		114		120		126		132		138		144	
Knit until (a) (length to armholes)	13½	*35*	14	*36*	14	*36*	14½	*37*	15	*38*	15	*38*	16	*41*
Dec to – st (across chest)	86		88		90		94		98		104		108	
Knit until (b) (length to neck)	17	*43*	17½	*44*	18	*45*	18½	*46*	19	*48*	19½	*49*	20½	*52*
Dec to – st (shoulder)	28		29		30		30		32		34		36	
BACK														
Knit until (c) (length from back neck to hips)	21½	*55*	22	*56*	22½	*57*	23	*58*	23½	*60*	24	*61*	25	*64*
SLEEVES														
Cast on – st (cuff welt)	58		60		60		62		68		70		72	
Inc to – st (sleeve width at biceps)	84		84		84		84		96		96		96	
Knit until (d) (length of sleeve seam)	17½	*45*	18	*46*	18	*46*	18	*46*	18½	*47*	18½	*47*	19	*48*
ROUND NECKBAND														
Left-side neck	28		28		28		28		30		30		30	
Back neck	30		30		30		34		34		36		36	
Total	110		110		110		114		120		122		122	
V NECKBAND														
Left-side neck	36		36		36		36		40		40		40	

VARIATIONS PHOTOGRAPHED IN COLOUR

Broken cable sweater (facing page 24)
Chest size: 86cm(34in.)
Yarn: 13 balls (40g) Sirdar 'Double crepe' double-knit, shade 260 (Medoc) (55% nylon, 45% acrylic)
Stitch pattern: 'chalice' (112 st for back and front)
Note: Pick up 99 st for collar and knit 7cm of rib on 4 double-ended needles.

Blue lace waistcoat (between pages 24/25)
Chest size: 91cm(36in.)
Yarn: 7 balls (50g) Pingouin 'Corrida 4' double-knit, shade 519 (sky blue) (60% cotton, 40% acrylic)
Stitch pattern: 'zigzag ribbons' (123 st for back and 59 st for fronts); Van Dyke edging (18 repeats)
Note: Opening can be worn at back or front. Stitches at bottom of bands decreased to follow shape of edging.

(a) Set-in sleeve: Child size Chart

Chest sizes	in. 19	cm 48	in. 20	cm 52	in. 22	cm 57	in. 24	cm 61	in. 26	cm 66	in. 28	cm 71	in. 30	cm 76
FRONT														
Cast on – st	62		70		76		80		86		92		98	
Knit until (a) (length to armholes)	$6\frac{1}{4}$	*16*	7	*18*	8	*20*	$9\frac{1}{2}$	*24*	11	*28*	12	*31*	13	*33*
Dec to – st (across to chest)	46		52		58		62		66		72		78	
Knit until (b) (length to neck)	$7\frac{1}{2}$	*19*	9	*23*	10	*26*	12	*30*	14	*36*	15	*40*	16	*42*
Dec to – st (shoulder)	13		14		18		20		20		21		24	
BACK														
Knit until (c) (length from back neck to hips)	$10\frac{1}{2}$	*27*	12	*31*	$13\frac{1}{2}$	*34*	$15\frac{1}{2}$	*39*	$17\frac{1}{2}$	*43*	19	*48*	$20\frac{1}{2}$	*52*
SLEEVES														
Cast on – st (cuff welt)	34		38		42		44		46		48		50	
Inc to – st (sleeve width at biceps)	52		52		54		56		58		62		66	
Knit until (d) (length of sleeve seam)	$5\frac{1}{4}$	*13*	$7\frac{1}{2}$	*19*	9	*23*	$10\frac{1}{2}$	*27*	$12\frac{1}{2}$	*32*	$14\frac{1}{2}$	*37*	$16\frac{1}{2}$	*42*
ROUND NECKBAND														
Left-side neck	23		25		28		28		28		28		29	
Back neck	24		24		22		22		26		30		30	
Total	88		92		96		96		100		104		106	
V NECKBAND														
Left-side neck	26		28		28		30		30		32		34	

Fair Isle slipover (between pages 24/25)
Chest size: 107cm(42in.)
Yarn: Patons 'Diploma' double-knit (50g balls) (60% wool, 40% acrylic)
Main colour: 3 × mid-brown (6714)
Contrast: 2 × cream (6750), 2 × light fawn (6718), 2 × grey (6711), 2 × Saxe blue (6725)
Stitch pattern: 'hearts and flowers' (140 st for front and back)

(b) Raglan sleeve pattern instructions

Written instructions sizes read as follows:
48-57cm(61-76cm:81-91cm:97-112cm)
19-22in.(24-30in.:33-36in.:38-44in.)

FRONT

Welt

Using smaller needles 3¼mm(no. 10), cast on the required no. of st from the size chart. ◧
Knit in chosen rib for at least 4cm(1½in.). ⬅

Main pattern

Change to larger needles, 4mm(no. 8), and chosen st patt. Knit until work measures (a) from cast-on edge (see chart). ⬅
Choose neck shaping and proceed accordingly.

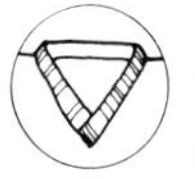

V neck – armhole and neck shaping

Maintain st patt while shaping as follows:
Mark centre of work with contrast thread.Cast off 4(6:6:8) st from side edge for armhole, work across to centre, turn work. Next row: dec 1 st at both neck and raglan edges, then dec 1 st every full alt row until 2 st remain.
Cast off. Work other side to match.

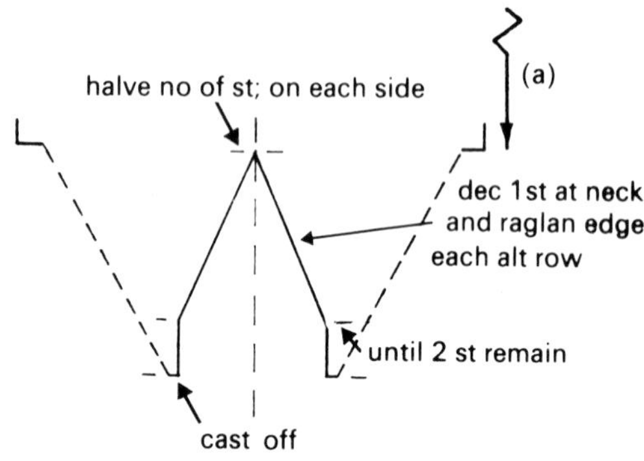

2.6 Pattern B: V neck detail (front)

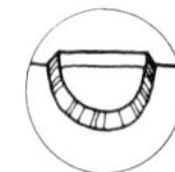

Round neck – armhole and neck shaping

Maintain st patt while shaping as follows:
Cast off 4(6:6:8) st from side edge(s) for armhole. Then dec 1 st at side edge(s) on next and foll alt rows. ★
Continue shaping in this way until front measures (b) from cast-on edge. ⬅

Round neck – neck shaping

★★ Work across row and slip central 18(24:26:30) st onto a st holder. ◧★★
Then at neck edge dec 1 st next row and foll alt rows until 7 st remain.
Continue shaping raglan only until 2 st remain.
Cast off.
Work other side to match.

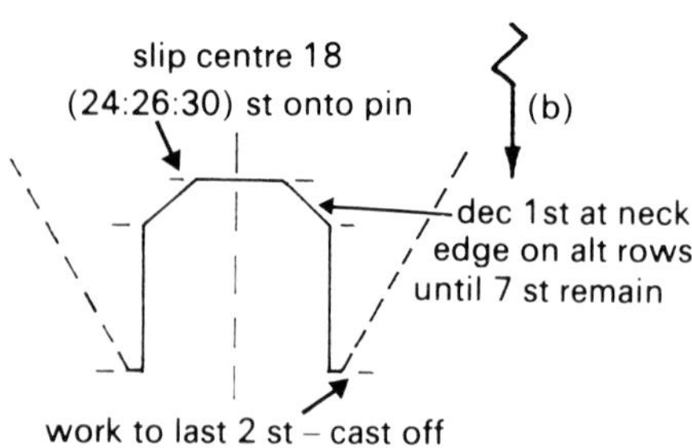

2.7 Pattern B: round neck detail (front)

Shirt neck – armhole and neck shaping

Maintain st patt while shaping as follows:
Cast off 4(6:6:8) st from side edge for armhole. Next row dec 1 st at side edge, then while working across slip central 6(6:8:8) st onto a safety pin. Shape raglan by dec 1 st on next and every foll alt row.
Follow round neck pattern from ★ BUT change instructions marked from ★★ ... to ... ★★ as follows:
Work across row and slip 6(9:9:11) st from neck edge onto a safety pin. Otherwise work as given.

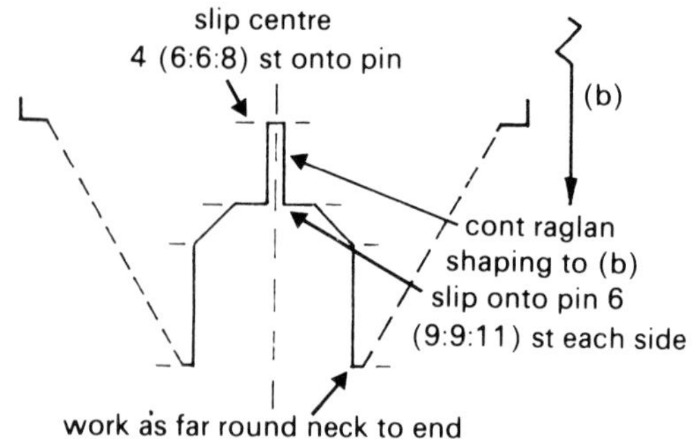

2.8 Pattern B: shirt neck detail (front)

Yoke neck

Maintain st patt while shaping as follows:
Cast off 4(6:6:8) st from side edge(s).
NB: for some children's sizes (48cm/19in. and 61cm/24in.) yoke neck starts here.

For all other sizes: dec 1 st at side edge(s) on next and foll alt row until 54(72:90:108) st remain. Slip all st onto a spare needle ★★★ until back and sleeves are completed with necessary modifications.

Yoke shaping – for jumper

1st row: with RS facing pick up and k row as follows: from left sleeve, k2tog, k to last sleeve st, ktog with first st of front, k to last front st, ktog with first st of right sleeve, k to last sleeve st, ktog with first st of back, k remaining st of back.

Yoke shaping – for cardigan

1st row: with RS facing pick up and k row as follows: start with right front, k to last front st, ktog with first st of right sleeve, k to last sleeve st, ktog with first st of back, k to last back st, ktog with first st of left sleeve, k to last sleeve st, ktog with first st of left front, k to end.

To give 180(234:288:342) st in all.

2nd-8th row foll dec as shown on graph patt, working dec by k2tog tbl, every 4 rows as indicated. Rep these 8 rows for 4(4:5:5) repeats. To give 100(130:128:152) st.

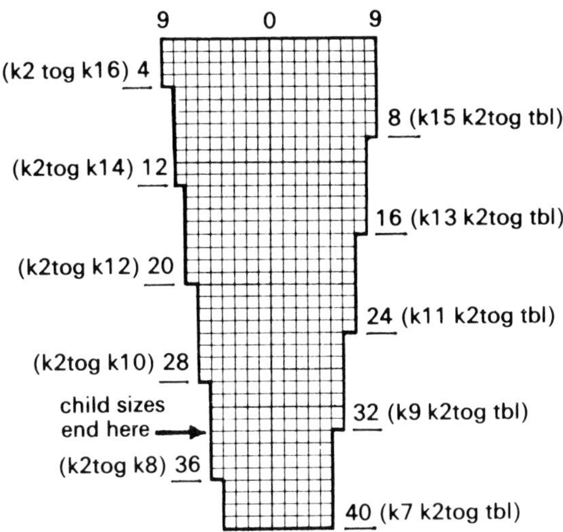

2.9 Pattern B: graph for yoke neck shaping

Neckband

Proceed for sizes as follows: working on smaller needles

48-57cm/19-22in.	– (k10,k2tog) rep to last 4 st; k4	(92 st)
61-76cm/24-30in.	– (k6, k2tog) rep to last 2 st; k2	(114 st)
81-91cm/32-36in.	– (k14,k2tog) rep to last st;	(120 st)
97-112cm/38-44in.	- (k7, k2tog) rep to last 8 st; k8	(136 st)

Work in chosen rib for at least 3cm($1\frac{1}{4}$in.).

Cast off with larger needle or suspended method (see p. 65).

BACK

Body

Follow pattern for round neck to ★

Yoke neck ONLY:

for this version work until ★★★

Raglan shaping

Maintain st patt and raglan shaping until back measures (c) from cast-on edge. ⬅

Check remaining no. of st against totals shown on chart.

Slip remaining st onto a st holder for neckband.

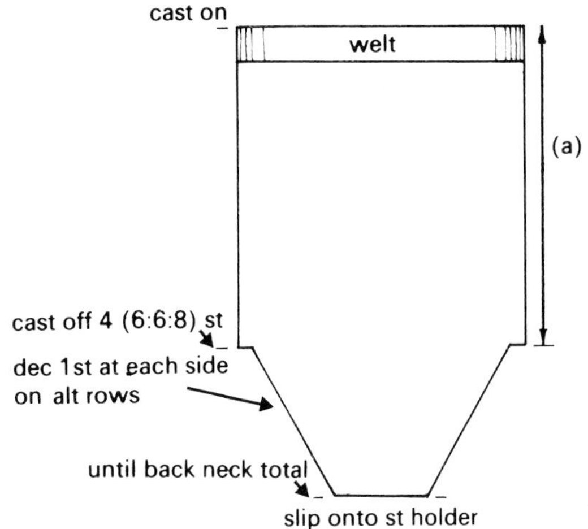

2.10 Pattern B: diagram for back

SLEEVES

Cuff welt

Using smaller needles cast on required no. of st from chart and knit in chosen rib for at least 4cm($1\frac{1}{2}$in.). ⬅

Sleeve shaping

Change to large needles and main st patt. Maintain this while inc 1 st at each end of next and foll 8th row until sleeve bicep total is reached (see chart).

Yoke neck ONLY:

These totals differ and require a single extra inc on small child and small adult sizes to give necessary total.

All

Continue until work measures (d) complete sleeve seam length (see chart). ⬅

Raglan

Maintain st patt while shaping as follows:

Cast off 4(6:6:8) st at beg of next 2 rows for armhole.

Then dec as given for front.

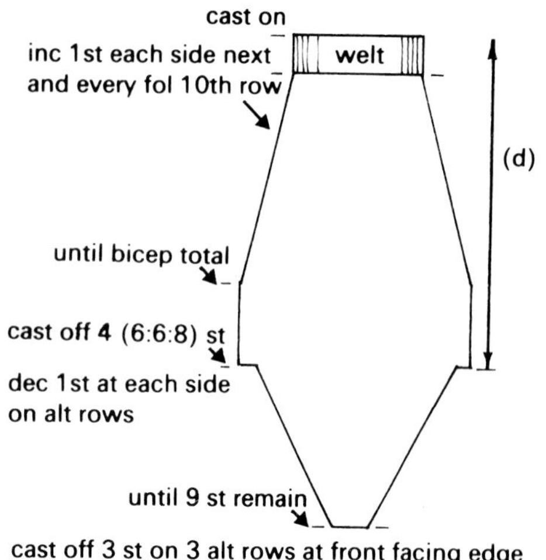

2.11 Pattern B: diagram for sleeve

Yoke neck ONLY:
Slip onto a spare needle when you have 38(47:56:65) st left.

Otherwise
Continue to dec until 9 st remain ★★★★
Next row: with RS facing cast off 3 st on this and foll alt row until 3 st remain. Cast off.
Work second sleeve to ★★★★. To get opposite shaping to sleeve crown, start with WS facing and dec as given.

BANDS

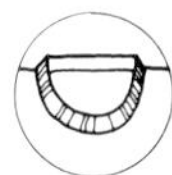

Round neck

After blocking work (see p. 75) sew up raglan, leaving seam of back to left sleeve open. Press seams. With RS facing and using smaller needles pick up evenly and k st from sleeve head and from left-side neck (see chart for no.); k18(24:26:30) st from front neck st holder; pick up and k st from right-side neck and right sleeve head to match left; k st from back neck st holder. To give total number of st required: check totals given on chart. Work in chosen rib for at least 3cm($1\frac{1}{4}$in.).
Cast off in rib using larger needle or suspended st method (see p. 65).

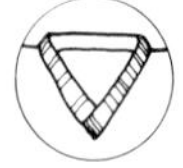

V neck

These instructions involve no dec at the apex of the V. The sides of the V overlap at the point. To finish follow instructions on p. 70.
After blocking work (see p. 75) sew up as given for round neck.

Left-side band
With RS facing using smaller needles pick up evenly and k st required from sleeve head and left-side neck (see chart). Work chosen rib for at least 2.5cm(1in.). Cast off in rib by an elastic method.

Right-side band
With RS facing using smaller needles pick up and k st from right-side neck and right sleeve head as for left side; then k st from back neck st holder. Check your total by adding V-neck left-side to round-neck, back total from chart.Work to match left-side band.

VARIATIONS PHOTOGRAPHED AND REPRODUCED IN COLOUR

Jacquard cardigan (facing page 16)
Chest size: 71cm(28in.)
Yarn: Patons 'Diploma' double-knit (50g balls) (60% wool, 40% acrylic)
Main colour: 3 × navy (6703)
Contrast: 2 × turquoise (6734), 2 × electric blue (6740), 2 × sea blue (6723), 2 × yellow (6736)
Stitch pattern: 'stars and mountains' (90 st for back)

Yoke-neck sweater (facing page 17)
Chest size: 66cm(26in.)
Yarn: 5 balls (50g) Wendy 'Shetland' double-knit, shade 393 (Mountain Dew) (100% wool – machine washable) at least 25g each of 3 colours miscellaneous double-knit
Stitch pattern: stocking stitch with 'leaf and berry' (without lattice) on yoke (11 st for leaf in first repeat, 9 st in second)
Note: I worked an extra berry between motifs on first repeat and on last row before neck rib; on cuffs alternately a single and then triple berry into every sixth stitch above the rib.

(b) Raglan sleeve: Adult size chart

Chest sizes	in. 32 / *cm 81*	in. 34 / *cm 86*	in. 36 / *cm 91*	in. 38 / *cm 97*	in. 40 / *cm 102*	in. 42 / *cm 107*	in. 44 / *cm 112*
FRONT							
Cast on – st	108	114	120	126	132	138	144
Knit until (a) (length to armholes)	13½ *35*	14 *36*	14 *36*	14½ *37*	15 *38*	15 *38*	16 *41*
Knit until (b) (length to neck)	17 *43*	17½ *44*	18 *45*	18½ *46*	19 *48*	19½ *49*	20½ *52*
BACK							
Knit until (c) (chosen length from back neck)	21½ *55*	22 *56*	22½ *57*	23 *58*	23½ *60*	24 *61*	25 *64*
Back neck – no. st held on st holder	36	36	38	40	42	44	46
SLEEVES							
Cast on – st (cuff welt)	57	59	61	63	65	67	69
Inc to – st (sleeve width at biceps)	75	81	85	89	93	97	101
Yoke neck	74	80	86	83	89	95	101
Knit until (d) (length of sleeve seam)	17½ *45*	18 *46*	18 *46*	18 *46*	18½ *47*	18½ *47*	19 *48*
ROUND NECKBAND							
Left-side neck	14	14	14	16	16	18	19
Sleevehead	9	9	9	9	9	9	9
Back neck	36	36	38	40	42	44	46
Total	108	108	110	120	122	128	132
V NECKBAND							
Left-side neck	30	32	34	37	40	43	46

(b) Raglan sleeve: Child size chart

Chest sizes	in. 19	*cm 48*	in. 20	*cm 52*	in. 22	*cm 57*	in. 24	*cm 61*	in. 26	*cm 66*	in. 28	*cm 71*	in. 30	*cm 76*
FRONT														
Cast on – st	62		70		76		80		86		92		98	
Knit until (a) (length to armholes)	$6\frac{1}{2}$	*16*	7	*18*	8	*20*	$9\frac{1}{2}$	*24*	11	*28*	12	*31*	13	*33*
Knit until (b) (length to round neck)	$7\frac{1}{2}$	*19*	9	*23*	10	*26*	12	*30*	14	*36*	15	*40*	16	*42*
BACK														
Knit until (c) (length from back neck to hips)	$10\frac{1}{2}$	*27*	12	*31*	$13\frac{1}{2}$	*34*	$15\frac{1}{2}$	*39*	$17\frac{1}{2}$	*43*	19	*48*	$20\frac{1}{2}$	*52*
Back neck – no. of st held on holder	18		22		24		26		28		30		32	
SLEEVES														
Cast on – st (cuff welt)	35		37		41		43		47		51		55	
Inc to – st (sleeve width at biceps)	49		51		55		59		61		65		71	
Yoke neck	46		54		62		55		61		63		69	
Knit until (d) (length of sleeve seam)	6	*13*	$7\frac{1}{2}$	*19*	9	*23*	$10\frac{1}{2}$	*27*	$12\frac{1}{2}$	*32*	$14\frac{1}{2}$	*31*	$16\frac{1}{2}$	*42*
–] Neck to wrist														
ROUND NECKBAND														
Left-side neck	14		14		15		14		14		15		15	
Sleevehead	8		8		8		8		8		8		8	
Back neck	18		22		24		26		28		30		32	
Total	80		82		86		94		96		100		102	
V NECKBAND														
Left-side neck	18		20		22		24		27		30		34	

These sketches show possible variations using basic pattern B. The instructions allow for opening and neck changes but also for working the shaping all at once as a yoke (see photograph facing p. 17).

Diamond cardigan

Yarn: miscellaneous balls of brushed mohair
Basic pattern C, Chapter 2

Reversible jacket

Yarn: Wendy 'Shetland' chunky
Basic pattern C, Chapter 2

Inset: reverse side of jacket

Basic pattern C can be worked not only as a jacket but also lengthened to form a coat or dressing gown or worked without sleeves as a body warmer. It knits up quickly in 'chunky' type yarns.

(c) Jacket pattern instructions

These instructions are general to the six given sizes and may be knitted in a variety of tensions – all of which apply to 'chunky' weight yarns. There are 6 different tensions given: 13, 14, 15, 16, 17, 18 st over 10cm(4in.). In order to follow the instructions for the size you want and the tension you wish to knit to, some simple calculations will need doing. For example, on the back (the first piece to knit) you will have to increase 1 st each side a number of times, over 7(10:14) rows to give the required total. You must decide which rows to make the increases on. If you are knitting chest 71-76cm(28in.-30in.) with a tension of 16 st this is easy, because you have 10 rows to inc 20 st – that is, 2 st each row. But if you are knitting the same size but with a tension of 14 st you will need to inc 14 st over 10 rows. As the st should be evenly inc at each side this means 7 st over 10 rows, which you can work out on a piece of graph paper. As you can see this gives a slight curve to the shaping.

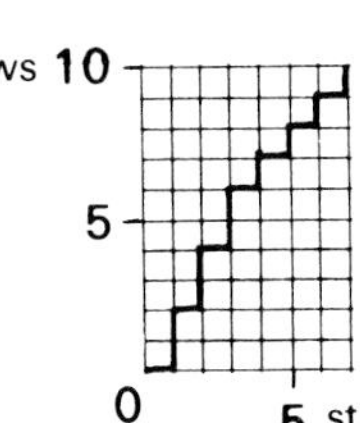

2.12 Using the graph to plan a decrease of 7 st over 10 rows; the graph shows 1st inc each end of rows 1,3,5,7,8,9,10.

To help you to do these calculations, included in the instructions are blank graphs for you to draw on (using pencil – so you can change your mind) to show what you will do about inc or dec for the size and tension you are knitting.

Adjust body length as required. The jacket back length measurements given on the chart are only intended as a guide. To adjust the sleeves, check by measuring the person with arms down – from base of neck at shoulder to wrist bone. This measurement is given on the chart as shoulder + arm. Add to or subtract from this amount to give you what you want. Do bear in mind that with larger sizes and a heavy weight of yarn the knitting will stretch over the shoulder and so it is worth measuring the length of your knitting as it hangs from the needle – rather than flat.

BACK

Welt

Using smaller size of needles 5mm(no. 6), cast on required no. of st (see chart) and knit chosen rib for at least 2cm($\frac{3}{4}$in.). ★★ 🡄

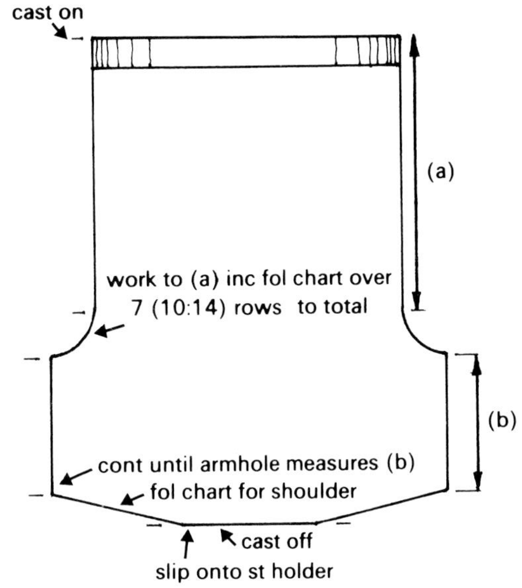

2.13 Pattern C: diagram for back

Sizes charted:					
53-59cm	61-66cm	71-76cm	81-89cm	92-99cm	102-112cm
(21-23in.)	(24-26in.)	(28-30in.)	(32-35in.)	(36-39in.)	(40-44in.)

Tensions:

13 st × 17 rows	14 st × 17 rows	15 st × 17 rows
16 st × 18 rows	17 st × 18 rows	18 st × 18 rows

In the written instructions brackets are used for the sizes as follows:

53-59cm and 61-66cm (71-76cm and 81-89cm:92-99cm and 102-112cm)
21-23in. and 24-26in. (28-30in. and 33-35in.:36-39in. and 40-44in.)

Main pattern
Change to larger needles 6mm(no. 4) and chosen st patt. Knit until work measures (a) from cast-on edge for jacket (see chart). ⬅

Armhole shaping
Maintain st pattern. Make inc as needed over next 7(10:14) rows. Use graph to calculate:
Inc 1 st each end rows =

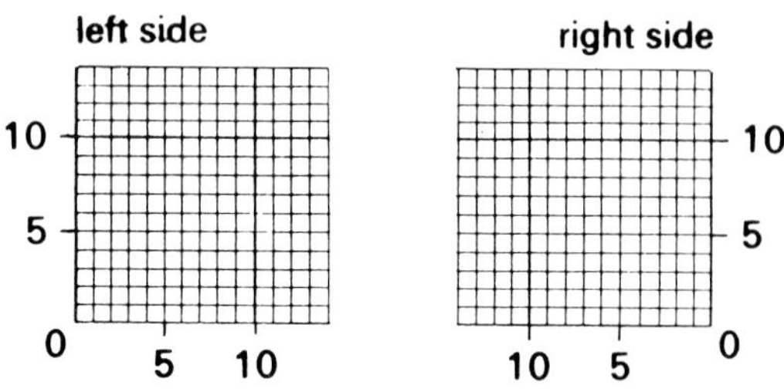

2.14 Pattern C: graph for planning armhole increases

Armhole
Maintain st patt and work until armhole measures required amount from end of shaping (b) (see chart).

Shoulder shaping
Maintain st patt while casting off given no. of st over the next few rows as stated on chart. The approx back length is given (without adjustments).
Slip remaining st onto a st holder for back neck.

FRONTS

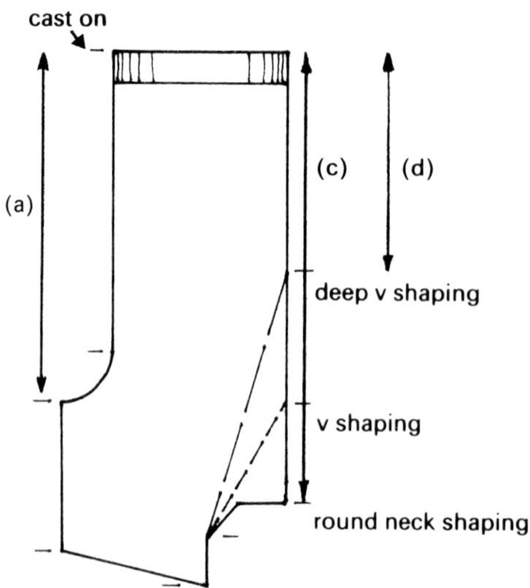

2.15 Pattern C: diagram for front

Welt
Using smaller needles cast on required no. of st (see chart) and knit welt as for back.

Main pattern
Change to larger needles and work main patt until front measures (d) for deep V neck (see ★★★) or same as back (a).

Armhole shaping
Maintain st patt and make inc according to your graph above, at side edge only, to give required no. of st (see chart). ★
Choose neck style and proceed accordingly:

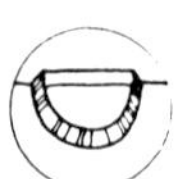

Round neck
Work until front measures (c) from cast-on edge. Maintain st patt while shaping as follows. At neck edge slip required no. of st onto st holder. Work to end row.
Next and following 4 rows, dec 1 st at neck edge each row. To check your total add the no. of st on st holder + 5 and take away from the number of st you had after inc for armhole.

Total st after armhole inc is ....

st holder .... + 5 ....

no. on your needle = ______

Round neck – shoulder edge
Follow instructions for back BUT cast off on alt rows at shoulder edge only.

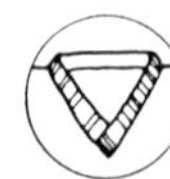

Deep V neck
When work measures (d) from cast-on edge proceed as follows: ★★★
Use the graph to plan how to make the dec for your size and tension. The chart gives the no. of rows over which to make the dec. Work the dec on the neck edge only and continue while shaping the armhole from when the work measures (a) or the same as back, as follows:

Deep V neck – armhole shaping
At side edge inc as planned for back to give the total on chart – less any dec for neck shaping.
Continue shaping at neck edge – following your chart to end. Then work should measure (b) from end of armhole inc.

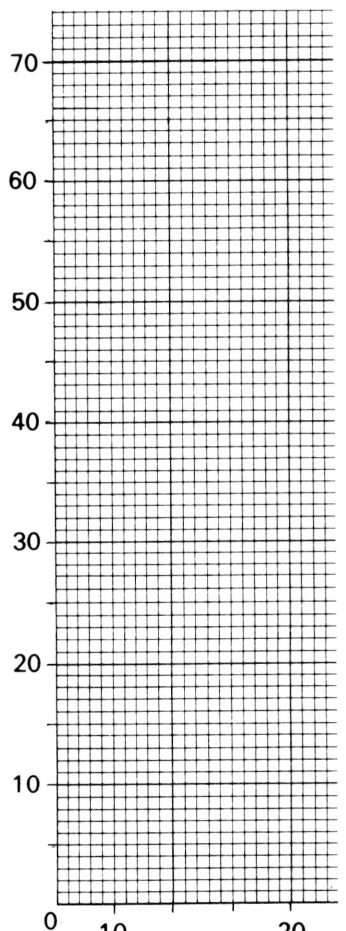

2.16 Pattern C: graph for planning deep V-neck shaping

Deep V neck – shoulder shaping
Follow inst given for round neck.

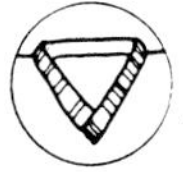

V neck
From ★ use the above graph to plan your shaping over the required no. of rows for your size and tension. Make your dec at neck edge only. Check when you have finished dec that your total equals the no. of st you had when armhole inc ended, less the no. you had to dec for neck: i.e.

Total st after armhole inc	....
no. dec for neck	minus ....
no. on your needle	= ______

V neck – shoulder shaping
Follow inst given for round neck.

SLEEVES

Cuff welt
Cast on with smaller needles no. of st required (see chart). Knit in chosen rib for at least 2½cm(1in.) ⬅

Main pattern
Change to larger needles and main st patt. Shape by inc 1 st each end of next and foll required no. of rows – see chart.To give required total no. of st (see chart). Work till sleeve measures (e) from cast-on edge. ⬅

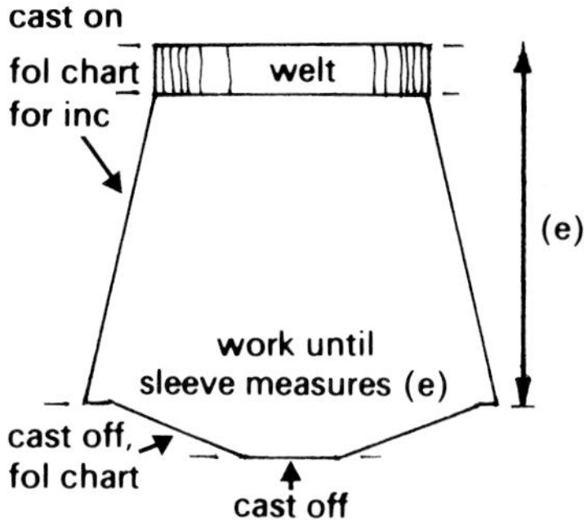

2.17 Pattern C: diagram for sleeve

Sleeve crown
Maintain st patt while casting off required no. of st over next appropriate no. of rows – see chart.Cast off remaining st.

VARIATIONS PHOTOGRAPHED IN COLOUR

Diamond cardigan (between pages 32/33)
Chest size: 61–66cm(24–26in.)
Tension: 10cm square = 18 st × 18 rows, 7mm needles
Yarn: 14 miscellaneous 25g balls of brushed mohair (e.g. Sirdar 'Nocturne')
Stitch pattern: jacquard version of 'pyramids' (64 st for back)

Reversible jacket (between pages 32/33)
Chest size: 92–99cm(36–39in.)
Tension: 10cm square = 18 st on 6mm needles
Yarn: 26 balls (50g) Wendy 'Shetland' chunky, shade 360 (Wood Bracken) (100% wool – machine washable)
Stitch pattern: 'castellations' (105 st on back, 57 st on front)
Note: For neck and front bands, I worked a rib, doubled it over and back-stitched it down so that the jacket could be reversible.

(c) Jacket: Size chart

Tension 10cm = 18 st × 18 rows

Chest sizes	in. 21/23 *cm 53-59*	in. 24/26 *cm 61-66*	in. 28/30 *cm 71-76*	in. 32/35 *cm 81-89*	in. 36/39 *cm 92-99*	in 40/44 *cm 102-112*
BACK						
Cast on – st	60	66	76	94	104	116
Knit until (a) (Jacket) length to armhole shaping	6½ *16*	8½ *22*	12 *31*	13½ *34*	14 *35*	15 *38*
Inc – st over 7 rows/total st	14/74	14/80				
Inc – st over 10 rows/total st			22/98	22/116		
Inc – st over 14 rows/total st					28/132	28/144
Knit until armhole measures (b) from end of inc	6½ *17*	7 *18*	7½ *19*	8 *20*	8½ *21*	9 *23*
For shoulders cast off – st	11	8	8	10	8	10
beg next – rows	4	6	8	8	12	10
To leave at back neck – st	30	32	34	36	36	44
Back length overall (jacket)	15¾ *40*	19 *48*	21½ *55*	25½ *65*	27½ *70*	29½ *75*
FRONT						
Cast on – st	32	36	40	50	56	62
Inc – st over 7 rows/total st	7/39	7/43				
Inc – st over 10 rows/total st			11/51	11/61		
Inc – st over 14 rows/total st					14/70	14/76
ROUND NECK						
Starts (c) (length from cast-on edge)	12½ *32*	15¾ *40*	18 *46*	22 *56*	23½ *60*	25½ *65*
Slip onto st holder	12	12	15	15	16	16
V NECK						
Starts end armhole inc Dec – st/over – rows	17/28	17/28	21/34	21/34	24/38	24/38
DEEP V NECK						
Starts (d) (length from cast-on edge)	5½ *14*	8½ *22*	8½ *22*	12½ *32*	13 *33*	15 *38*
Dec – st/over – rows	17/38	17/38	21/66	21/66	24/74	24/74
SLEEVES						
Cast on – st (cuff welt)	32	36	40	44	48	50
Inc 1 st each end of foll – row	4	5	5	6	5	5
To give – st	56	60	64	68	76	80
Knit-until (e) (length of sleeve seam)	12 *30*	14 *35*	16½ *42*	17¼ *44*	17¼ *44*	17¼ *44*
Sleevehead cast off – st	7	7	6	6	6	6
at beg of next – rows	7	7	9	9	11	11
Cast off remaining st	7	11	10	14	10	14
(shoulder + arm) CB Neck to wrist	21 *53*	24½ *62*	28¾ *73*	32¼ *82*	33½ *85*	34¼ *87*

Tension 10cm = 17 st × 18 rows

in. 21/23 *cm* *53-59*	in. 24/26 *cm* *61-66*	in. 28/30 *cm* *71-76*	in. 32/35 *cm* *81-89*	in. 36/39 *cm* *92-99*	in. 40/44 *cm* *102-112*
56 6½ *16* 14/70 6½ *17* 7 6 28 15¾ *40*	64 8½ *22* 14/78 7 *18* 8 6 30 19 *48*	74 12 *31* 20/94 7½ *19* 10 6 34 21½ *55*	90 13½ *34* 20/110 8 *20* 12 6 38 25½ *65*	100 14 *35* 26/126 8½ *21* 11 8 38 27½ *70*	110 15 *38* 28/138 9 *23* 12 8 42 29½ *75*
30 7/37	34 7/41	39 10/49	47 10/57	52 13/65	57 14/71
12½ *32* 11	15¾ *40* 11	18 *46* 14	22 *56* 14	23½ *60* 15	25½ *65* 15
16/28	16/28	19/34	19/34	21/38	21/38
5½ *14* 16/38	8½ *22* 16/42	8½ *22* 19/66	12½ *32* 19/70	13 *33* 21/74	15 *38* 21/74
30 4 54 12 *30* 7 7 5 21 *53*	34 4 60 14 *35* 7 7 11 24½ *62*	38 4 62 16½ *42* 6 9 8 28¾ *73*	40 5 64 17¼ *44* 6 9 10 32¼ *82*	44 5 70 17¼ *44* 6 11 4 33½ *85*	48 5 64 17¼ *44* 6 11 8 34¼ *87*

Tension 10cm = 16st × 17 rows

in. 21/23 *cm* *55-59*	in. 24/26 *cm* *61-66*	in. 28/30 *cm* *71-76*	in. 32/35 *cm* *81-89*	in. 36/39 *cm* *92-99*	in. 40/44 *cm* *102-112*
52 6½ *16* 12/64 6½ *17* 10 4 24 15¾ *40*	58 8½ *22* 12/70 7 *18* 11 4 26 19 *48*	68 12 *31* 20/88 7½ *19* 10 6 28 21½ *55*	82 13½ *34* 20/92 8 *20* 8 8 28 25½ *65*	92 14 *35* 26/118 8½ *21* 14 6 34 27½ *70*	104 15 *38* 26/130 9 *23* 12 8 34 29½ *75*
28 6/34	32 6/38	36 10/46	44 10/54	48 13/61	54 13/67
12½ *32* 10	15¾ *40* 10	18 *46* 12	22 *56* 12	23½ *60* 15	25½ *65* 15
15/26	15/26	18/32	18/32	20/36	20/36
5½ *14* 15/30	8½ *22* 15/32	8½ *22* 18/46	12½ *32* 18/48	13 *33* 20/52	15 *38* 20/52
28 4 50 12 *30* 6 7 8 21 *53*	32 5 54 14 *35* 6 7 12 24½ *62*	34 6 56 16½ *42* 5 9 11 28¾ *73*	38 6 60 17¼ *44* 6 9 6 32¼ *82*	42 5 66 17¼ *44* 6 9 12 33½ *85*	44 5 70 17¼ *44* 7 9 7 34¼ *87*

(c) Jacket: Size chart   Tension 10cm = 15 st × 17 rows

Chest sizes	in. 21/23 *cm 53-59*	in. 24/26 *cm 61-66*	in. 28/30 *cm 71-76*	in. 32/35 *cm 81-89*	in. 36/39 *cm 92-99*	in 40/44 *cm 102-112*
BACK						
Cast on – st	48	54	64	78	86	98
Knit until (a) (Jacket) length to armhole shaping	6½ *16*	8½ *22*	12 *31*	13½ *34*	14 *35*	15 *38*
Inc – st over 7 rows/total st	10/58	12/66				
Inc – st over 10 rows/total st			14/78	18/96		
Inc – st over 14 rows/total st					24/110	20/118
Knit until armhole measurers (b) from end of inc	6½ *17*	7 *18*	7½ *19*	8 *20*	8½ *21*	9 *23*
For shoulders cast – st	8	10	8	8	10	14
beg next – rows	4	4	6	8	8	6
To leave at back neck – st	26	26	30	32	30	34
Back length overall (jacket)	15¾ *40*	19 *48*	21½ *55*	25½ *65*	27½ *70*	29½ *75*
FRONTS						
Cast on – st	26	30	34	42	46	52
Inc – st over 7 rows/total st	6/32	6/36				
Inc – st over 10 rows/total st			9/43	9/53		
Inc – st over 14 rows/total st					12/58	12/64
ROUND NECK						
Starts (c) (length from cast-on edge)	12½ *32*	15¾ *40*	18 *46*	22 *56*	23½ *60*	25½ *65*
Slip onto st holder	9	9	13	13	15	15
V NECK						
Starts end armhole inc Dec – st/over – rows	14/26	14/26	17/32	17/32	18/36	18/36
DEEP V NECK						
Starts (d) (length from cast-on edge)	5½ *14*	8½ *22*	8½ *22*	12½ *32*	13 *33*	15 *38*
Dec – st/over – rows	14/30	14/32	17/46	17/48	18/52	18/52
SLEEVES						
Cast on – st (cuff welt)	26	30	32	36	38	42
Inc 1 st each end of foll – row	5	5	6	6	5	5
To give – st	46	50	52	56	62	66
Knit until (e) (length of sleeve seam)	12 *30*	14 *35*	16½ *42*	17¼ *44*	17¼ *44*	17¼ *44*
Sleevehead cast off – st	6	6	6	5	6	6
at beg of next – rows	7	7	7	9	9	9
Cast off remaining st	4	8	10	2	8	12
(shoulder + arm) CB Neck to wrist	21 *53*	24½ *62*	28¾ *73*	32¼ *82*	33½ *85*	34¼ *87*

Tension 10cm = 14 st × 17 rows

in. 21/23 *cm 53-59*	in. 24/26 *cm 61-66*	in. 28/30 *cm 71-76*	in. 32/35 *cm 81-89*	in. 36/39 *cm 92-99*	in. 40/44 *cm 102-112*
46	52	60	72	82	92
6½ *16*	8½ *22*	12 *31*	13½ *34*	14 *35*	15 *38*
10/56	12/64				
		14/74	18/90		
				22/104	22/114
6½ *17*	7 *18*	7½ *19*	8 *20*	8½ *21*	9 *23*
8	10	12	8	12	14
4	4	4	8	6	6
24	24	26	26	32	30
15¾ *40*	19 *48*	21½ *55*	25½ *65*	27½ *70*	29½ *75*
25	28	32	38	43	48
6/31	6/34				
		9/41	9/47		
				11/54	11/59
12½ *32*	15¾ *40*	18 *46*	22 *56*	23½ *60*	25½ *65*
9	9	12	12	13	13
13/26	13/26	16/32	16/32	17/36	17/36
5½ *14*	8½ *22*	8½ *22*	12½ *32*	13 *33*	15 *38*
13/30	13/32	16/46	16/48	17/52	17/52
26	28	30	34	36	38
5	6	7	7	6	6
44	46	50	54	58	62
12 *30*	14 *35*	16½ *42*	17¼ *44*	17¼ *44*	17¼ *44*
5	6	6	5	6	6
7	7	7	9	9	9
9	4	8	9	4	9
21 *53*	24½ *62*	28¾ *73*	32¼ *82*	33½ *85*	34¼ *87*

Tension 10cm = 13 st × 17 rows

in. 21/23 *cm 53-59*	in. 24/26 *cm 61-66*	in. 28/30 *cm 71-76*	in. 32/35 *cm 81-89*	in. 36/39 *cm 92-99*	in. 40/44 *cm 102-112*
42	48	56	68	76	84
6½ *16*	8½ *22*	12 *31*	13½ *34*	14 *36*	15 *38*
10/52	10/58				
		16/72	16/84		
				20/96	20/104
6½ *17*	7 *18*	7½ *19*	8 *20*	8½ *21*	9 *23*
8	9	8	10	12	10
4	6	6	6	6	8
20	22	24	24	24	24
15¾ *40*	19 *48*	21½ *55*	25½ *65*	27½ *70*	29½ *75*
23	26	30	36	40	44
5/28	5/31				
		8/38	8/44		
				10/50	10/54
12½ *32*	15¾ *40*	18 *46*	22 *56*	23½ *60*	25½ *65*
8	8	11	11	12	12
12/26	12/26	15/32	15/32	16/36	16/36
5½ *14*	8½ *22*	8½ *22*	12½ *32*	13 *33*	15 *38*
12/30	12/32	15/46	15/48	16/52	16/52
24	26	28	32	34	36
5	6	7	7	7	6
42	44	46	50	54	58
12 *30*	14 *35*	16½ *42*	17¼ *44*	17¼ *44*	17¼ *44*
5	5	6	5	5	6
7	7	7	9	9	9
7	9	4	5	9	4
21 *53*	24½ *62*	28¾ *73*	32¼ *82*	33½ *85*	34¼ *87*

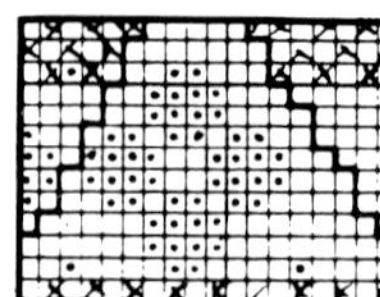

3
Pattern writing

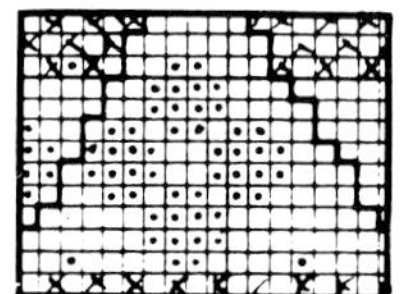

Introduction

Writing patterns seems like a very complex process - all those 'k1, p2tog to end of row ... cont in this way till work measures 60cm from cast-on edge', and so on. They don't need to be so detailed, as you may know if you have ever seen or used any French knitting patterns, such as those produced by Elle magazine or the Pingouin yarn company. British patterns have always been more detailed and it is difficult to move away from this amount of information when the consumer has come to expect it. The prospect of writing instructions in such detail seems rather off-putting and is really not necessary. I think all one needs is a diagram with added written notes about shaping, of the sort given for each of the basic patterns in Chapter 2 (see p. 24). What the diagram looks like is determined by the shape of garment you have designed and what size it will need to be to fit the person you are making it for.

There are several different ways to work out this relationship of fit to style or shape. Some are easier than others. In this Chapter I give accounts of a number of different possibilities. They are, in order of increasing difficulty:

A a simple example of garment design based on a series of squares and rectangles whose sizes are related to basic body measurements; with a number of other ideas for garments based on the same shapes – none of which requires any shaping during knitting;

B a pattern taken from an existing garment, in this case a jersey fabric child's dress, then converted into a knitting pattern;

C a pattern based on a dressmaker's flat pattern;

D a more complex piece of pattern drafting for a classic raglan garment working from basic body measurements; with the body measurement formula needed for set-in sleeve and dropped shoulder styles;

E a picture jacket whose shape was determined by the size of the motifs used to decorate it;

F a design inspired by the nature of a yarn and stitch combination, and developed through a series of sketches.

Each of the patterns is given in sufficient detail for you to be able to use it to knit any of the garments illustrated – if you happen to want to make it in the sizes given. (If you want a different size you can try altering the pattern!) The aim of presenting the patterns in this way is to de-mystify the process of pattern writing. By studying the pattern description of the method you want to try, I hope you will be able to apply it and so write a similar one for yourself. The descriptions are given in general terms, step by step. The calculations I have used for rows and stitches are given as examples to illustrate the principles.

As well as these detailed accounts there are instructions for measuring the body – the starting point for any piece of knitting; details of how to fit stitch patterns with a particular multiple of stitches to written instructions for a specified number of stitches; and also instructions for calculating how much yarn you may need for your ideas.

HOW TO MEASURE

Use a tape measure and keep to one unit of measurement – do not mix centimetres and inches or you will get confused. Use the blank tables on p. 42 to fill in and record them as you go. If you are measuring yourself you will need help with some parts of the body. It is best to measure people standing in a relaxed position, not stiff and 'to attention'. Keep a record of measurements over underclothes and then amend these if you are making an outer garment by measuring over the clothes that would be worn underneath it. This will give you a better starting point for adding 'ease' (see next section p. 43).

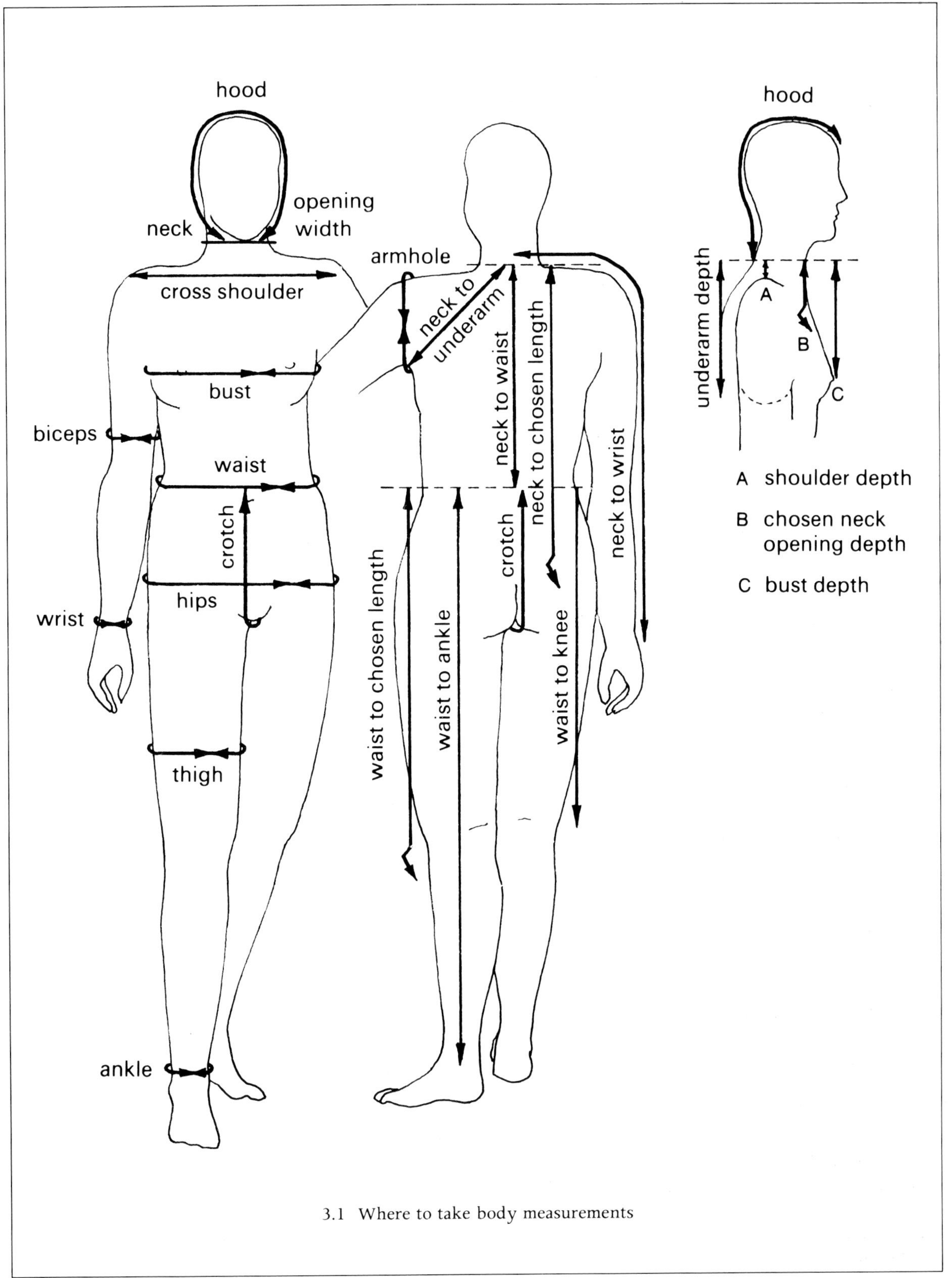

3.1 Where to take body measurements

MEASURING TABLE TO FILL IN AND KEEP

		Name	Name	Name	Name
FRONT-VIEW DRAWING	chest/bust waist hips hood *neck opening cross shoulder biceps wrist hip depth thigh ankle crotch (measure from waistline at front between legs and up to waistline at back)				
BACK-VIEW DRAWING	neck to wrist neck to underarm neck to waist waist to ankle waist to knee armhole shoulder depth (to give slope) *neck to chosen length *waist to chosen length				
SIDE-VIEW DRAWING	bust depth underarm depth (from neck point) *neck depth shoulder depth				

EASE ALLOWANCES

This is the term used to describe an amount that is added (or sometimes subtracted for very tight-fitting styles) to give the garment the desired fit and to allow the body to move comfortably in it. For those familiar with pattern cutting the allowance is not such a critical part of pattern drafting for knitted fabric as it is for woven cloth, as most knitted fabrics stretch. The figures given in the table opposite are intended as a guide and should be added or subtracted from half the measurement for the appropriate part of the body (e.g. $\frac{1}{2}$ chest + ease).

In order to decide how much ease to allow you need to know how loose or tight you want the garment and also whether your chosen knitted fabric

TABLE OF EASE GUIDELINES

	SIZES		FIT		
	in.	*cm*	tight	medium	baggy
CHEST AND HIPS	19–30	*48–76*	up to −2%	0 to 3%	4 to 6% or more
	32–38	*81–97*	up to −4%	4 to 8%	6 to 10% or more
	40–44	*102–112*	up to −4%	5 to 10%	8 to 12% or more
ARMHOLE, BICEPS AND WRIST	19–30	*48–76*	up to −1%	2 to 6%	10% or more
THIGH AND ANKLE	32–38	*81–97*	up to −2%	6 to 12%	20% or more
	40–44	*102–112*	up to −3%	10 to 20%	30% or more

will stretch. Check that your tension sample does stretch across the direction that will be used round the chest and elbow. If it does not you will have to allow for this in your ease calculation. In some cases the so-called ease allowance is a function of the design and not associated with fit. But it is wise to check the pattern to make sure the body will fit into it. For example, always check that the neck to underarm measurement can be accommodated; check that if the garment is longer than the waistline it will actually fit comfortably over the hips; that if the neck opening is small the circumference is not smaller than the person's measurements at the base of the neck – if the neck opening is as tight as this you will almost certainly have to include some kind of fastening, as the head is unlikely to pass through without it.

If you are not sure about how much ease to allow it is a good idea to try comparing the measurements of existing garments with those of the person they fit. This will help you to visualise the relative effect of allowances of, say, plus 2% or plus 10%.

Example of calculating a percentage ease allowance

Taking the information from the ease guide table for a garment of average fit on a chest size of 85cm (32in.) an ease allowance of 4% to 8% is recommended. If I choose to add 5%, the figure for ½chest + 5% is calculated thus:

cm	in.
½ of 85cm is 42.5	½ of 32in. is 16
1% of 85 is .85	1% of 32 is .32
so 5% is 5 × .85 = 4.25	so 5% is 5 × .32 = 1.6
added to ½bust = 46.75	added to ½chest = 17.6
so work to 47cm	so work to 17½in

FITTING STITCH PATTERNS TO A SPECIFIED NUMBER OF STITCHES

Most stitch patterns are worked over a particular number of stitches. This means that when you are planning to use one you will need to work out how to repeat it. The simplest method is to plan to knit with a number of stitches that is exactly divisible by the number needed for a repeat of the pattern. For example, double moss stitch is worked over 4 st (row 1: k2, p2 repeated to end row; row 2: p the k st and k the p st; the rows may be doubled to give a 4-row repeat). For a garment using this stitch it is easiest to be knitting with a multiple of 4 st – say 48 st – which divided by 4 gives 12 repeats. If at all possible see whether you can slightly adjust the number of stitches you need for the piece in order to achieve this. As a general rule do not adjust the total number of stitches round the chest by more than 3cm(1¼in.) either larger or smaller than your original measurements or you will alter the fit. Using the above example again: for the front of a child's jumper

36cm(14in.) were needed for the chosen size, worked with a tension of 24 st over 10cm(4 in.) – this gave a total of 86 st. In order to get a total that was divisible by 4 the pattern was written with 88 st for the front and back – the extra four stitches giving an additional 1.5cm($\frac{5}{8}$in.) round the chest. This method of adjustment works best for patterns with a relatively small number of stitches in the repeat.

For larger stitch patterns

If it is not possible to adjust the total so that it can be divided evenly an alternative is to see whether one part of the garment can be knitted with an even number of repeats. If this is the case start by knitting this section until you are familiar with the stitch pattern and feel confident enough to try knitting it over the additional stitches. Another thing to try – if the styling permits – is to start a section of the garment with an even number of repeats and then gradually increase to the required number of stitches.

Stitch pattern repeats on Aran patterns

Aran style patterns are traditionally worked with a side or edge panel of moss or trinity stitch so that this can be shaped easily without affecting the central cable, trellis or bobble patterns. For raglan-style garments this is not possible and shaping will involve half cables and the like.

Stitch pattern repeats on jacquard or Fair Isle work

These can be easily adjusted either by the above method of altering the number of stitches or by indicating the row start and finish on the stitch pattern grid.

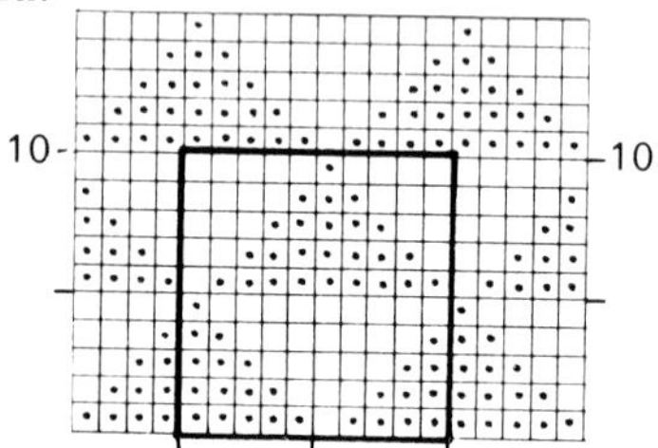

3.2 On this grid the start and finish points are shown with a heavy vertical line (see p. 79, working from grids).

Calculating amounts of yarn

There is no sure way of working out in advance exactly how much yarn you will need. This is difficult for a number of reasons. Yarn is sold in standard-weight balls, hanks or cones, most commonly weighing 25g, 50g or 100g.

Each quality, not only thickness and fibre type but brand and even dye colour within a range will vary in the length you will get for a given weight. (Dark colours retain more dye and so have a shorter length-to-weight ratio than pale colours.) So it is important that your calculations are based on the exact colour and type you intend to use.

So that you can be sure of obtaining enough yarn from the same dye lot it is worth either buying too much and returning unused balls later or asking the shop to reserve a quantity, if you are a quick knitter, while you make your calculations. If you can, the best thing to do is to knit the whole back of the garment keeping a record of how much yarn it takes. On the basis of this you can estimate fairly accurately how much more will be needed for the remaining sections. If you cannot do this, then knit up a complete ball and calculate from this. It is worth bearing in mind that you use more yarn on a k1, p1 type rib than on most stitch patterns. Measure the section you have been able to knit and work out how many square cm(in.) it has produced. Then, ignoring shaping and treating the remaining sections as rectangles add up how many square cm (in.) for the whole garment. By dividing your total by the first ball amount, you will get an approximate amount for the whole.

Example

This pattern is described in detail on p. 46. The total for the body is 100 x 50 = 5000 sq cm; the

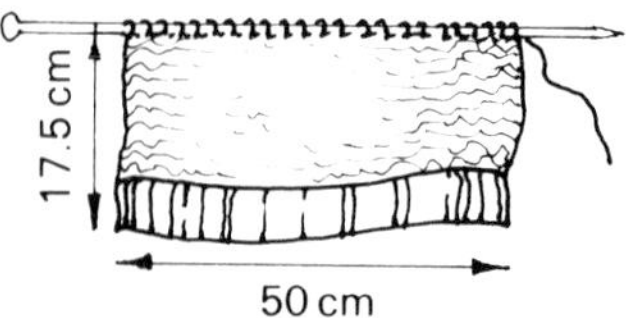

3.3a What was knitted from the first ball of yarn

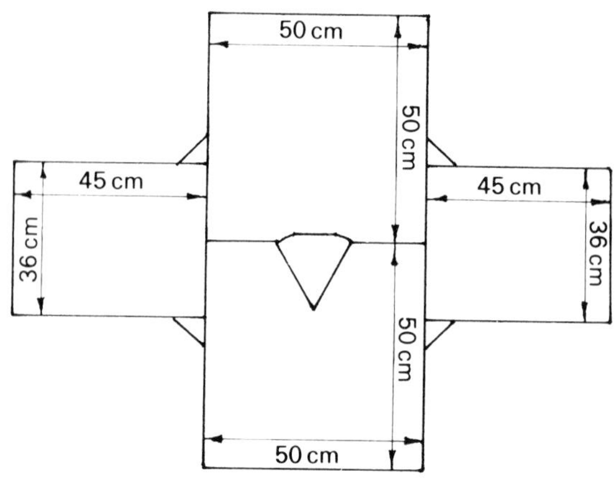

3.3b The pattern broken down into simple squares and rectangles to make calculating easier

sleeves 2 x 45 x 36 = 3240; giving 8240 sq cm in total (ignoring the underarm and neck shaping that more or less cancel one another out). The first ball knitted up the back 17.5cm. The number of square centimetres of back worked with first ball is 17.5 x 50 = 875. So 8240 ÷ 875 = 9.4 balls.

It is always wise to be generous in calculating your amounts – there is nothing worse than trying to cope with working an odd ball of a different dye lot in a self-coloured garment.

What to do with different dye lots

If you have only one or two balls of the different dye lot on a single coloured garment the easiest thing to do is to work the ribbing or welts with the contrast colour. This may mean unpicking welts to rescue the original colour of yarn, in order to finish the main-stitch pattern sections. Ribbing cannot be unravelled from the bottom up, so follow the instructions in the knitting techniques section for pulling out a strand (see p. 68). Then pick up the bottom loops of the main-pattern section on smaller-size needles and work the welt downwards. Then unravel the original rib and treat the yarn as described in Chapter 6 (see p. 95) to remove the wrinkles. If you do not bother with this, you risk the possibility of the section worked in wrinkled yarn showing up when compared with the rest of the work.

All-in-one-piece top with V-neck opening at back

Having decided on the style of garment, make a sketch if you can, showing your idea complete as it will look when worn and a diagram to show how it will be made. My first example is for a garment based on simple squares and rectangles that can be knitted in one piece – with the minimum amount of shaping.

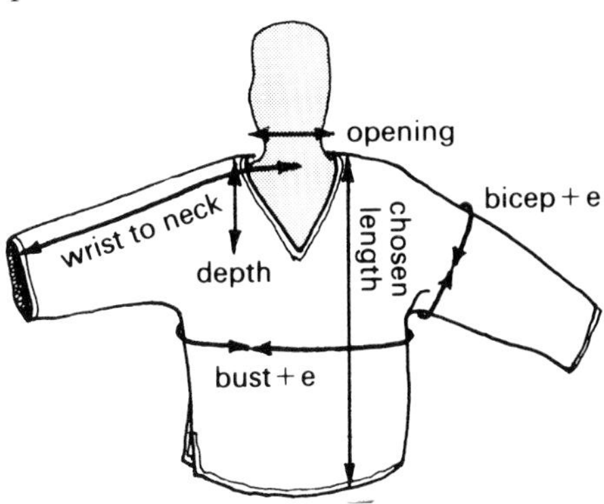

3.4 The arrows show where the measurements were taken for drafting the pattern

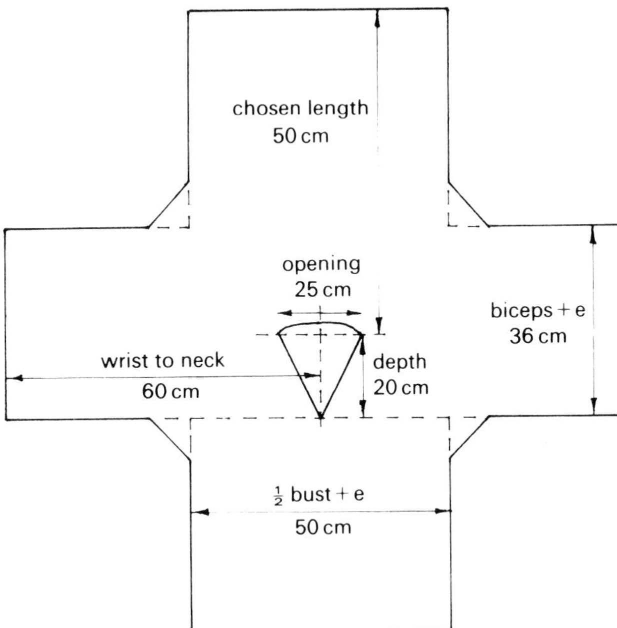

3.5 A scale diagram showing how the measurements are used to create the shape

Further ideas for garments involving no shaping and other styles worked in one piece are given after the pattern instructions.

My design had two squares for front and back, with about 15% ease allowance, and two rectangles for sleeves, each 36cm wide. This made only a rather small underarm measurement so I added triangular gussets for extra armhole depth. The neck opening was placed just before the halfway point of the work.

To knit the garment I chose a beaded lace stitch worked in a brushed mohair.

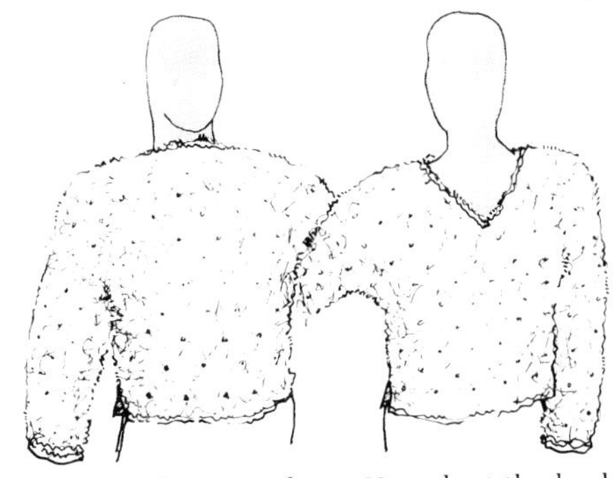

3.6 The finished jumper has a V neck at the back

Beaded cat's paw stitch Multiple of 6

Beadwork: the beads are threaded onto one ball of yarn and used for rows 1, 2, 9 and 10 where they appear on the forward facing loop of the k stitch, adjusted evenly, marked **k1**. (Non-beaded rows worked with another ball.) See Chapter 4 for more on beadwork techniques.

yonB = yarn carrying bead on needle

Row	
1	k3 *k2tog yonB k4 rep from * to last 3 st, k2tog yonB k1
2	p1 *k1 p5 rep from * to last 5 st, **k1** p4
3	k2 *k2tog yon k1 yon k2tog k1 rep from * to last 4 st, k2tog yon k2
4 to 8	p even numbered rows, k odd rows
9	*k2tog yonB k4 rep from * to end
10	p4 ***k1** p5 rep from * to last 2 st, **k1** p1
11	k2 yon k2tog *k1 k2tog yon k1 yon k2tog rep from * to last 2 st, k2
12 to 16	p even rows k odd rows

I tried the stitch pattern twice before arriving at a satisfactory tension on 6mm needles of

10cm = 16 st × 18 rows

i.e. 1cm = 1.6 st × 1.8 rows

I first added a few more details to the pattern and then multiplied each of the cm measurements by the appropriate figure to produce the diagram below.

I calculated the armhole shaping like this. I wanted the gusset to measure about 7 or 8cm; in terms of st this would mean 12 or 13, in rows 12 to 14. To make life simple I chose to inc 12 st over 12 rows – that is 1 st each row for 12 rows.

The neck shaping was more complex and required a graph:

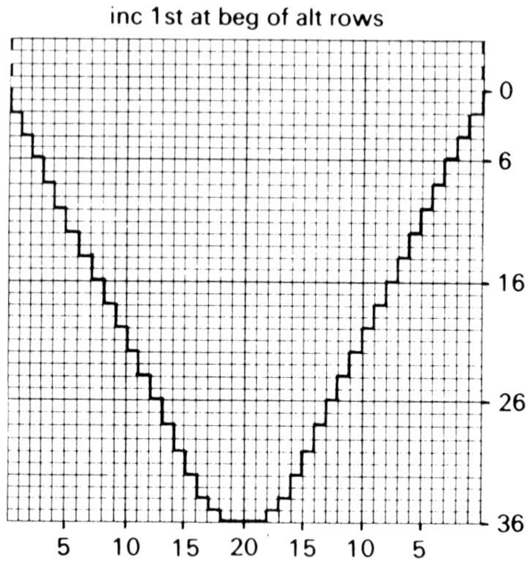

3.8 Graph showing the increases for the V neck – work from the top

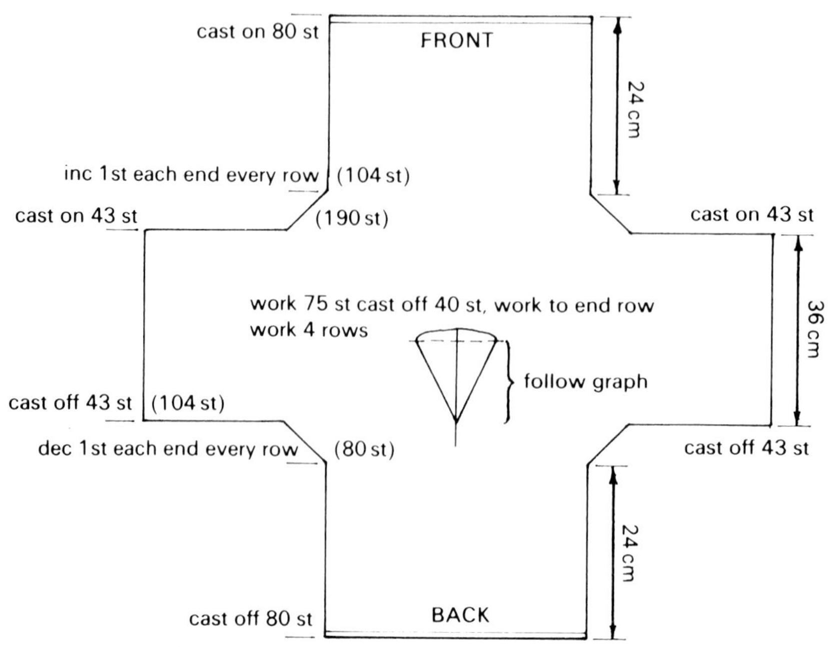

3.7 Diagrammatic pattern for all-in-one top

The neck hole was positioned on the front, 2 rows before the halfway point. Having slipped the neck st onto a holder the first side of the neck opening was worked, with increases as given on the graph. The second side was worked to match, before work continued on all the stitches to finish the back. To finish the cuff and neck openings I picked up stitches and worked 4 rows of garter stitch before casting off. By trial and error I used: 36 stitches for the cuff and 30 st on each side of the neck + the 40 from the st holder, making 100 st in all.

Colour photograph facing page 48
Beaded sweater
Chest size: 86–91cm(32–36in.)
Yarn: 12 balls (25g) Sirdar 'Nocturne' brushed mohair, shade 561 (Blue Spar) (77% mohair, 13% wool, 10% nylon) 3 of balls pre-threaded with the approx. 220 beads needed
Note: The V neck was designed to be worn at the back but can, of course, be worn at the front.

A Other ideas based on squares and rectangles

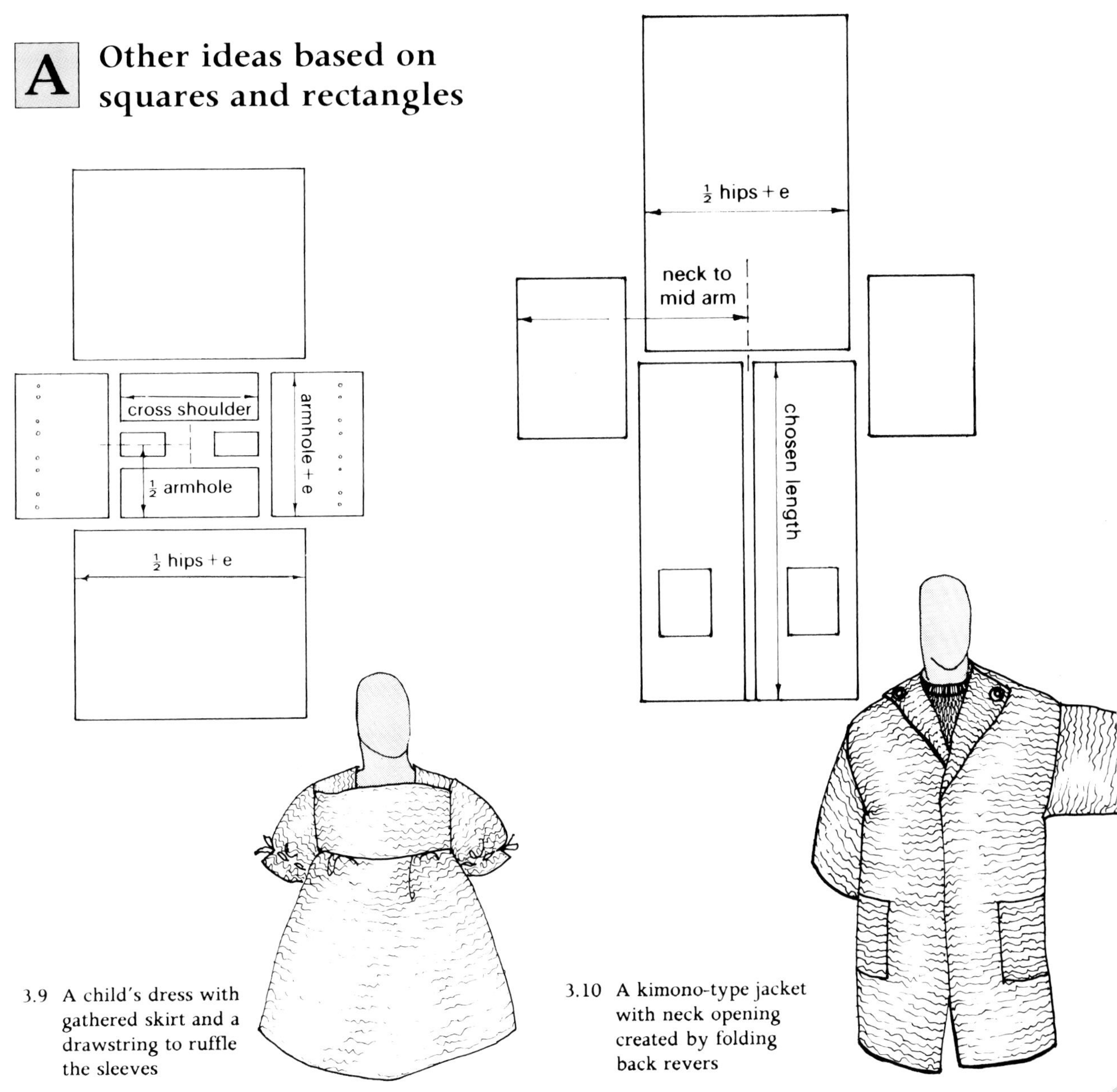

3.9 A child's dress with gathered skirt and a drawstring to ruffle the sleeves

3.10 A kimono-type jacket with neck opening created by folding back revers

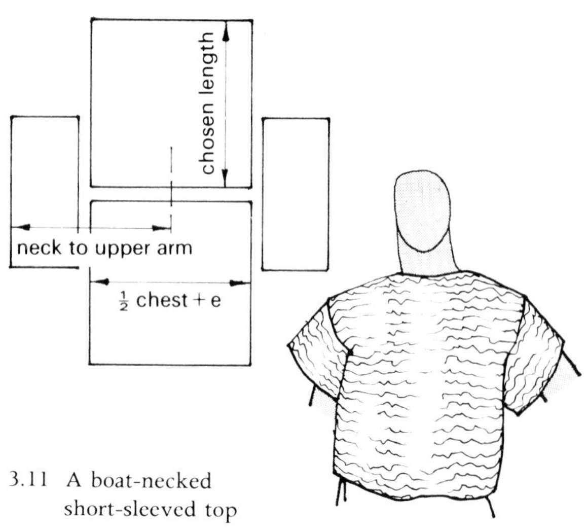

3.11 A boat-necked short-sleeved top

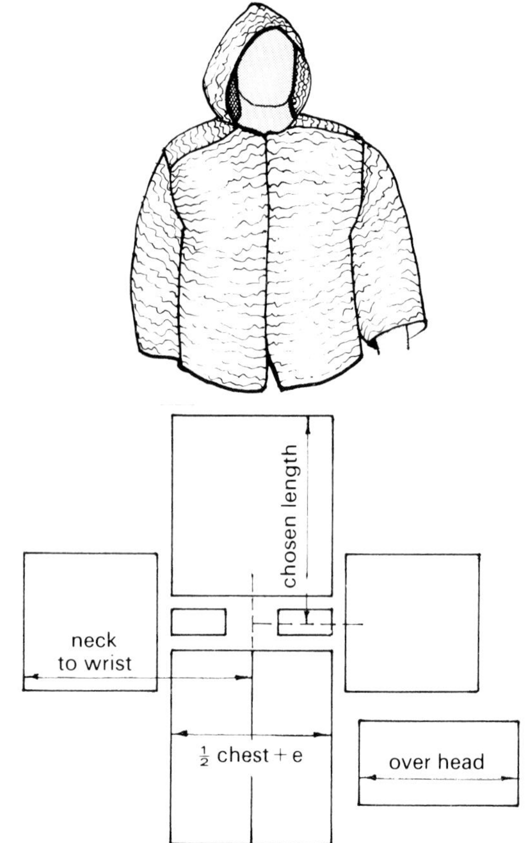

3.12 A jacket with shoulder sections (to avoid shaping) and a hood

Figs 3.9–3.14 show some ideas for garments made entirely from simple squares or rectangles – with no shaping needed during knitting. The body measurements you will need to take are indicated on the sketches. To turn them into pattern instructions simply multiply the number of cm(in.) you need for each section by the tension for your chosen stitch pattern. For example, if your tension is 10cm = 24 st x 30 rows or 1cm = 2.4 st × 3 rows and you want to knit a rectangle 50cm wide and 60 cm long then:

50 x 2.4 = 120 st to cast on
60 x 3 = 180 rows to knit before casting off

Figs 3.13 and 3.14 show two basic styles that can be knitted in one piece – like the beaded top, example A (colour photograph facing page 48). If you choose to work a pattern of this sort in larger sizes you may have problems with numbers of stitches. For children's sizes they are really great because the number of stitches needed either from wrist to wrist (when worked bottom up) or lengthwise over the shoulder (when worked sideways), as the stitches will fit onto an ordinary 35cm(14in.) knitting needle. For larger sizes it is possible to use a circular needle, knitting to and fro, to get the extra length. Use the same method described in the pattern example A to calculate rows, stitches, etc.

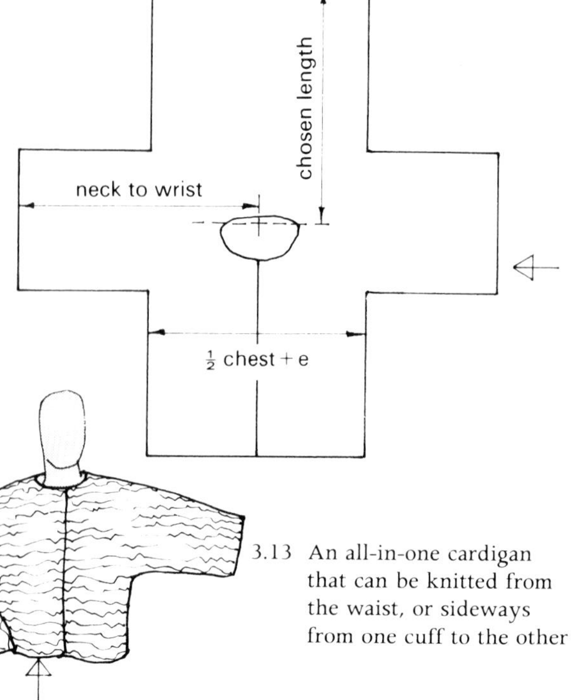

3.13 An all-in-one cardigan that can be knitted from the waist, or sideways from one cuff to the other

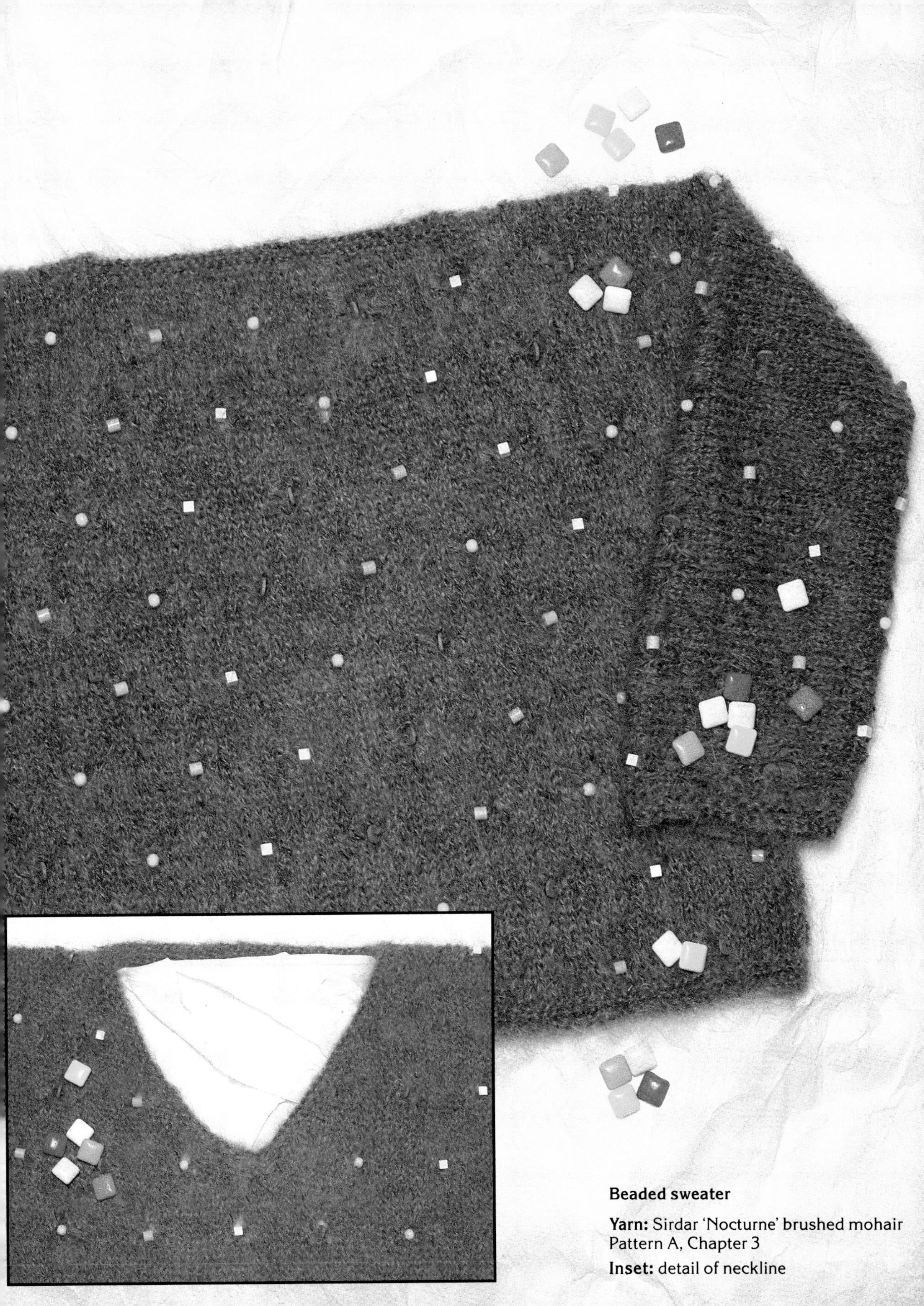

Beaded sweater

Yarn: Sirdar 'Nocturne' brushed mohair
Pattern A, Chapter 3

Inset: detail of neckline

Aran dress

Yarn: Pingouin 'Confort'
Pattern B, Chapter 3

Random-striped baby suit

Yarn: miscellaneous double-knit
Pattern C, Chapter 3

Toddler's jacquard jacket

Yarn: Patons 'Diploma' double-knit
Pattern D, Chapter 3

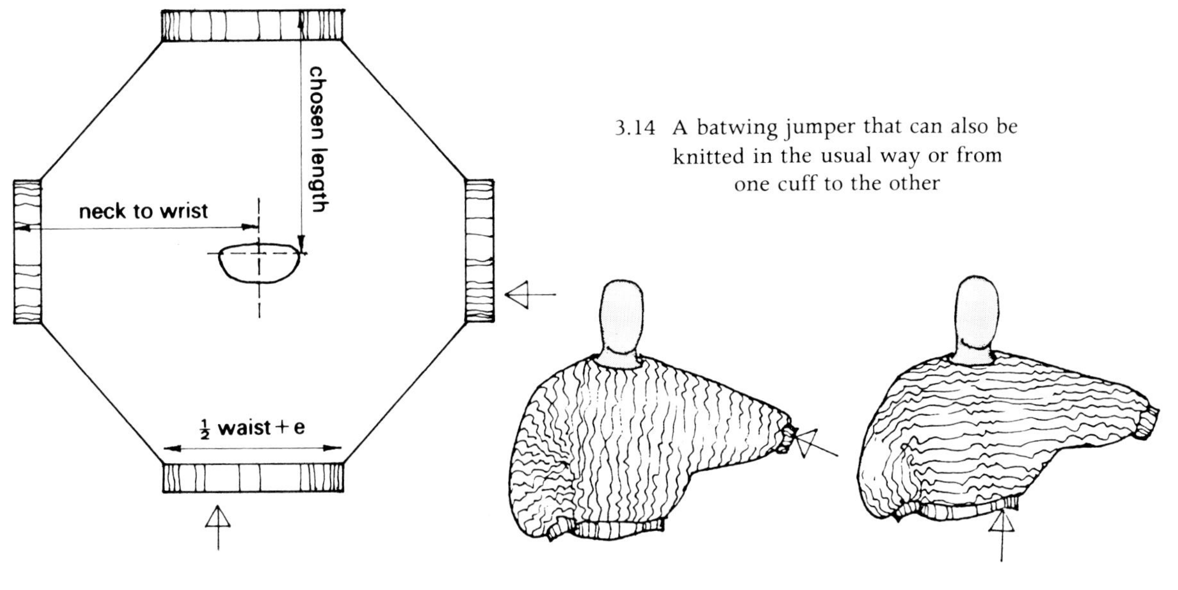

3.14 A batwing jumper that can also be knitted in the usual way or from one cuff to the other

Child's Aran dress

a pattern taken from an existing garment

The shaping for this pattern was all worked out by calculating the numbers of rows and stitches required to match the sizes taken from the dress. I wanted to knit the dress using cable motifs chosen from the Stitch Dictionary (see p. 87). I arranged them according to their widths to give me the sizes I needed for each section of the dress. I included sections of double moss stitch to make shaping easier on the front and sleeves.

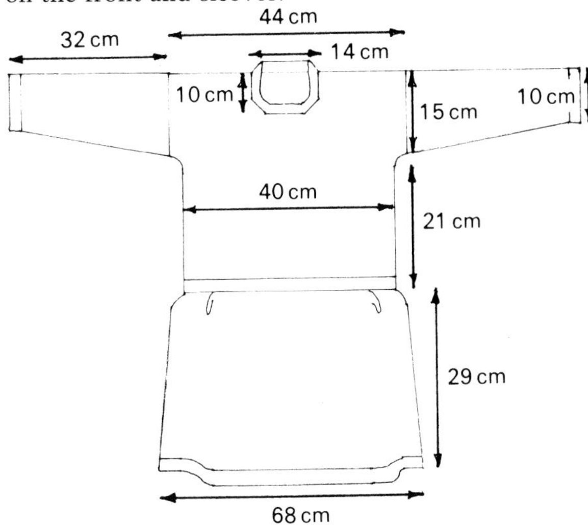

3.15 The measurements of the dress on which the pattern was based

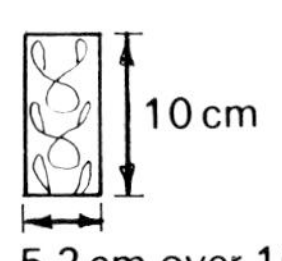

Hearts
5.2cm over 16 st

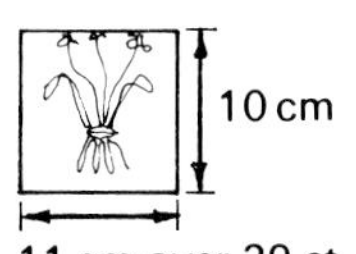

Ears of corn
11cm over 29 st

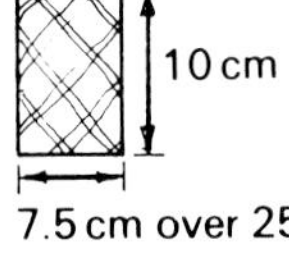

Celtic trellis
7.5cm over 25 st

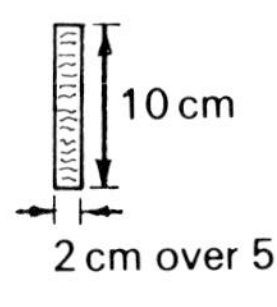

Ladder
2cm over 5 st
Multiple of 5 st
row 1 k1tbl, k3, k1tbl
2 p5
3 k1tbl, p3, k1tbl
4 p5
5 as row 1
6 p1, k3, p1

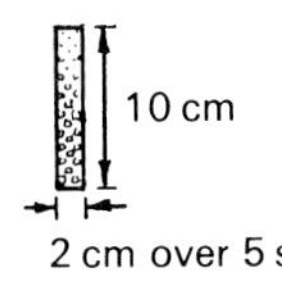

3.16 Tensions achieved for the chosen Aran motifs

Double moss
2cm over 5 st
Multiple of 4 st
row 1 p2 k2
2 p2 k2
3 k2 p2
4 k2 p2

I came up with the following arrangement, after several tries. To separate the motifs I included 2 stitches of reverse stocking stitch in places (called 'purl' in the table opposite). The welts were worked on fewer stitches in garter stitch.

To make knitting the various cable patterns alongside one another easier I recommend copying them out and sticking them together side by side so that you can see how the rows of each motif relate to one another.

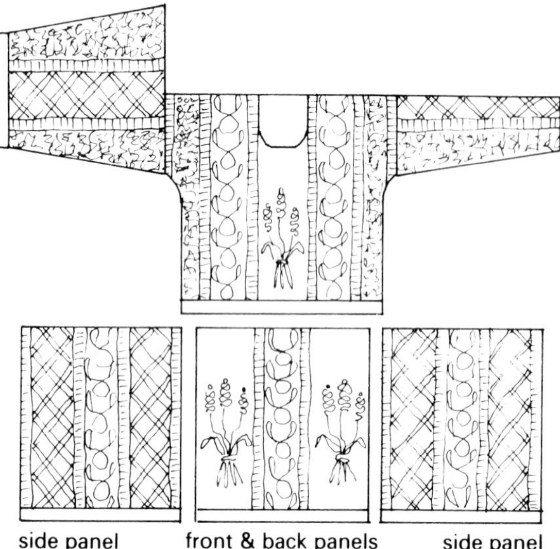

3.17 Drawing shows how the motifs were used on the sections of the dress

Sleeves

Cast on 43 st with 3¼mm(no. 10) needles and work in garter st for 9 rows. Next row inc 12 st evenly along the row to give 55 st. Change to 4mm(no. 8) needles and work patterns as given in table on p. 51 opposite.

Work pattern while inc 1 st each side every 6 rows until there are 75 st. Cont in patt until work measures 32cm from cast-on edge. Work second sleeve to match.

Skirt front and back panels

Cast on 76 st with 3¼mm(no. 10) needles and work 8 rows garter st. Next row inc into every 7th st to give 86 st. Change to 4mm(no. 8) needles and work pattern as shown in table on p. 51 (start corn on 6th row).

When the corn motif is finished continue in reverse stocking st on the side sections until work measures 29cm from cast-on edge. Keep panels on a spare needle or length of contrast yarn.

Skirt side panels

Work welt as given for front and back panels but inc into every 4th st to give 96 st. Change to larger size needles and work as shown in table p. 51:

Work until panels measure 29cm from cast-on edge (I found this was a few more rows than the front panels). Keep st on spare needle. Sew up the side seams of the 4 panels and press gently.

Bodice back

Using 3¼mm(no. 10) needles with RS facing working from centre of side panel to opposite centre of side panel, k2tog to give 91 st. Work 9 rows of garter st. Next row inc 18 st evenly across row. Change to larger size needles and work as shown in table opposite (start corn on 10th row).

Work pattern until it measures 18cm from end of garter st waistband. Shape armholes by inc 1 st of ladder motif at beg of next 10 rows, to give 119 st. Cont in pattern: when corn finishes, work reverse stocking stitch on centre section, until straight section of armhole measures ★ 15cm. Cast off 45 st at beg of next 2 rows. Slip central 29 st onto a st holder.

Bodice front

Work as for back bodice to ★, straight section of armhole measures 6cm. Neck shaping: work 52 st, slip central 15 onto a st holder, work to end of row. At neck opening dec 1 st each alt row 7 times to give 45 st. Work until armhole matches back and cast off all 45 st. Work second side of neck to match first.

Neckband

Sew up left shoulder. With RS facing and 3¼mm(no. 10) needles pick up and k 29 st from back neck st holder, 20 st from front left-side neck, 15 st from front neck st holder, 20 st from right-side neck to give 84 st in all. Work 4 rows of garter stitch, cast off loosely using the suspended st method or larger size needles.
Press and sew up.

Colour photograph between pages 48/49

Aran dress

Chest size: 66–71cm(26–28in.)
Yarn: 10 balls (50g) Pingouin 'Confort', shade 164 (Cinnamon) (50% wool, 40% acrylic, 10% mohair)

Sleeves

Double moss	Ladder	Purl	Celtic trellis	Purl	Ladder	Double moss	
8	5	2	25	2	5	8	=55 st

Skirt front and back panels

Ears of corn	Ladder	Purl	Hearts	Purl	Ladder	Ears of corn	
29	5	1	16	1	5	29	=86 st

Skirt side panels

Ladder	Purl	Celtic trellis	Purl	Ladder	Purl	Hearts	Purl	Ladder	Purl	Celtic trellis	Purl	Ladder	
5	2	25	2	5	1	16	1	5	2	25	2	5	=96 st

Bodice back

Double moss	Ladder	Purl	Hearts	Purl	Ladder	Ears of corn	Ladder	Purl	Hearts	Purl	Ladder	Double moss	
12	5	1	16	1	5	29	5	1	16	1	5	12	=109 st

C Striped baby suit

based on an existing flat pattern

As an example of this way of working I chose a baby garment because babies are difficult to measure in advance! I got a Babygro-type pattern intended for jersey fabric. As you can see from the diagram it had integral envelope feet and front flaps.

The measurements are quoted without seam allowance as knitting seams are sewn edge to edge. There is no need to worry about ease as this will have been included by the pattern drafter. I wanted to work the garment in odd balls of double-knit yarn and to avoid darning in ends and unnecessary seams I decided to combine the front and back sections and work the body as one.

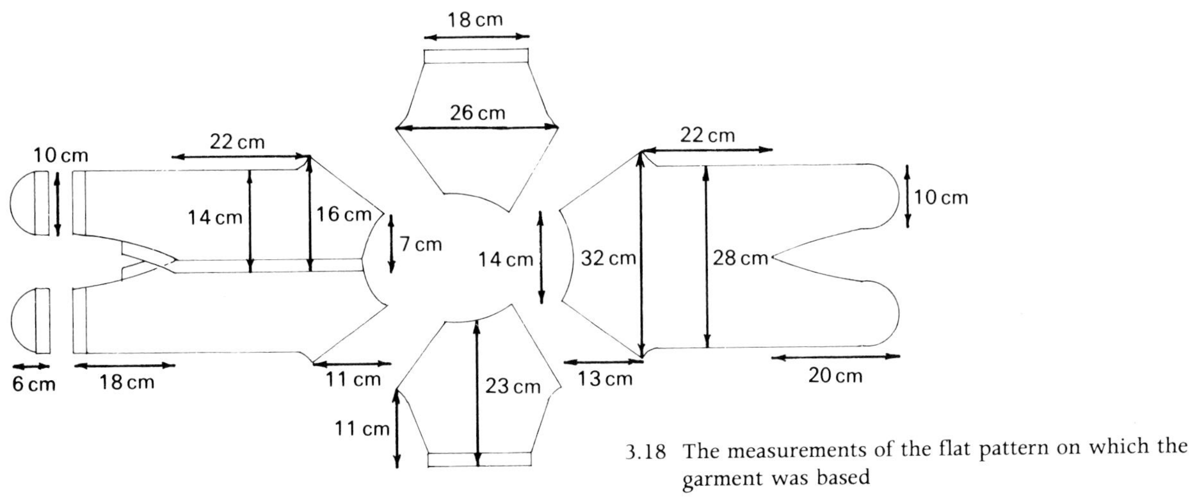

3.18 The measurements of the flat pattern on which the garment was based

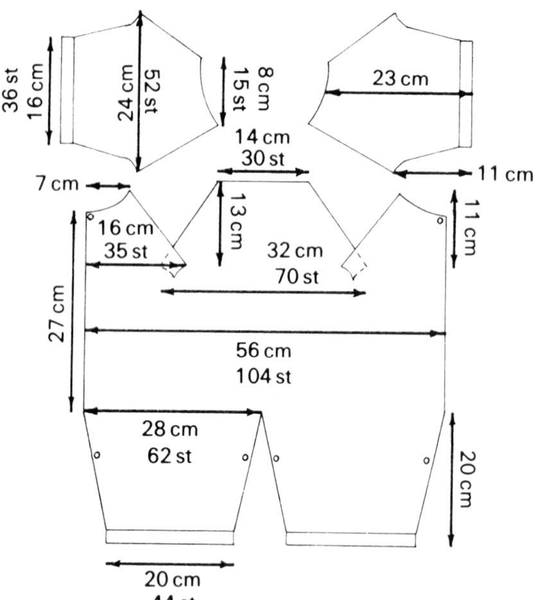

3.19 The shape, measurements and stitch and row totals actually used. Dots show where to start and end when you pick up stitches for flaps

This diagram shows the final sizes of the sections. The dotted lines indicate the overlap between the underarm increases. I have narrowed the sleeves as compared with the original, omitted the foot envelopes in favour of a ribbed welt, and added vertically picked-up front, back and neck welts.

My stitch pattern is worked with nine odd balls of double-knit yarn, in stocking stitch, one row in each colour. I used 4mm needles and got a tension of 22 st × 30 rows over 10cm square. The basic numbers of rows and stitches have been included on the diagram.

Front and back as one

Leg section: cast on 44 st with $3\frac{1}{4}$mm(no. 10) needles and work in rib for 9 rows. Change to larger needles and main pattern. Inc 1 st each end of next and foll 6th row to give 62 st. Cont till leg measures 20cm from cast-on edge. Work second leg to match. Combine and work across whole body, from centre front to centre front until work measures 45cm from cast-on edge, finishing with a p row. Next row divide work with right centre front facing:

Right front

Row 1 of underarm shaping: k across 30 st, inc into next st, to give 32 st. Turn work. With an extra needle work on this section as follows: inc 1 st on 3rd, 5th and 6th rows at side edge. Work 1 row without shaping, giving 35 st. *Raglan shaping*: dec 1 st at side edge each alt row for 24 rows until 23 st remain. *Neck shaping*: maintain shaping at side edge while shaping for neck as foll – slip central 10 st onto a st holder, then dec 1 st each row at neck edge 5 times leaving 5 st. Cont to shape raglan as usual till 2 st remain. Cast off.

Back section

Row 1 of underarm shaping: inc into first st, work 60, inc into next st to give 64 st. Turn work. Using spare needle work on the back sections as follows: inc 1 st on 3rd, 5th and 6th rows at each edge, work 1 row without shaping, to give 70 st.
Raglan shaping: dec 1 st at beg of each row till 30 st remain. Slip onto a st holder.

Left front section

Row 1 of underarm shaping: inc into first st, work 30 giving 32 st. Turn work and foll instructions given for right front, shaping on opposite sides.

Sleeves

With $3\frac{1}{4}$mm(no. 10) needles cast on 36 st. Work rib for 9 rows. Change to larger sized needles and work in stocking stitch while shaping as follows: inc 1 st each end of every 4th row, to give 44 st. Continue without shaping till work measures 11cm from cast-on edge. Underarm shaping: inc 1 st at each end of next and foll 3rd, 5th and 6th rows, work 1 row without shaping, 52 st. *Shape raglan*: dec 1 st at beg of each row till 18 st remain. Then at back edge cont to dec while at front edge cast off 5 st three times – to leave 1 st, cast off. Work second sleeve with shaping on opposite sides.

Left front flap

With RS facing and smaller needles pick up and k 8 st over each 9 row repeat, till 76 st on needle. Work in rib for a row. Make buttonholes on 3rd row by working to last 20 st; then yon p2tog, work 10, yon p2tog work 6. Work 2 more rows rib. Cast off loosely.

Right front flap

With RS facing starting from same point on leg as left front flap ended, pick up and k 76 st. Work 1 row rib. 3rd row make buttonholes as foll: work 6 (yon p2tog work 10) rep brackets to last 10 st; yon p2tog work 8. Work 2 more rows rib. Cast off loosely.

Back flap

Start from same point on pattern as for front flaps, pick up and k 8 st over each of 9 rows of pattern to give 44 st. Work 4 rows rib, cast off loosely.

Neckband

Press pieces following instructions from Chapter 5 and sew up raglans and underarm seams. With RS facing and $3\frac{1}{4}$mm needles pick up and k 3 st from front flap; 8 from slipped st; 7 from dec on side neck; 15 st from sleeve top; 20 st from back neck; 15 st from 2nd sleeve; 7 from other side neck; 8 from slipped st and 3 from second front flap, to give 86 st in all. Work 4 rows of rib. Next row make buttonhole as follows: work to last 4 st; p2tog yon work 2. Work 3 more rows of rib. Leaving long ends of yarn sufficient to chain st down edges of neckband to meet cast-off row of front flaps, cast off in the same colour as used for the front flap cast-off row.

Sew up leg seams and overlap front flap on top of back flap. Finish all ends and sew on buttons.

Colour photograph between pages 48/49

Random-striped baby suit
To fit 3–6 month old baby
Yarn: 9 balls (50g) miscellaneous double-knit
Note: To avoid problems, select yarns with similar washing instructions.

Toddler's jacquard jacket

to demonstrate complex pattern drafting using basic body measurements

At the end of this section you will find four diagrams that show the body measurements you will need in order to draft patterns like those in Chapter 2.
raglan sleeve pattern (see p. 28)
set-in sleeve pattern (see p. 23)
simple square shoulder
dropped shoulder (see p. 33)
I chose to make a child's cardigan jacket for age 2-4 years based on the raglan pattern and used the diagram above to take the following measurements:

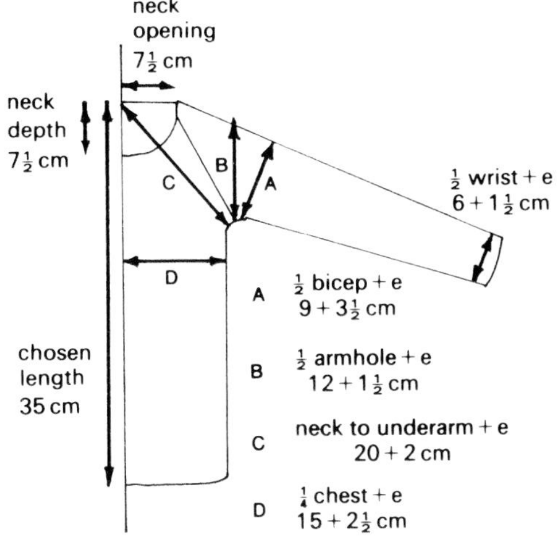

3.20 The drafting diagram shows the body measurements that I took

Then I made a sketch to scale, using squared paper (1 square = 5cm). To knit the jacket I chose a Fair Isle pattern, shown on the grids on p. 54, with flowers and windmills. It was worked in a main colour and three contrast colours with double-knit superwash wool and 4mm(no. 8) needles. The tension achieved was 10cm = 22 st x 24 rows. The next stage was to place the motif or Fair Isle pattern. My motif conveniently measured 5cm wide so it fitted easily. I chose to place the motif with a half repeat at the side seam edge in order to have a complete repeat on either side for the front opening. On the sleeve I chose to place the motif centrally so the pattern would show effectively from the side.

Once the scale pattern was made I calculated the number of stitches I would need and wrote them onto the diagrams. Because the garment was so small I decided to make a detailed graph to work out the shaping for the raglan and sleeve seams. To do this I marked out on my graph paper a rectangle of 77 by 27 squares for the front and back.

On the top edge I marked the 33 centre squares with a line to show the stitches to be left for the back neck. Then I did a similar thing for the sleeves; a rectangle 55 by 85 squares; I marked the central 33 stitches for casting on the cuff and the 11 stitches for sleeve head; I also marked the beginning of the armhole shaping at row 56.

The next thing was to decide how to decrease for the raglan. In my design the shaping on the body and the sleeve was the same; 22 stitches each side over 27 rows. It is usual to start a raglan by casting off a few stitches before starting to shape; I chose 5 leaving 17. I then drew a line diagonally up from the 5 cast-off stitches to the back neck stitches. Then I drew over it in steps to represent the individual decreases. I followed the same method to calculate the neck – drawing a rough curve – then changing it into a stepped line. Then I worked out the sleeve seam shaping to give an un-shaped bicep section.

To make it easier for myself I chose to mark the Fair Isle pattern onto the graphs – this is a good tip to follow if you are in doubt.

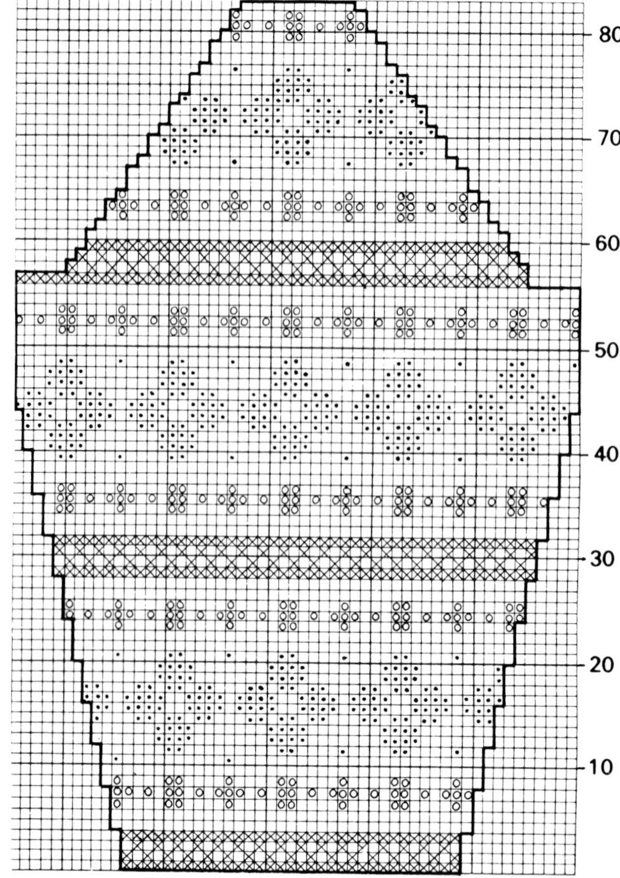

3.21 Detailed grid of sleeve shaping with the Fair Isle detail

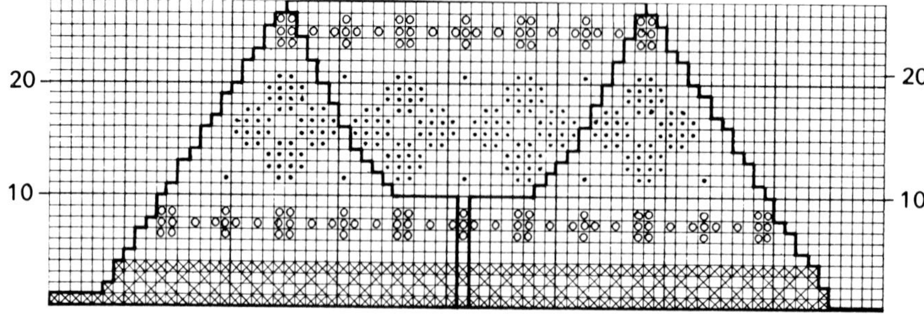

3.22 A combined grid showing the raglan shaping detail and the Fair Isle motif for the back and fronts

Once the chart is drafted it is easy to knit straight from it. I feel it is a waste of effort to write out in words what you can see clearly from your diagram. Leave the detail until you need it, then it is easy to count up how many stitches you should have or how many rows you should have knitted, and so on. In my example, the problem of coping with the split motifs on the body section may be made clearer by writing it out as follows.

The back
For my cardigan I started on the back with 77 st, and using $3\frac{1}{4}$mm (no. 10) needles worked eight rows single moss st (row 1 kl pl to last st, kl; row 2 purl knit st and knit purl st. Changing to 4mm (no. 8) needles I started (with the right side of the work facing) on a k row, reading from right to left: (see detail of chart 1) work from stitch 5, half repeat; six full repeats; to stitch 6. On the next row, purl, read from left to right of chart: work from stitch 6, half repeat; six full repeats; to stitch 5. Continue in this way until you have completed two repeats of the Fair Isle motif. Then shape raglan following the chart. Cast off all remaining st.

Right front
Cast on 39 st and work band. Using the left-hand side of the chart and reading it as before: on a k row work 3 repeats; then to stitch 6 of next half repeat. On a purl row work from stitch 6 half a repeat and then 3 repeats. Continue as for back, shape raglan and neck from chart.

Left front
Cast on 38 st and work band. Using the right hand side of the chart, reading as before: on a knit row work from stitch 5 of half repeat; then 3 repeats. On a purl row work 3 repeats then to stitch 5 on a half repeat. Continue as right front.

Sleeves
Cast on 33 st, work band. Work from chart as before.

Colour photograph facing page 49

Toddler's jacquard jacket
Chest size: 48–60cm(19–23in.)
Yarn: Patons 'Diploma' double-knit (50g balls) (60% wool, 40% acrylic)
Main colour: 2 × fawn (6717)
Contrast: 1 × A (green, 6766); 1 × B (pink, 6761); 1 × C (blue, 6763)

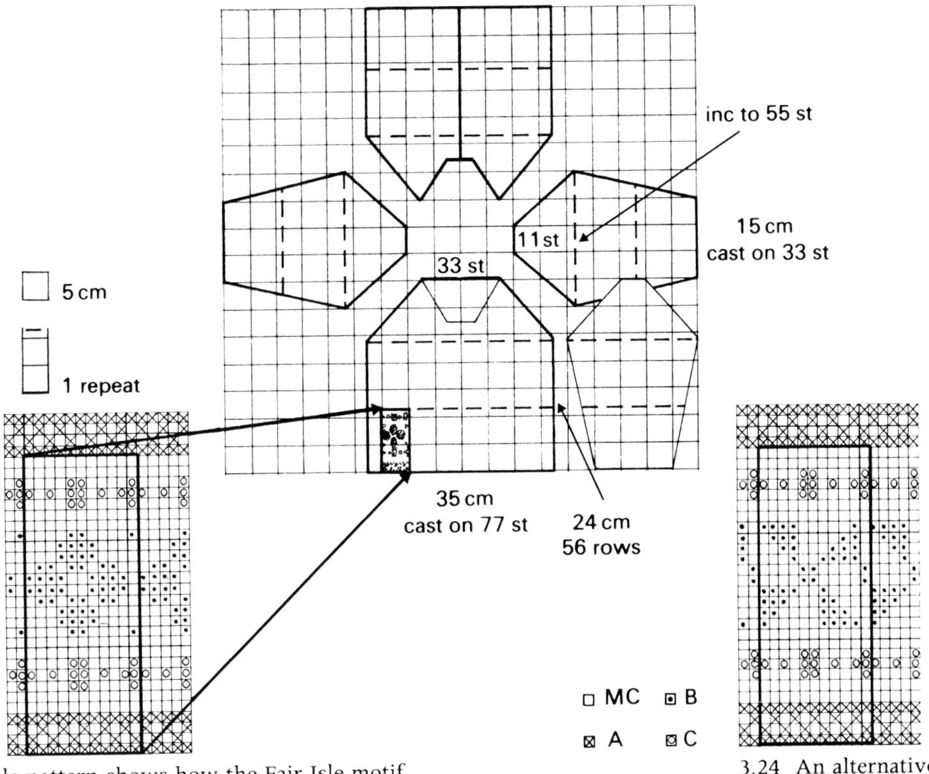

3.23 The scale pattern shows how the Fair Isle motif will repeat and the grid to work from

3.24 An alternative windmill motif grid

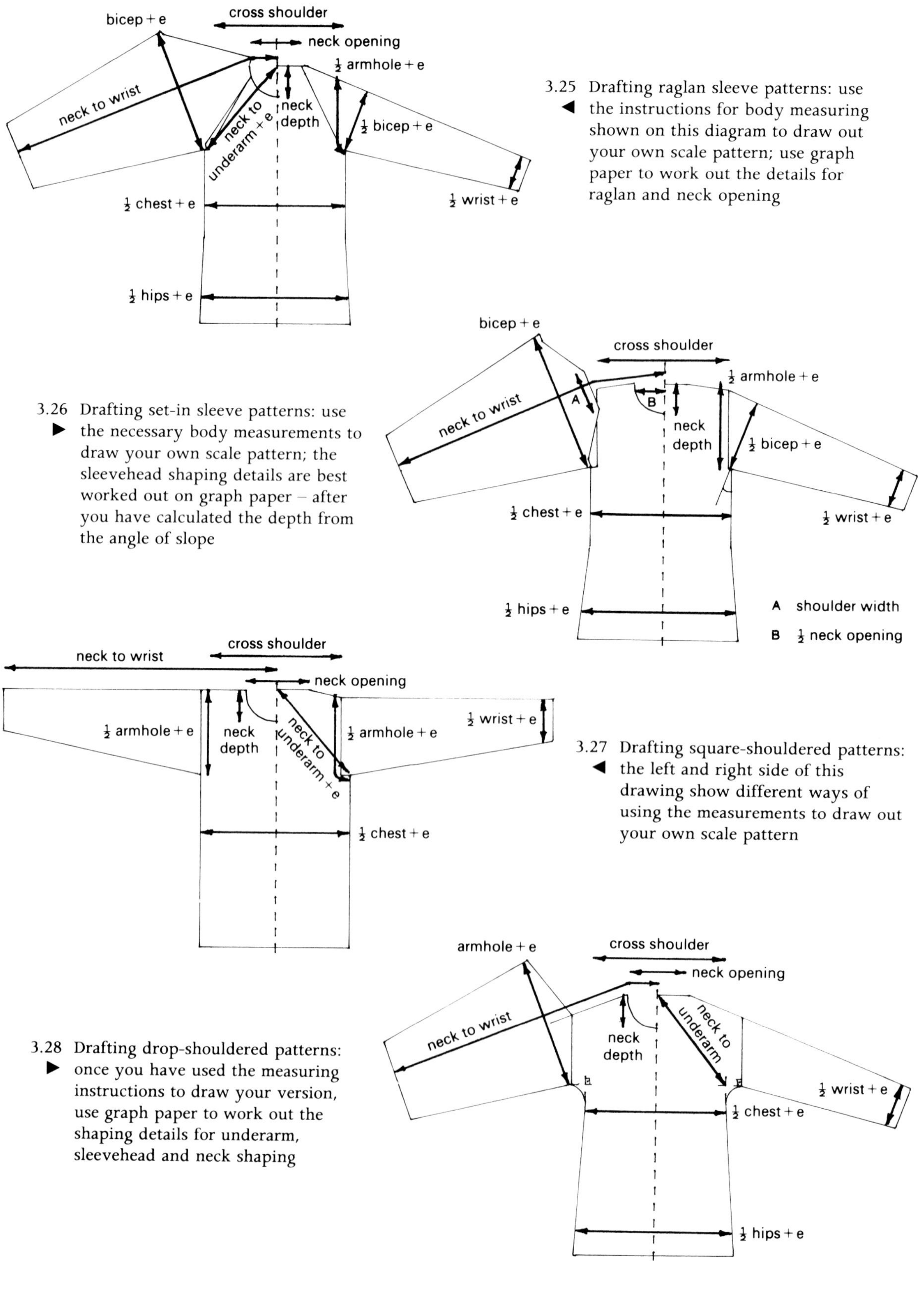

3.25 Drafting raglan sleeve patterns: use ◀ the instructions for body measuring shown on this diagram to draw out your own scale pattern; use graph paper to work out the details for raglan and neck opening

3.26 Drafting set-in sleeve patterns: use ▶ the necessary body measurements to draw your own scale pattern; the sleevehead shaping details are best worked out on graph paper – after you have calculated the depth from the angle of slope

3.27 Drafting square-shouldered patterns: ◀ the left and right side of this drawing show different ways of using the measurements to draw out your own scale pattern

3.28 Drafting drop-shouldered patterns: ▶ once you have used the measuring instructions to draw your version, use graph paper to work out the shaping details for underarm, sleevehead and neck shaping

Baroque jacket

Yarn: Bee Bee 'Mohair Random' and Yarn Store 'Natural British Wool' Pattern E, Chapter 3

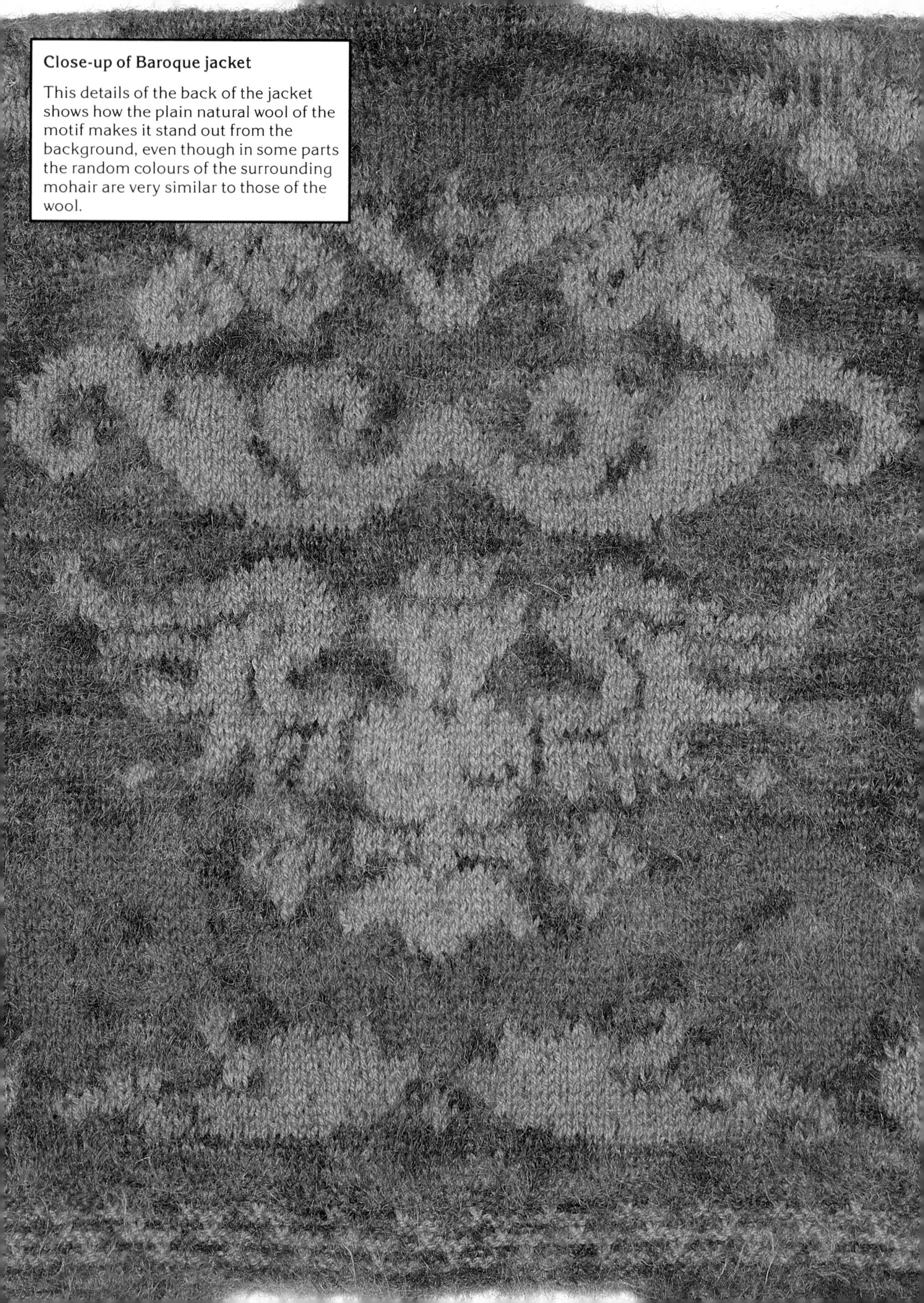

Close-up of Baroque jacket

This details of the back of the jacket shows how the plain natural wool of the motif makes it stand out from the background, even though in some parts the random colours of the surrounding mohair are very similar to those of the wool.

Double-breasted jacket

Yarn: Pingouin 'Ruban', 'Jarre' and 'Orage'
Pattern F, Chapter 3

Close-up of double-breasted jacket

This detail shows a full repeat of the stitch pattern used. The effect is best when the jacket is knitted in similar shades of one colour.

E Baroque jacket

shape based on jacquard motifs

The idea for this garment started with my finding some space-dyed mohair on a market stall in Knaresborough (from Bee Bee wools). I then decided to use a number of coloured wools that picked up the main shades in the mohair. I chose a natural British wool in Aran thickness from the Yarn Store in London, in muted brown, blue, green and dark red. I wanted to use a jacquard design and the colour combination I had reminded me of old embroidery or carpets. I had a book of Baroque needlework designs (*Baroque Charted Designs for Needlework*, Dover, 1975) which seemed to provide the right kind of source material. I particularly liked the mythical man-beast combinations. I compiled a series of charts from my favourite images and started moving them around until I came up with an arrangement that would display the motifs to their best advantage. Then I knitted a tension sample on 5mm needles, using a simplified motif. I got 10cm = 18 st x 20 rows. I used a calculator to work out the sizes that the charts would knit up to in my yarn.

This gave me the minimum sizes for each of my proposed garment pieces. The resulting shape was a straight body with a simple over-lapping front opening, ties – called 'points' in the Baroque period – to fasten it, and fairly full sleeves with a wide cuff. I used the minimum amount of shaping, in order to make the knitting simple; in order to incorporate the wide twin-tailed merman on the back without a join, I shifted the side seam round towards the front. To

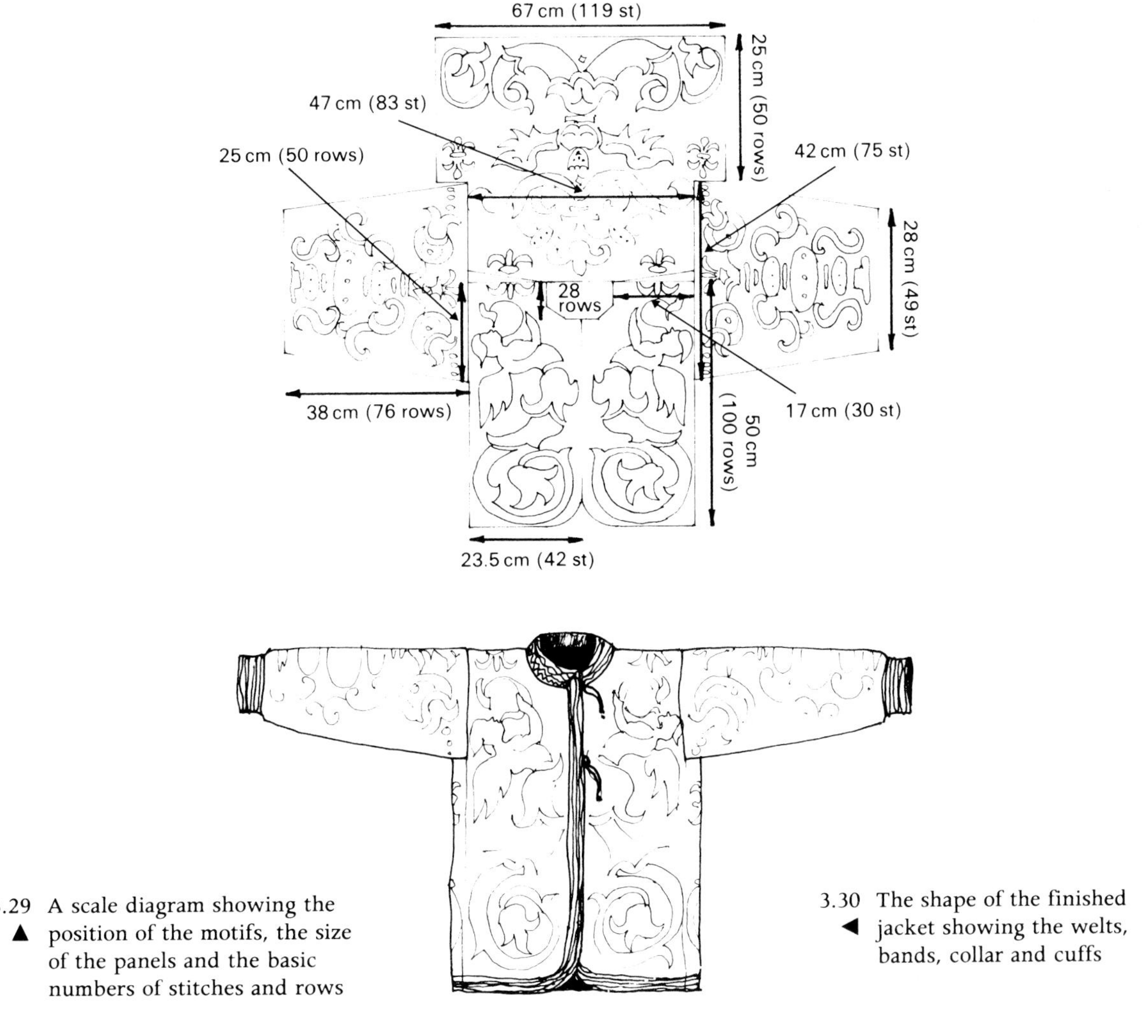

3.29 ▲ A scale diagram showing the position of the motifs, the size of the panels and the basic numbers of stitches and rows

3.30 ◀ The shape of the finished jacket showing the welts, bands, collar and cuffs

3.31 Grid for jacket back ▲

emphasise the serpentine quality of the winged merman on the front I curved the edge at the centre-front bottom corner. To get a neat finish and a curve on this front corner I picked up the hem and front edge in one and increased at the curve. I picked up the back edge and knitted it to match, but worked the cuff in the usual way. I also chose to use a mitred corner for the join between the front and neck bands. The bands were all worked in a version of pebble tuck stitch (see stitch dictionary for details).

The scale diagram showing the final dimensions of the garment and the placing of the motifs is given above. I have added the basic stitch and row figures to this but used the motif grid to work out the exact stitch-by-stitch shaping of the front edge and neck curves, and sleeve seams.

As the diagram already showed so much detail, to make the instructions clearer, I wrote them out as follows: (on all grids MC = random mohair)

Back

Cast on 119 st with $5\frac{1}{2}$mm (no. 5) needles and MC. Starting with a k row, work 2 rows of stocking stitch (stst). Read chart from right to left on k rows. Work two-tailed beast from chart using brown for upper tail, flower and fleur de lys; blue for tail fan, belt and wings; dark red for mid tail and skirt; green for hips, chest and head.

3.32 Grid for jacket sleeve ▼

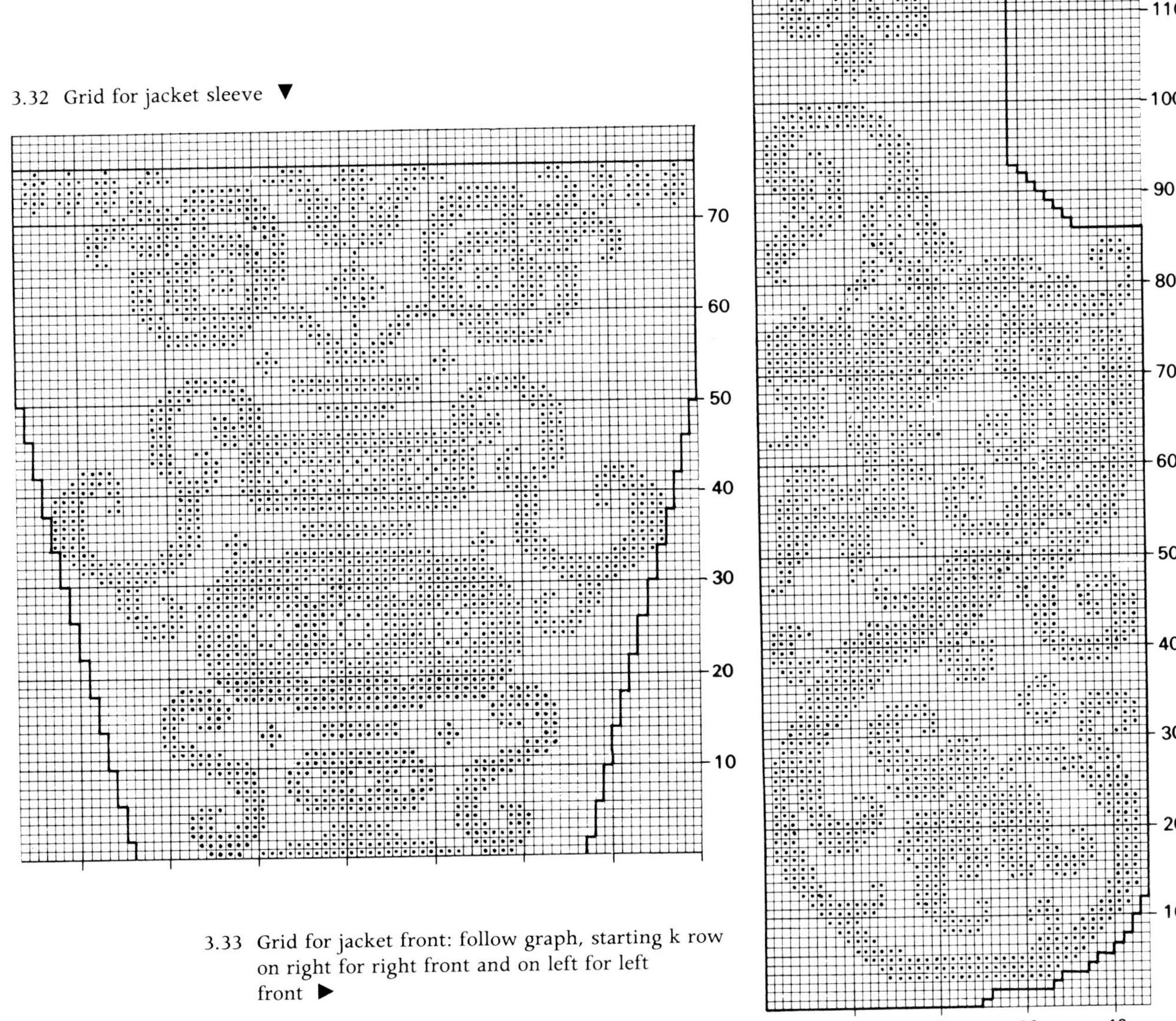

3.33 Grid for jacket front: follow graph, starting k row on right for right front and on left for left front ▶

Continue with fleur de lys and start acorn motif using dark red for centre point and brown for lower foliage. After 10 rows dec for armhole by casting off 18 st each side to give 83 st. Continue with acorn motif using dark red for central strips and top foliage; green for acorn nuts; brown for acorn cups and blue for stalks and the half fleur de lys on the shoulder.

Shape shoulders: work 1 row MC then cast off 14 st at the beg of next 4 rows to leave 25 st on st holder for back neck.

Back band: With RS facing pick up and k 110 st on $4\frac{1}{2}$mm (no. 9) needles in MC, next row k. Work pattern using colours as follows, changing next and every 2nd row: dark red, MC, blue, MC, green, MC, brown, MC, cast off with MC loosely.

Right front

Cast on 25 st with $5\frac{1}{2}$mm needles follow chart reading from right to left on k rows and shape accordingly. Working motifs as follows: green for mid tail and skirt; dark red for tail fan, wing and trumpet; blue for upper tail and hat; brown for flower and torso.

Left front

Work to match right but read chart in reverse, i.e. from left to right on k rows.

Front band:
With $4\frac{1}{2}$mm needles and MC pick up and k 25 st from cast-on edge, 22 st evenly round curve and 81 st from the 83 rows that form the straight part of the front edge, to give 128 st. Next row k. Work band as for back but inc 1 st on curved section every alt row 6 times while maintaining patt evenly, and at neck edge to form mitre corner.

Neck band:
Pick up 24 sts from each front, 25 sts from back neck st holder to give 73 sts. Work in pattern to match other bands but inc on alt rows at each end to form mitre corner.

Sleeves – both alike
Cast on 48 st with $4\frac{1}{2}$mm needles and MC, knit welt as given for back in reverse, finishing with the last two rows of MC. Change to $5\frac{1}{2}$mm needles, k row and inc 1 st into every 6th st to give 55 st, work 3 more rows of stst. Work pomegranate urn chart while inc 1 st every 4th row as shown on grid, using brown for the plinths and strips between sections, flowers next to pomegranates and centre top two flowers and the pollen; green for the urn handles, flower stalks and leaves; dark red for the flowers on either side of the lower sections of the urn and the pomegranate and its pollen. Work 4 rows of MC at end of grid.
Cast off in MC.

Colour photograph facing page 56

Baroque jacket
Chest sizes: 86–91cm(32–36in.)
Main yarn: 13 balls (25g) Bee Bee 'Mohair Random', brown/black
Contrast yarn for motifs: Yarn Store 'Natural British Wool' (100g hanks)
1 × blue (308) 1 × brown (310)
1 × green (307) 1 × red (311)

Woman's double breasted jacket

with textured effect

My inspiration for the stitch pattern came from the desire to use three different yarns together in a textural pattern. I tried several ideas before arriving at the chosen pattern – in it I have combined what I thought of as the best aspects of each yarn. That is, I like the right side of the linen mixture and the wrong side of the fluffy yarn when worked over stocking stitch and I wanted to use that with raised stripes of the viscose ribbon. I also wanted to work them in a predominantly vertical way. The resulting combination can be seen in the close-up photo facing p. 57. It is knitted as follows:

Stitch Pattern
Worked in three yarns: A = Ruban (viscose ribbon), B = Orage, C = Jarre

rows
1 and 2 Ak to end row
3 *Bk3, Ck3, rep from * to end
4 *Cp3, Bk3, rep from * to end
5 Ck1 *Bp3, Ck3, rep from * to last 5 st, Bp3 Ck2
6 and even rows unless specified, work in same colours as prev row, k the k st and p the p st
7 Ck2 *Bp3 Ck3, rep from * to last 4 st, Bp3 Ck1
9 Ck3 *Bp3 Ck3, rep from * to last 3 st, Bp3
11 Bp1 Ck3 *Bp3, Ck3, rep from * to last 2 st, Bp2
13 Bp2 Ck3 *Bp3 Ck3, rep from * to last st, Bp1
15 *Bp3 Ck3, rep from * to end
17 and 18A as rows 1 & 2
19 *Ck3 Bk3, rep from * to end
20 *Bk3 Cp3, rep from * to end
21 Ck2 *Bp3 Ck3, rep from * to last 4 st, Bp3 Ck1
23 Ck1 *Bp3 Ck3, rep from * to last 5 st, Bp3 Ck2
25 *Bp3 Ck3, rep from * to end
27 Bp2 *Ck3 Bp3, rep from * to last 4 st, Ck3 Bp1
29 Bp1 *Ck3, Bp3 rep from * to last 5 st, Ck3 Bp2
31 *Ck3 Bp3, rep from * to end
Rep these 32 rows.

It was worked using 6mm needles and gave a tension of 18 st x 20 rows over a 10cm square.

I made a number of sketches before deciding to use the stitch pattern horizontally for a jacket/cardigan style of garment. Then I drew up a scale diagram to show the final sizes and shapes of each part of the garment and converted these to basic numbers of stitches and rows.

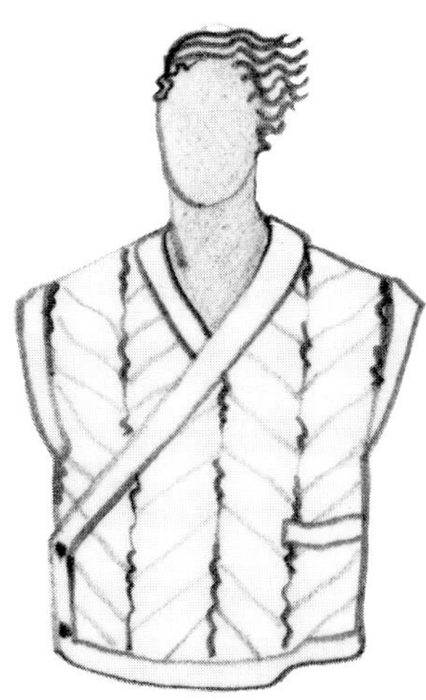

3.34 A preliminary sketch for a garment with the stitch pattern used vertically – knitted from the side

These I expanded to give myself the following pattern instructions:

Back

Cast on 93 st with 4mm needles and colour B. Work 7 rows of garter stitch. Change to 6mm needles and main pattern, continue till work measures 30cm or until 60 rows have been worked in main pattern. Shape armholes by dec 1 st at beg of each row for 6 rows, to leave 87 st. Continue until 10 rows of fourth repeat have been worked, when work should measure 52cm. For shoulders cast off 10 st at beg of next 6 rows leaving 27 st to transfer to a st holder.

Right front

Prepare pocket back; cast on 18 st with B on 6mm needles and work in stst for 7cm. Cast on 64 st and work mitre corner as given for left front but make dec at beg of rows. Change to larger needles and work in main patt until front measures 10cm or until $\frac{1}{2}$ a rep is completed. Work next 2 rows A. Next row with RS facing make pocket opening as follows: work 24 st in pattern; slip 18 st onto a st holder; work across prepared pocket back; cont to end row. Shape front edge for V neck as follows: dec 1 st at end of 2nd, 6th, 10th, 14th, and 16th rows of the st pattern. When work measures 30cm shape armholes by dec 1 st at side edge each alt row 3 times. Continue to dec in this way till 3 reps have been worked and 35 st remain. Shape neck every alt row for next 4 rows then cont while casting off 10 st each alt row from side edge 3 times.

Left front

Cast on 64 st with 4mm needles and B, work in garter st and for mitre corner dec 1 st at end of 2nd, 4th, 6th rows, work 7th row without dec. Change to larger size needles and main patt, dec 1 st at end of first row to leave 60 st. Cont in main patt until front measures 10cm from cast-on edge. Start shaping V neck, making dec at beg not end of each row, following instructions for right front to end.

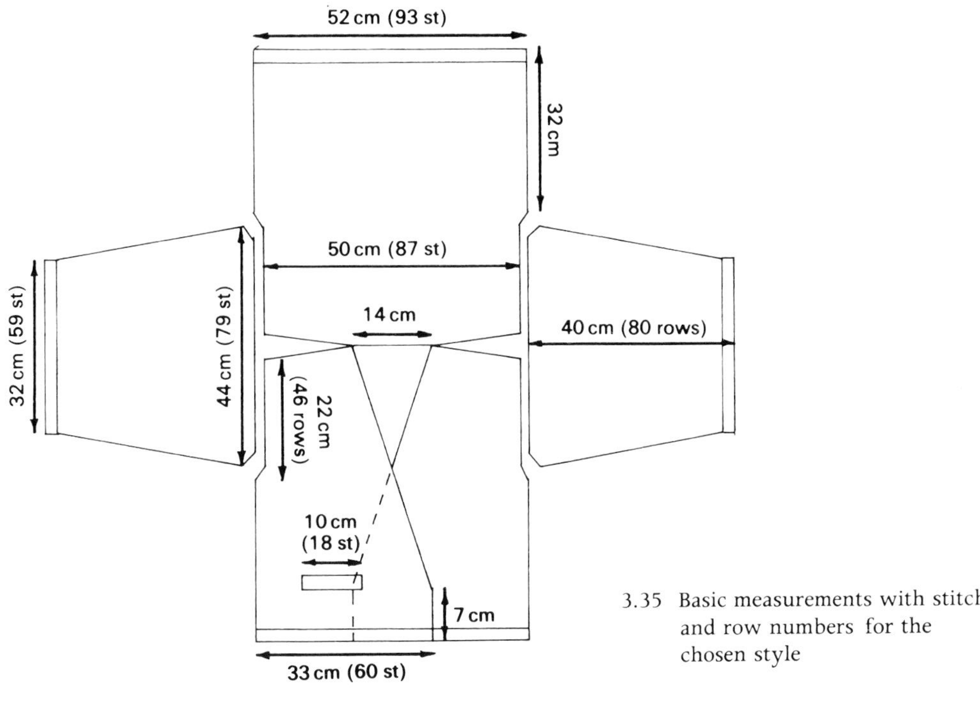

3.35 Basic measurements with stitch and row numbers for the chosen style

Sleeves

Cast on 57 st and work welts as given for back. Change to larger needles and main st pattern. Inc 1 st each end of next and every foll 6 rows to give 81 st. Cont in patt until 12 rows of 3rd rep have been worked. Shape sleeve crown as foll: dec 1 st at beg of next 6 rows.

Pocket edging

Using 4mm needles and B work 5 rows, cast off.

Right front edging

With WS facing and an odd fine knitting needle (e.g. 3mm) start at shoulder edge and slip edge st onto needle evenly (14 over each $\frac{1}{2}$ repeat) to give 98 in all. Turn work and using A and 4mm needles, knit 2 rows of garter st. Change to B, cont in garter st and inc into first st (at bottom corner for mitre) on next and foll alt rows for 7 rows. Cast off loosely.

Left front and back edging

Sew up left shoulder using back st. Use same technique as for right front, but start at bottom edge with WS facing; slip 98 st onto fine needle, then the 27 st from back st holder, to give 125 st. Turn and work as for given right front edging, but work inc into last st of alt rows for mitre.

Follow instructions given in Chapter 4 for pressing and finishing.

Colour photographs between pages 56/57

Double-breasted jacket

Chest size: 86–91cm(32–36in.)

Yarn: 4 balls (50g) Pingouin 'Ruban' shade 34
4 balls (50g) Pingouin 'Jarre' shade 16
5 balls (50g) Pingouin 'Orage' shade 117

4
Knitting hints and techniques

In this chapter you will find a number of descriptions and explanations of ways to make your knitting look professional. Also given are instructions for garment details that may help you to widen your design vocabulary or inspire you to try different things.

The descriptions are arranged in sections: the first group deals with techniques that are integral to any knitting, such as different ways of casting on, forming edges and casting off and their suitability for particular stitch patterns or parts of a garment. This section also includes shaping, hems and how to cope with working stitch patterns together that have different row tensions.

The second group consists of ideas and explanations for techniques you can use for garment design. It includes a section on picking up stitches, followed by ideas for pockets, bands, collars, hoods and buttonholes. The explanations are general as it is not feasible to specify, for example, the exact number of stitches needed for a polo-neck collar in all types of yarn, with every size of needle. But I hope they are sufficiently detailed for you to be able to broaden the scope of your designs.

The third group of descriptions is concerned with getting the best possible quality of finish for your garment. It describes pressing and blocking, stitching up and decoration. This may consist of tassels and cords, or embroidery or bead knitting. Embroidery can be used either to enhance or to elaborate a garment, or as a means of including a high level of detail in jacquard or picture knitting. The traditional skill of bead knitting is an easy technique that merits reviving. The written explanations are accompanied by illustrations to make them easier to understand, and some photographs showing their use.

CASTING ON

There are several methods of casting on, each of which gives different characteristics to the edge produced. This means that it is important to choose an appropriate method for a particular situation. The methods and their applications are given below:

Single-loop casting on

Use: a light edge for lace and fine knitting. Also used for unravelling at a later stage – see hems (pp. 66).

Method: start with a slip knot and short free end of yarn. With left hand make a loop – like upside down blanket stitch – tighten, repeat to desired number of stitches. (This stitch is deceptively simple and is difficult to knit evenly on the first row.)

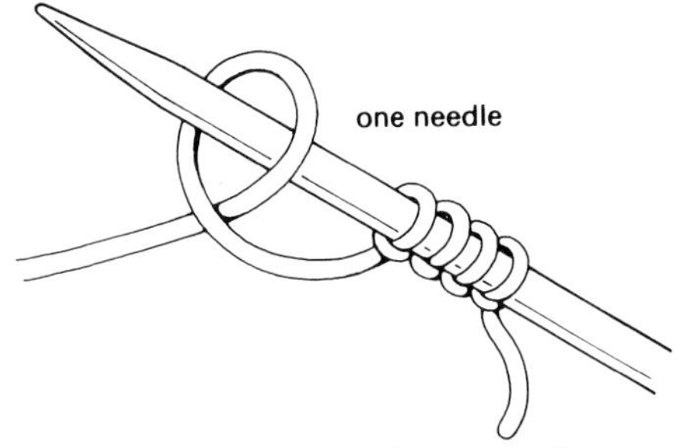

4.1 Single-loop casting on with one needle

Chain casting on

Use: an elastic loose edge used for lace and stretchy stitch patterns.

Method: make a slip knot with a short free end of yarn on LH needle. Put RH needle into loop, wind yarn round and pull loop through – as in knitting – transfer loop back to LH needle.

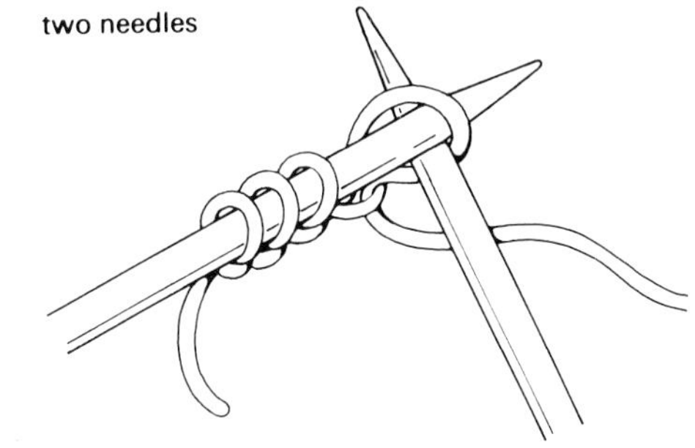

4.2 Chain casting on with two needles

4.3 Cable stitch casting on using two needles

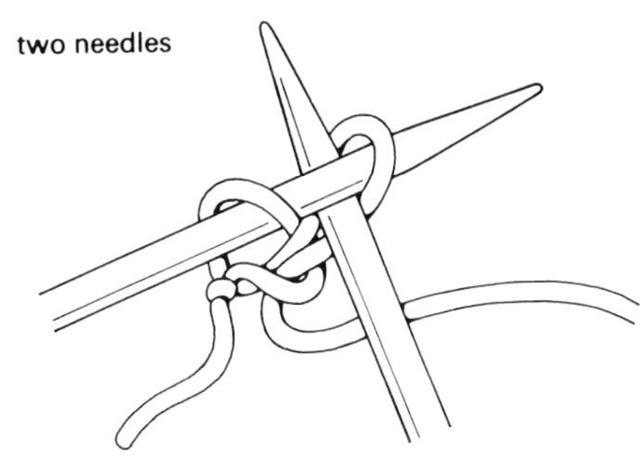

Cable-stitch casting on
Use: a firm edge that is very hard wearing – most commonly used for main edges.
Method: start first loop as for chain method but continue by inserting RH needle behind both sides of loop just created.

SELVEDGES

The selvedge is the finished side edge of the knitting and is formed by the first and last stitch of each row. How these are treated will affect the stability of the edge and so an appropriate technique should be chosen for the different parts of the work.

Chain selvedge
Use: gives elasticity useful when edge is to be picked up.
Method: there are several ways of working this, the most common is to slip a stitch at the beginning of each row – knitwise on k row and purlwise on a p row.

Moss-stitch selvedge
Use: gives a line of knobbly loops that make row matching easy in sewing up.
Method: k first and last stitch of all rows.

Seam selvedge
Use: when edge is to be joined to another selvedge and so must be firm and strong. (For sewing-up techniques, see vertical seaming p. 76.)
Method: first and last stitches are worked in stocking stitch.

Non-curling selvedge
Use: for stocking stitch, to help avoid edges curling under on purl side.
Method: the second and penultimate stitches are purled on k rows.

SHAPING

Various methods are used either to increase or decrease the number of stitches in the work in order to give it shape or to create stitch patterns.

Decreasing
The most common methods are given with their symbols – which can be used in graph planning of work. The dominant line in the symbol represents the direction in which the front stitch will slope.

 k2tog

 s1, k1, psso

 p2tog

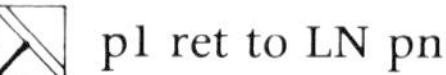 p1 ret to LN pnso

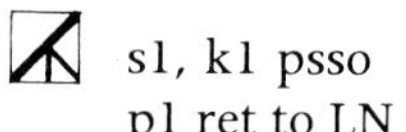 s1, k1 psso p1 ret to LN pnso

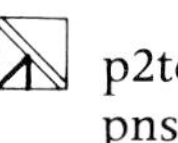 p2tog, ret to LN pnso

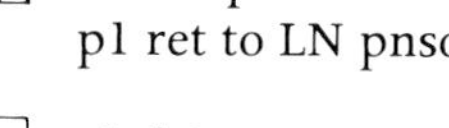 s1, k2tog, psso

 s1, p1 ret to LN pnso, ret to RN psso

 s2, k1, p2sso

Increasing
Both 'invisible' and 'visible' means are possible to increase the number of stitches. As a general rule invisible ways are used for shaping and visible ways for stitch patterns, such as lace effects.

Barred increase M1B This gives a moss stitch-like bar at point of increase produced by working into front and back of stitch. For symmetry, work 1 stitch sooner at the end of row, than at beginning of row.

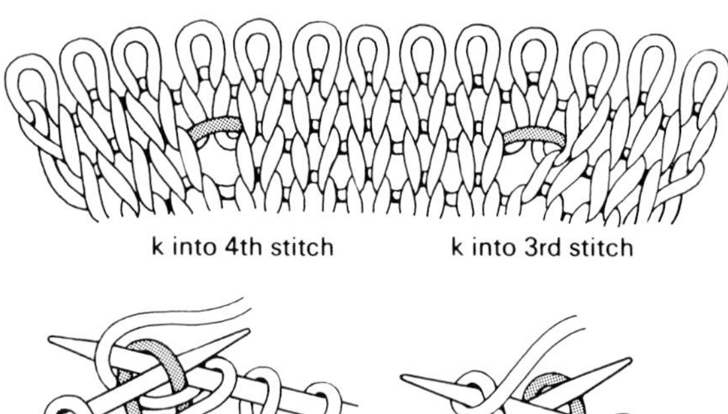

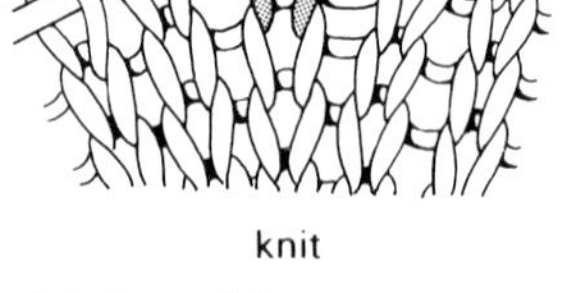

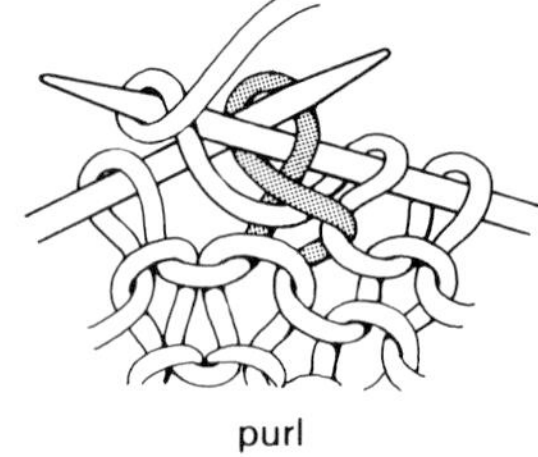

4.4 Barred increase M1B

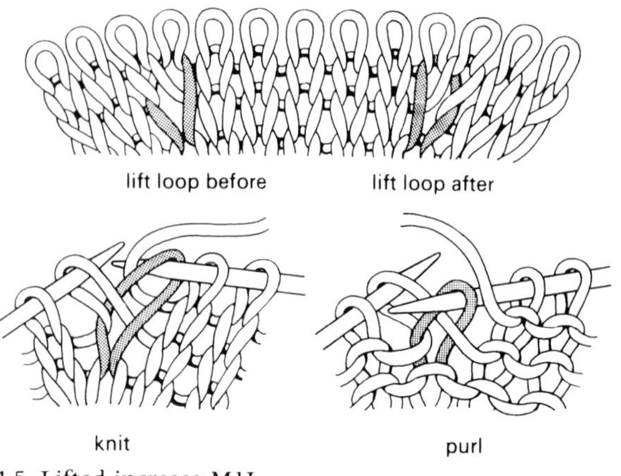

4.5 Lifted increase M1L

(continued on page 65)

EMBROIDERY AND SWISS DARNING

Most embroidery stitches can be worked on knitting. They are a useful way of elaborating a plain jumper or revamping a plain relic. Embroidery can also be used to camouflage stains or darns. Use a specialist embroidery book to give you detailed stitch explanations and ideas.

When embroidering on knitting it is easiest to treat the fabric as a loosely-woven cloth and work into the spaces between the stitches. Cross stitch can be worked over each whole stitch as shown below.

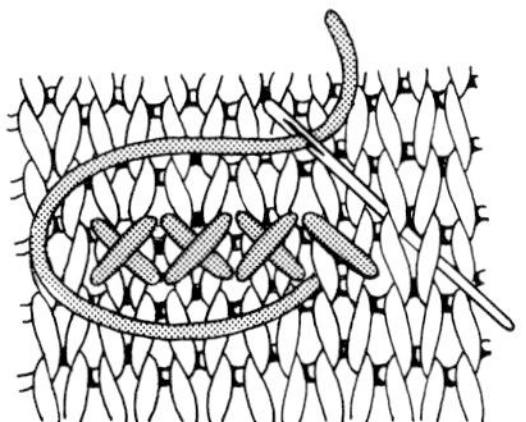

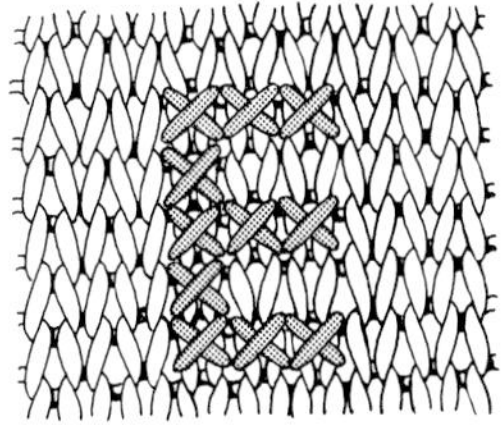

4.48

Swiss darning: This is a useful kind of embroidery specifically worked on knitting. It is usually worked over stocking stitch and may be employed for a variety of reasons. It is a useful technique for the addition of small details to a picture or jacquard design – for example, a third colour to a row that already uses two, or to add a small animal or initial motif to a child's sweater. More mundanely it can be used to reinforce areas of a sweater that suffer a lot of wear, such as the elbows.

The stitch is worked with a tapestry needle over the top of the existing stitches, to imitate them. It may follow a row or be worked in blocks. Use graph paper to plan your design – each square representing one knitted stitch.

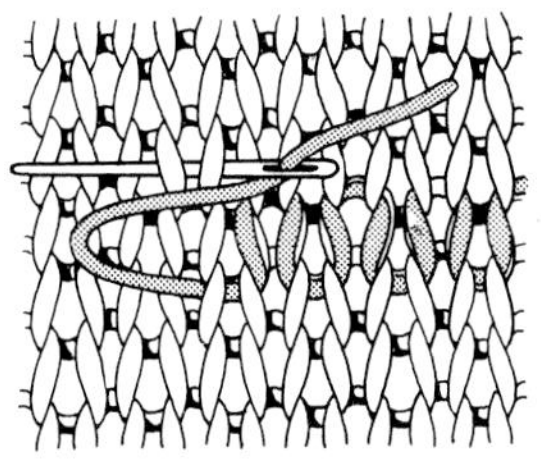

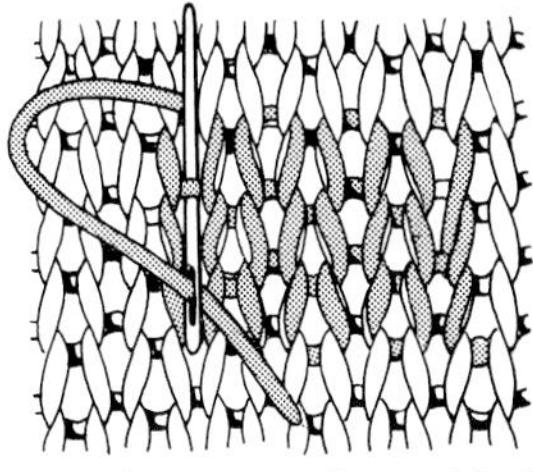

changing rows to form a block

4.49

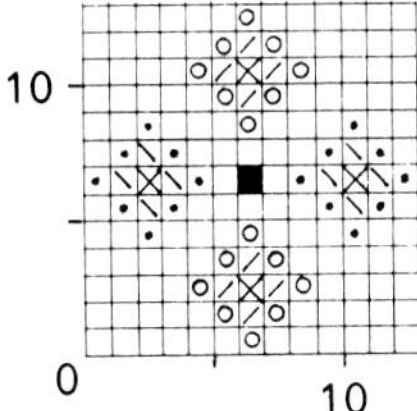

4.50 Grid for Swiss darning worked in five colours: the black centre square is worked as a knot stitch

BEADED KNITTING

A traditional way of decorating knitting, much loved by the Victorians, in which beads are worked in groups or patterns into the knitted fabric. The beads have to be threaded onto the yarn before it is knitted. When choosing beads it is best to ensure that they are slightly larger than the loops that make up the knitted fabric or else they may slip through to the back of the work. The two simplest ways of working are given below.

Garter stitch method

This is best for smaller beads. The beads are introduced on the second and each alternate row and are worked from the back of the fabric. All odd rows are knitted and form the right side of work. A bead is pushed up to the work after each k stitch, on the right-hand needle.

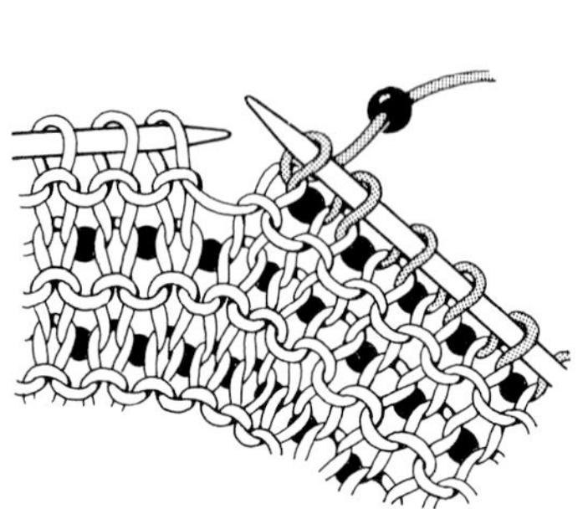

4.51

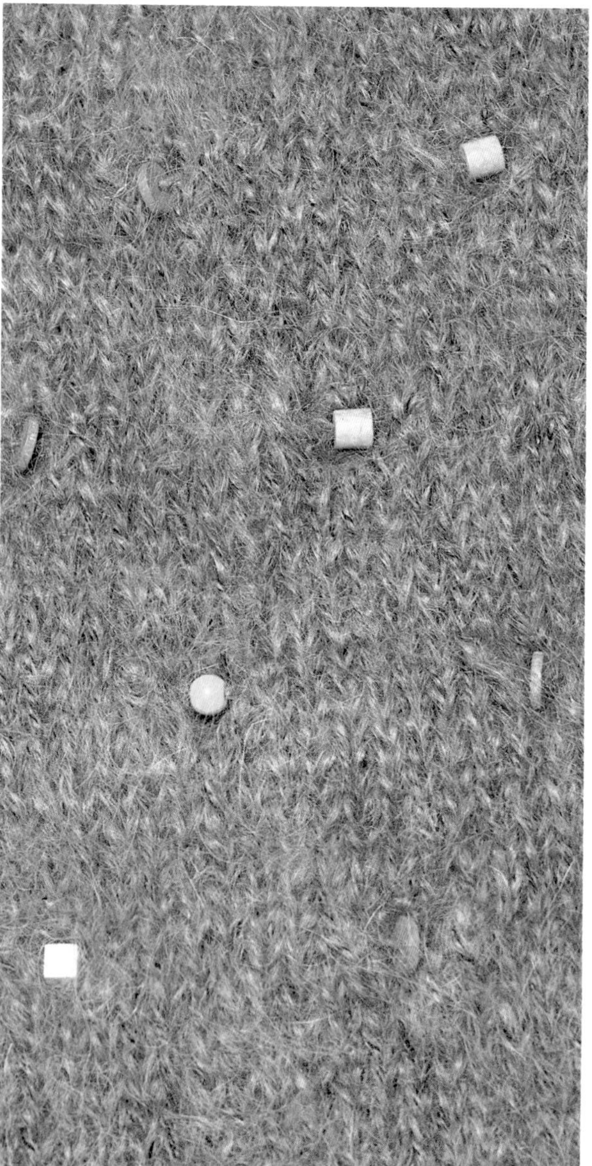

With this method the beads hang on the forward-facing loop between stitches. It is possible to cover the whole fabric in this way or else to introduce groups of beads in patterns, and even to work sections of beaded garter stitch within another stitch pattern.

Slip stitch method

This is suitable for larger beads. The beads are carried on a slipped loop to the front of the work, which is usually stocking stitch. On a k row the yarn is brought forward so the stitch that will be behind the bead can be slipped purlwise, the bead is pushed up to the work and then the yarn is taken back, and the next stitch is worked. This method is particularly suitable for introducing beads at fairly wide intervals.

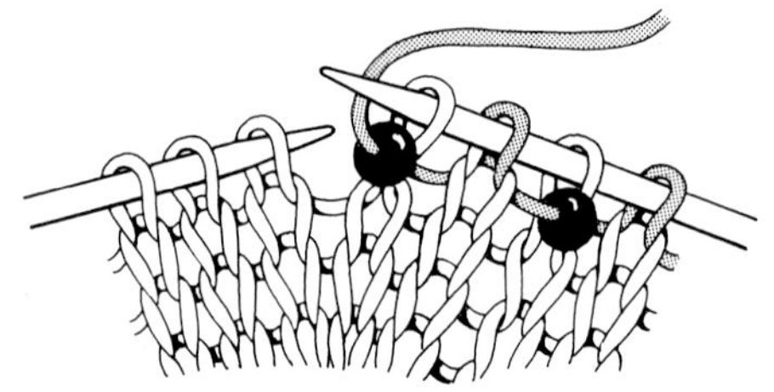

4.52

(continued from page 64)

Lifted increase M1L Lift 'worked' loop (see anatomy of stitch below) of previous row and k or p into it. For symmetry, work into loop of previous stitch at beginning of row and loop of next stitch at end of row.

Raised increase M1R This can be invisible or visible, the latter is just like a tighter version of a yon that has been knitted. For an invisible effect: insert left-hand needle below 'bar' between stitches from front to back, then either k or p through back loop. For visible effect: k or p into front of raised 'bar'.

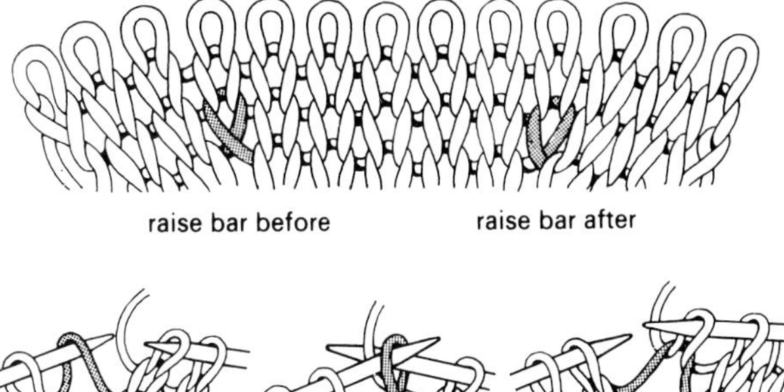

4.6 Raised increase M1R

Over yon This makes a visible increase as used for buttonholes, picot hems, eyelet holes and lace effects. Take the yarn forward and over the top of the needle – the next stitch must be worked.

ANATOMY OF A STITCH

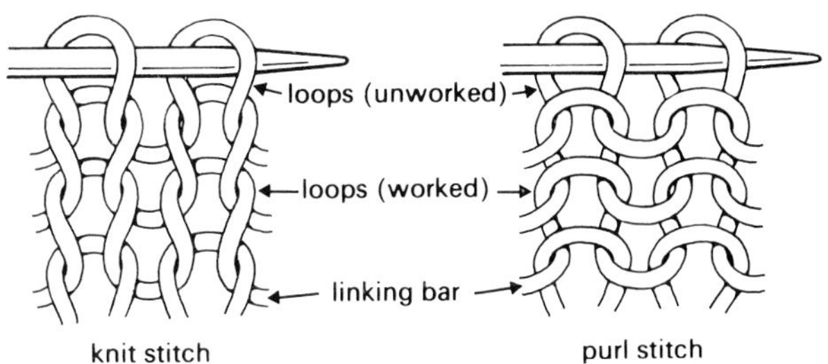

4.7 Anatomy of a stitch

CASTING OFF

As with casting on the choice of method should take account of function.

Standard casting off

Use: for firm stable edges.
Method: can be done using a crochet hook or needle. Always follow the working of the previous row – so k stitches are knitted before being drawn over and p stitches are purled.

Elastic casting off (suspended method)

Use: for edges that require elasticity – such as welts and bindings.
Method: either use a larger size of RH needle or use the 'suspended' technique in which the slipped or drawn-over stitch is retained on the tip of the LH needle until the next stitch has been worked, after which it is dropped, so the next loop can be drawn over. This controls the tension of the yarn and prevents the newly cast-off stitches from being pulled tight as subsequent stitches are knitted and drawn over.

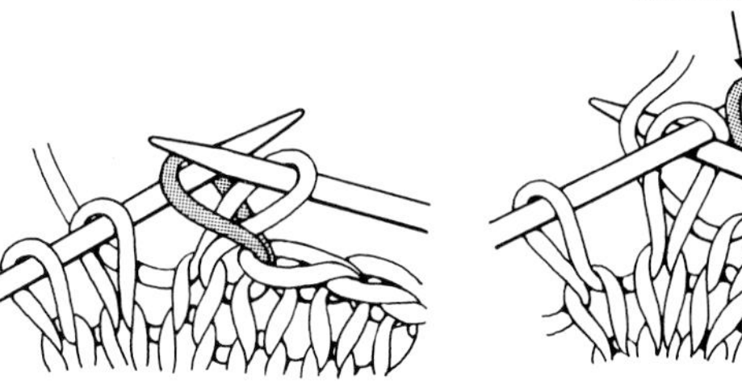

4.8 Suspended casting off

Temporary casting off

Use: to hold stitches that will later be picked up.
Method: thread up a tapestry needle with contrasting, smooth yarn. This is threaded through each of the stitches on LH needle.

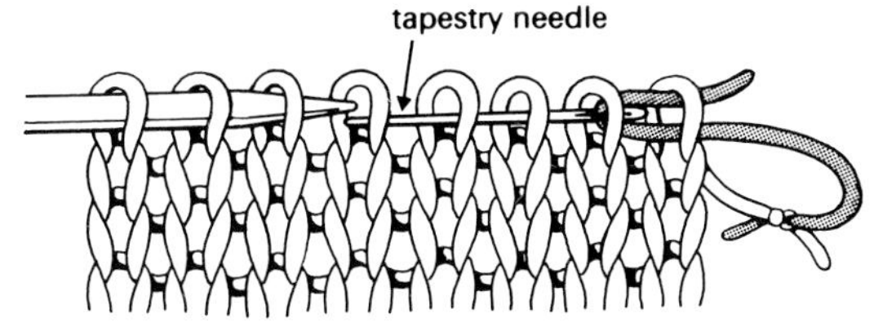

4.9 Temporary casting off

Invisible casting off

Use: for ribbed welts.
Method for single rib: worked in a similar way to grafting. Cut the yarn 3 to 4 times longer than length to be cast off. Using a tapestry needle sew knitwise into first k stitch and slip off needle, then
(1) purlwise into next stitch and from back to front through previous stitch, now dropped, pull yarn through.

(2) Insert needle into next k stitch on LH needle and p stitch (2 stitches), drop both stitches, pull yarn through. Continue in this way, keeping an even tension until all are cast off.

Method for double rib: this is most easily done by twisting the second k stitch with the first p stitch of each pair, so that the stitches are presented as for single rib and can be worked in the same way. To do this using a cable needle, slip the first k stitch onto RH needle; second onto cable needle and leave to front of work; slip first p stitch onto RH needle; slip k stitch from cable needle onto RH needle; slip second p stitch onto RH needle. The stitches on RH needle should now be ordered k,p,k,p reading R to L. Continue in this way till all stitches have been slipped – if the last 2 stitches are k, then k two stitches together to maintain the single rib pattern. Cast off as given above for single rib.

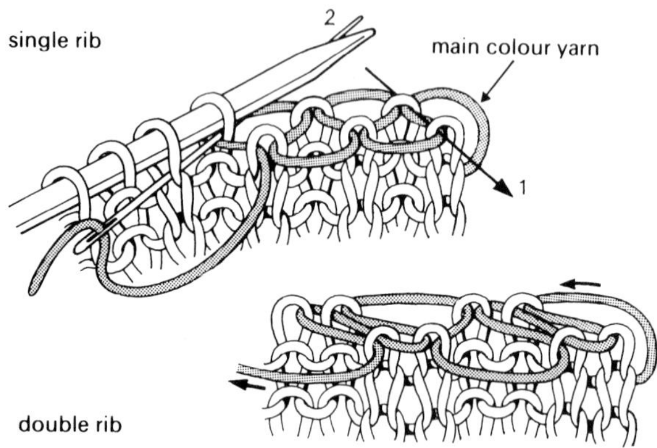

4.10 Invisible casting off methods

HEMS

Knitting usually uses some kind of stitch pattern to begin or end work as a folded hem can easily be too bulky. If you want a hem then try to avoid this by knitting the section that will be folded behind either with a smaller-sized needle or with a finer yarn. If the main section is knitted in a stitch pattern, use stocking stitch for the hem return and do not forget to measure the length rather than count rows. It helps to make a neat fold if the row at which the actual fold is to be made is knitted in reverse stocking stitch.

Hem at the beginning of the work Cast on with the single loop method – after a couple of rows unravel cast-on edge, a few stitches at a time, and slip stitches onto a fine double-ended needle. Continue knitting, using chosen method to mark fold, until an even number of rows have been worked or hem is the same length as right side. Fold the work in half and knit together stitches from both needles, to give maximum elasticity.

Hem at end of work Mark fold row and work hem. Then break off a length of yarn about 3 to 4 times as long as edge. Using a tapestry needle, oversew each loop off needle to the back bar of a stitch from row on main piece.

Picot edge Mark fold as follows:
Row 1: *k2tog yon; repeat from * to last stitch: k1
Row 2: p row

Scallop edge for 4 to 8 rows at fold line (the fold will come in the centre of chosen number of rows).
For a multiple of 5 + 4 st:
First row: *k4 sl yon k4; repeat from * to end row
Next and subsequent rows (except last): p4 *sl yon p 4; repeat from * to end row
End row of section: p4 *p slipped stitch and all yon as one stitch, p4; repeat from * to end row. When pressing encourage the scallops to show by gently pulling them downwards.

Tubing or casing for elastic This can be formed by making a narrow hem to thread it through. This can also be done at the start of a rib:
Cast on half the number of stitches needed for the rib using the single-loop method. Knit at least 4 rows stocking stitch (to give twice the width of the elastic), unravel the cast-on edge and slip onto a fine needle.
Next row: in rib k1 from first needle, p1 from second – continue in this way until all stitches are ribbed.

For casing not on ribbed edge use as many stitches as needed for main section and work hem as given above, knitting stitches together at beginning of work or oversewing them at end of work.

WORKING TWO OR MORE STITCH PATTERNS WITH DIFFERENT ROW TENSIONS TOGETHER

Coping with differing tensions caused by knitting a number of stitch patterns across a piece can cause problems if not allowed for in advance. The easiest way of dealing with it is to knit a few extra rows of the tighter-tensioned stitch section as needed. This can be done by eye or calculated precisely as shown in Fig 4.11.

In the example over 30 rows pattern A measures 10cm and B measures 12cm. This means that more rows of A will be needed over the 12cm of B to give a constant-seeming tension. If there are 30 rows of A in 10cm then 1cm = 3 rows, so we will need 2cm extra or 6 rows. For these extra rows to be knitted inconspicuously, they must be spaced two at a time evenly over the length – every 10th row in this case. Knit across the row to end of tighter section, turn work and knit back across tight section only, turn work and knit across to end of row. Next row knit across as usual. In this way the tight section is knitted an extra 2 times and a seemingly constant tension is achieved.

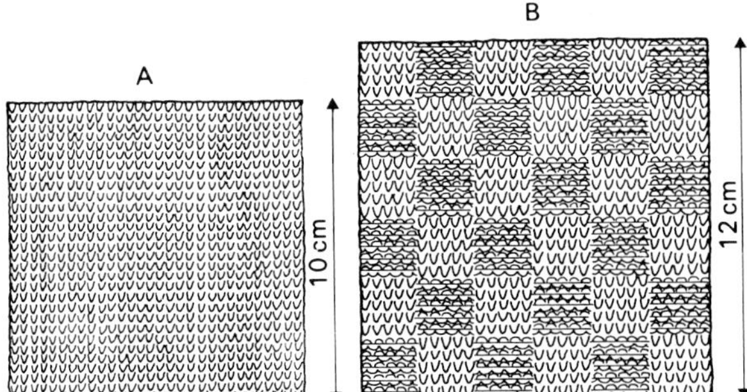

4.11 Tension squares each 30 rows long but measuring different lengths

PICKING UP STITCHES

Stitches need to be picked up so that further knitting can take place, usually at the edge of the work and sometimes in other places.

Picking up stitches for a neckband or collar The most important point about this is that the stitches should be picked up evenly and without any lumps or holes. To plan from where the stitches will be picked up, start by taking away the number of stitches on stitch holders or temporarily cast off, from the total number needed for the neck. Divide the remaining number of stitches so that they are equally allocated to the remaining edges. In the example 100 stitches need to be picked up for a round neckband. 60 stitches are ready on stitch holders and so a further 40 need to be picked up from the remaining edges – 20 on each side of the front neck.

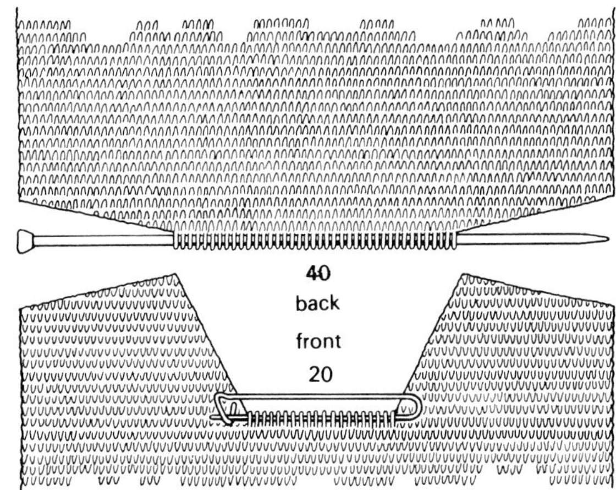

4.12 When working out how many stitches to pick up for neck, first count how many are left on stitch holders

To do this evenly use safety pins to divide up the sides into 2cm (or some other convenient measurement). In each section 5 stitches need picking up. To do this painlessly, use a fine knitting needle and, with the wrong side facing, insert needle into work and slip an appropriate number of loops onto the needle between two safety pins. On a chain selvedge work between chain and first stitch.

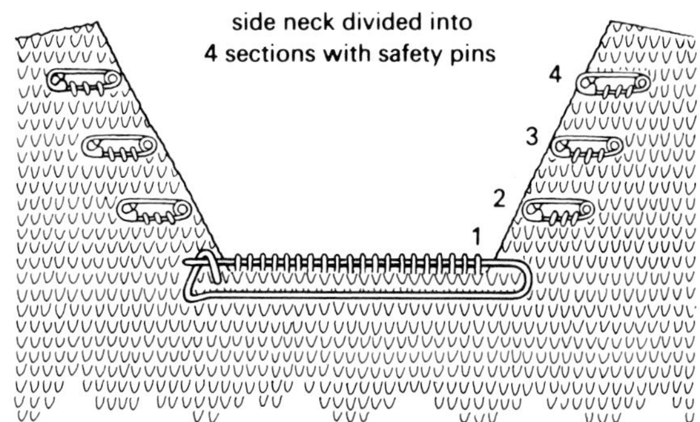

4.13 Then divide up remaining neck opening into sections with safety pins

If you pick up too many loops they can easily be dropped when the first row is knitted onto them. If the loops you pick up seem very loose they can be twisted if you knit into the back on the first row. When you have all the stitches ready with the right side of work facing and appropriate sized needles, knit as required the stitches from each of the various holders or needles.

Picking up stitches from a vertical edge If you know how many stitches need to be picked up, use the same technique described above of dividing with pins. If not, 3 stitches for every 4 rows is a rough guide for stocking stitch or a ribbed edging. If you plan to pick up a vertical edge, use a chain selvedge. This will give 3 stitches for 2 chains – 1 stitch being picked up from the tight division between chains.

Picking up stitches from a horizontal edge These should be picked up direct to give the best results – not from a cast-off edge. Try to plan ahead and leave stitches to be picked up on safety pins, stitch holders or a strand of wool. If this is not possible carefully unravel the cast-off edge and knit the stitches directly. This will ensure maximum elasticity.

If the tension is the same as that already used, pick up each existing stitch; if not, increase or decrease accordingly.

Picking up stitches not at an edge Mark the length to be picked up either with safety pins or contrasting wool (particularly useful for curves and diagonals).

For a horizontal pick up, use the fine needle technique: with right side facing, start at left and pick up the side loop of each stitch across length.

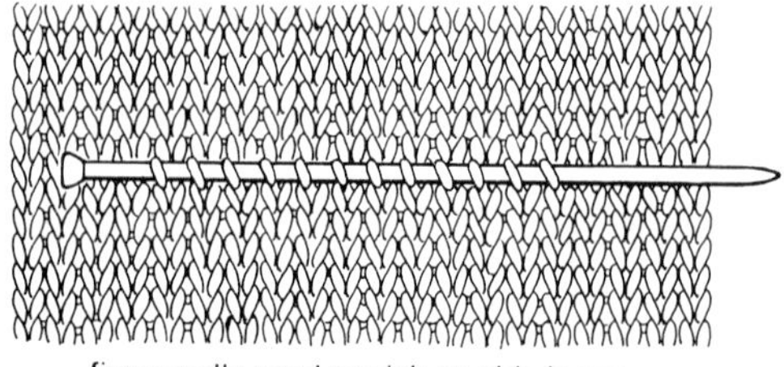

4.14 Picking up stitches in the centre of work: horizontal method

For a vertical length use same method but pick up only enough loops to achieve the desired tension. This should be calculated in advance by measuring the length to be picked up.

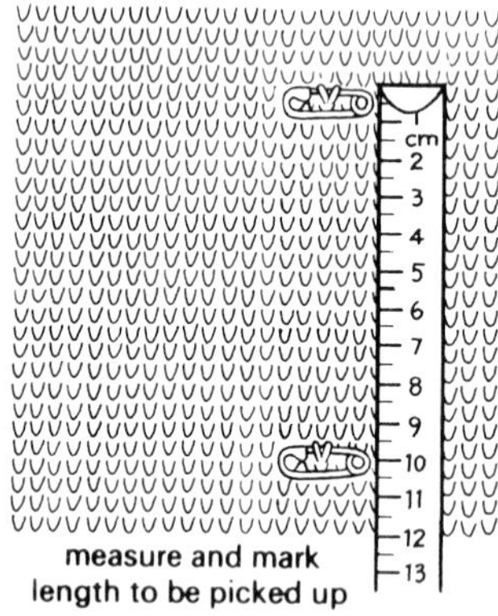

4.15 Vertical picking up: calculating how many loops over the chosen length

In the example this is 10cm. In the stitch pattern to be knitted on the picked up stitches there should be 20 stitches over 10cm. The existing knitting used 18 rows for the 10cm and so all except 2 loops will need to be picked-up. The missed loops should be spaced out evenly for the best results.

For stitches at an angle follow the method described for vertical picking up.

POCKETS

There are two types of pocket: one is integral and must be allowed for in knitting the section in which it occurs; the second is added to the garment by being worked separately and stitched on or knitted on picked-up stitches. Either type may be a single layer or lining which is stitched to the main fabric or a separate bag or pouch attached only at its mouth.

Integral pockets

Horizontal, opening along a row: these can be knitted at a later stage providing the pocket position is marked in advance. Do this by knitting the stitches that will form the pocket opening in a contrasting yarn, with the main yarn looped at the back. This method is particularly useful in complex stitch patterns where a break could be distracting.

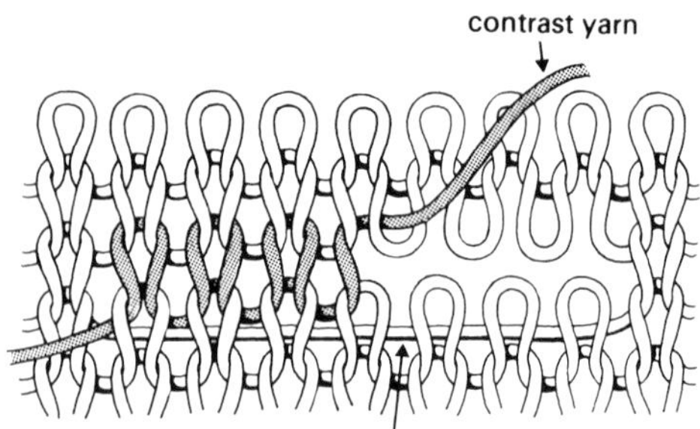

4.16 Marking a horizontal pocket opening for later working

When you are ready to make the pocket, gently pull out the contrast yarn and slip the stitches from below and above onto a needle or stitch holder. Work your chosen pocket on them. More often a pocket lining is knitted in advance, with 2 more stitches than the gap, in stocking stitch. The extra stitches are knitted together with the stitch at each side of the gap, to avoid holes at the corner. A binding or welt is knitted on the gap stitches, usually at a later stage.

Another method is to knit an extra length, long enough to be doubled over to form the pocket, on the stitches from the gap. If you do this, increase 1 stitch at each side of the pocket section. When the pocket is long enough, at each side pick up the corner stitch from the first row of the pocket and knit it together with the two edge stitches or pocket end row – to get back to the original number of stitches.

Both these types of pocket need some kind of binding or welt to finish the edge and to stop the pocket from stretching or sagging.

Vertical pocket opening: to work this type of opening it is necessary to use an additional ball of yarn to work the section to one side of the pocket. When you reach the start of the opening, turn work and knit a piece long enough to form the opening. Leave stitches on a stitch holder or spare needle. Join in spare yarn at base of pocket opening on second side and work to match first.

It is possible to use this technique to form a diagonal opening by decreasing on one side of the pocket opening and increasing by a similar amount on the other.

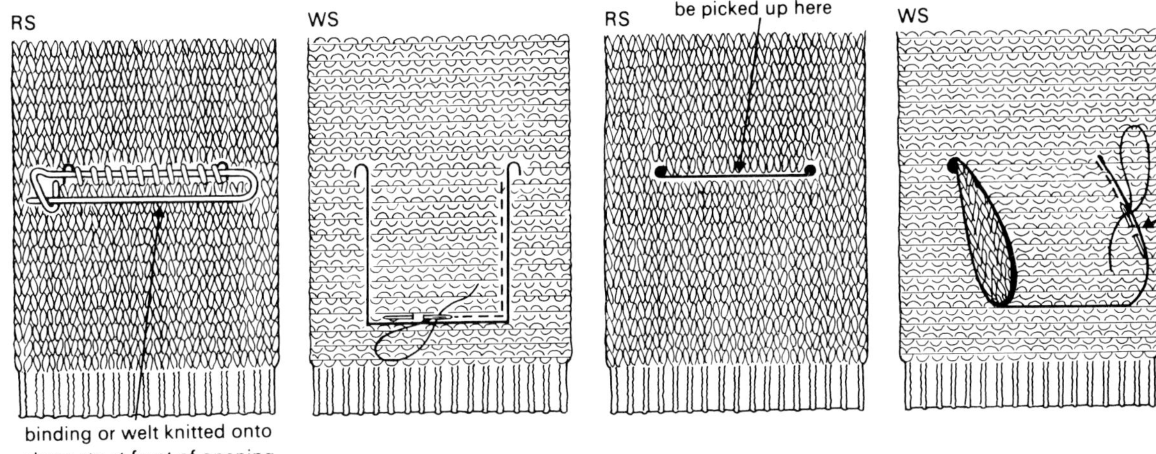

4.17 Working a single pocket lining onto an opening

Continuous pocket worked during course of knitting

Additional pockets

Patch pockets These are knitted as a complete piece, in any shape, and are then stitched carefully in place. They can be used to mask stains or holes in older garments – which may account for their name.

Side-seam pockets If you plan in advance to have a side seam pocket it is a good idea to incorporate an integral pocket edging or welt in the front of the garment.

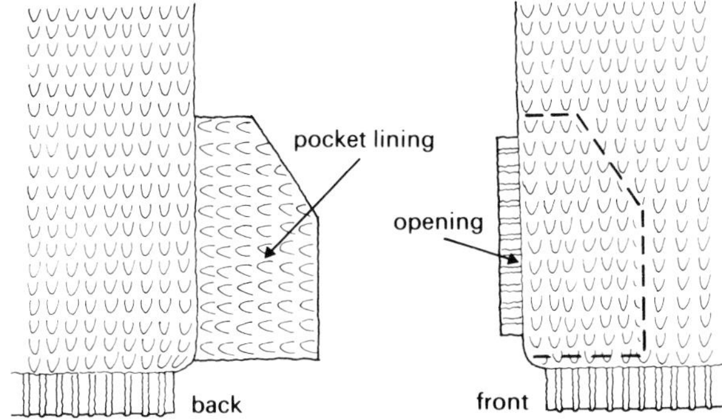

4.18 Side pocket can be either picked up and knitted sideways or knitted and then stiched on afterwards

If this is not appropriate to the design, then work some kind of binding – either by picking up and knitting a few rows (which may be turned inwards to reinforce the edge invisibly) or by crocheting the edge. The pocket lining may also be an integral part of the back of the garment. Cast on extra stitches and shape the top edge. If not, the stitches can be picked up at the side of the work vertically and knitted to desired shape.

Kangaroo pouch pockets These can be worked as a patch pocket.

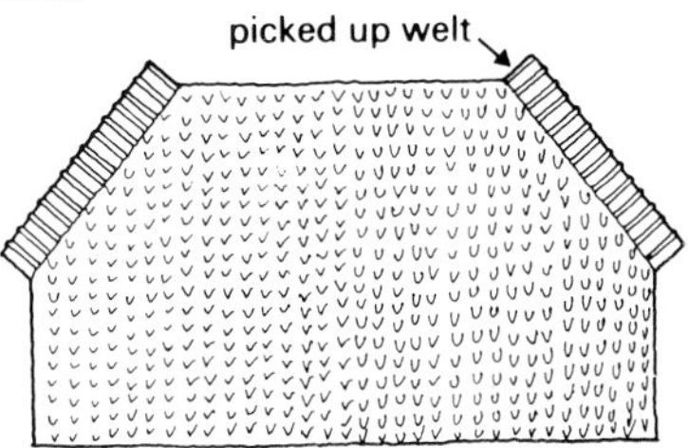

4.19 Kangaroo pouch pocket worked separately

To give a neater finish to top edge, knit the pocket in advance but do not cast off top edge – leave stitches on a spare needle. Then work garment front to length of pocket top, then work across row to position of pocket, knit together stitches from pocket top and front, work to end row.

FRONT AND NECKBANDS

Front bands

Front bands are used to finish the fastening edges of a garment and may be knitted in several ways. They are usually worked on smaller needles or use a stitch pattern that will produce a stable edge – most commonly rib, garter stitch and moss stitch.

Integral border is knitted at the same time as the garment section which is to be edged. A certain number of stitches are constantly knitted to form a band in a stitch pattern that is slightly denser (more rows per cm) than the main fabric, to ensure a firm unpuckered edge. If the main work is stocking stitch this could be single moss stitch or twisted rib (k

stitches worked through back of loops). It is best to work a sample to check the suitability of your choice.
Vertical band is worked afterwards with finer needles and seam selvedges and is then joined on. Always work the band for the buttons first and leave on a safety pin – so that the length can be adjusted if necessary. Use safety pins to hold it edge to edge with the main front. With right side facing, work a vertical grafted seam, allowing for uneven row tension between the band and front. When you are happy with the band decide where the buttons should be and mark with safety pins. Check they are evenly placed by counting rows and make a note of where they come so that the buttonhole band can be knitted exactly from your calculations.
Horizontal band is where stitches are picked up vertically (see page 68) and a band knitted on. It is not easy to judge the exact number of stitches you will need for the effect you want, so do not be afraid to unpick and start again as many times as necessary to get the best results.
Corners – if the band turns a corner you will have to shape it so that it will lie flat.

Shaping corners on front and neck bands

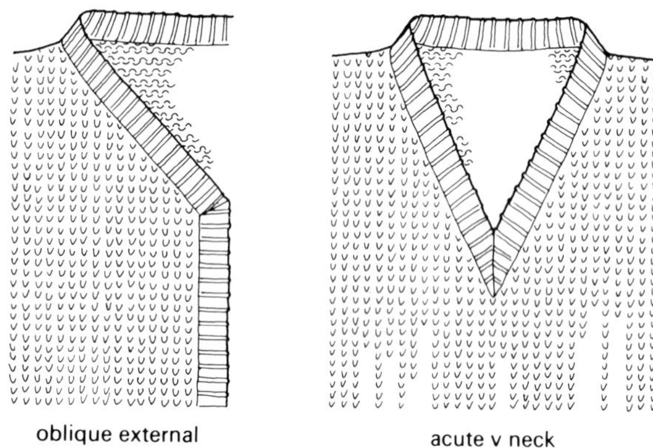

4.20 Band with an oblique external corner
V neck band with acute corner

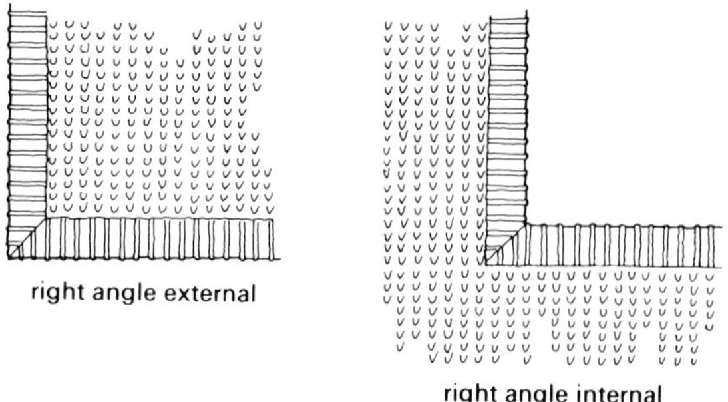

4.21 Band with an external right angular corner
Neck band with internal right angular corner

Oblique external Increase 1 stitch on alternate rows at apex.
Right angle external At beginning of work cast on enough stitches for full width, slip 2 stitches onto a safety pin at edge on alternate rows. Pick up stitches vertically and work band, picking up 2 stitches from safety pin on alternate rows – until all are incorporated and edge even. Cast off in pattern.
Right angle internal Leave horizontal stitches on holder until vertical side completed. Pick up stitches from vertical edges and stitch holder. (If you want to work an axis stitch pick up a stitch from the angle – and use a single decrease on either side of it on alternate rows.) Work a double decrease on alternate rows at corners.
Acute angle internal corners Work as for right angle internal but decrease every row. If the angle is very acute you may have to work a few extra decreases near the apex before casting off to avoid a wavy or protruding edge.

Neckbands – how to calculate the number of stitches

This is not easy to do, so be prepared to unravel and try again. As a rough estimate pin together the bottom edge ribbing and see how many stitches you need to get your head through. Then count the number of stitches you have available on stitch holders; see fig. 4.22 for how to decrease for different angles.
Total up the projected number of stitches obtainable by estimating like this and make sure it is at least equal to and preferably greater than the rough head size number. Follow method for picking up the stitches (see p. 68) and knit as desired.
Round neckband Follow instructions given to calculate the number of stitches and pick up the stitches needed. When using rib no shaping should be necessary providing the band does not exceed 5cm in height.
V neckband Follow instructions given to calculate the number of stitches and pick up those needed. Follow corner shaping described above.
Overlapping V neckband (not suitable for a very deep, acute V). For this the stitches to form the band are picked up in two stages. Traditionally the band is seamed at the left shoulder, so with the right side facing pick up and knit stitches along left front neck. Then the right neck and back are picked up and knitted. To sew up, taking care not to stretch the bands, on the wrong side catch the side edge of the right front band to base of first few picked-up

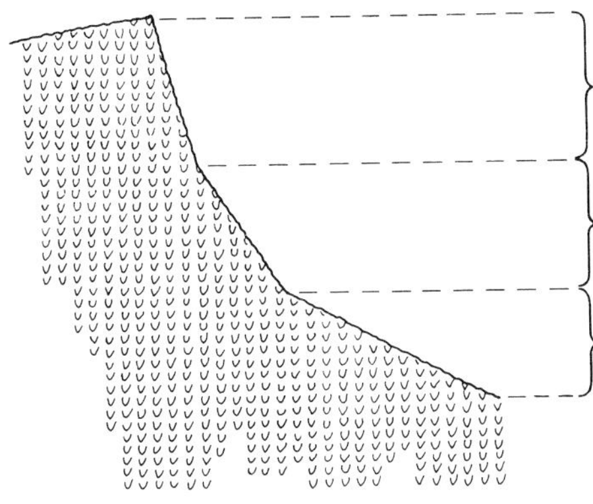

2 stitches over 3 rows – from vertical or angled edge

3 stitches over 4 rows – from shallow angle
(1 decrease each alternate row)

1 stitch over 1 row – from very shallow angle
(1 decrease or more every row)

4.22 Guide to calculating how many stitches to pick up along a shaped opening

stitches on the left front band. On the right side of work invisibly catch down the side edge of left band to base of picked-up stitches of right front band.

Overlapping V neckband: finished effect when sewn up

Doubled-over bands are used to give a reinforced or bulky edge. They may be knitted in a variety of stitches including stocking stitch which can be treated in jacquard to simulate patterned ribbon binding. If buttonholes are included in the band they must be knitted on both sides of the band and then stitched together to finish (use a buttonhole stitch to reinforce them). There are two main ways of finishing off the bands – neither involving casting off. For an invisible finish: pick up the stitches with the right side of work facing, knit the band and fold to the wrong side. Break the wool allowing 3 to 4 times length of edge, and using a tapestry needle, oversew each loop from the knitting needle onto the back of the base stitch of the picked-up row. For a visible finish: to imitate a commercial 'linked edge', the band is picked up with the wrong side of work facing and then folded over to the right side.

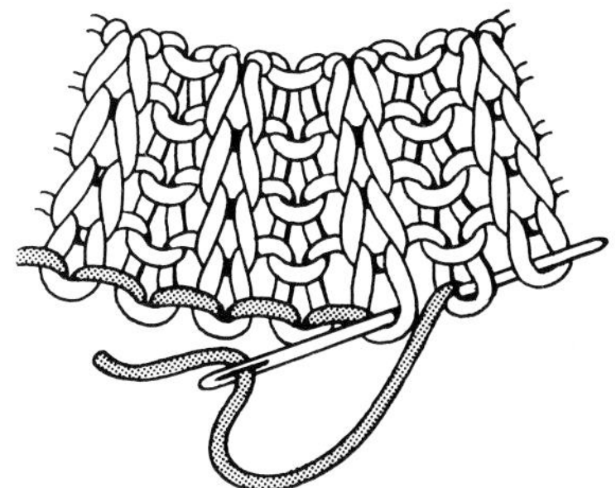

4.23 Doubled over band being stitched down

Allow wool 4 to 5 times length of the edge and using a tapestry needle backstitch up through next loop and back through previous loop. Continue in this way matching the stitches with the base of each previously picked-up stitch.

COLLARS

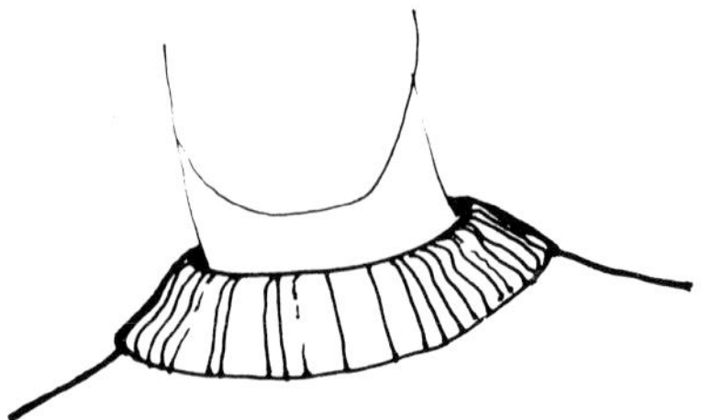

4.24 Crew neck

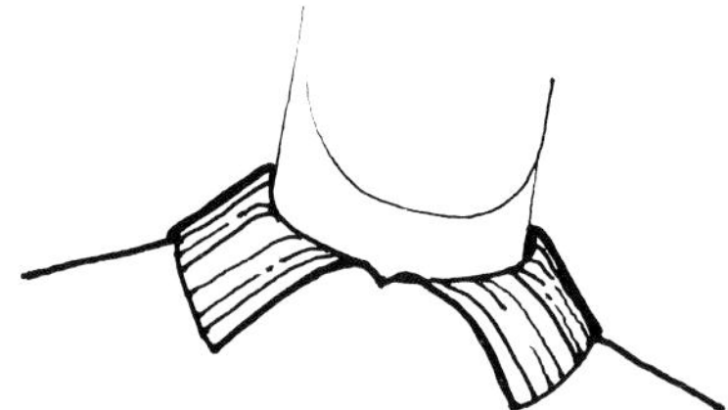

4.28 Straight collar

Crew neck

This is a deep round neckband – halfway to a polo neck – and often folded over. To get this to lie flat use three sizes of needle and work in k1,p1, rib. Start with needles that are only one size smaller than the main garment pattern and work one third of the finished length. (If you want to fold the neck this means one third of the final folded length, as the second side is knitted like the first but in reverse.) Change to next smaller size of needle and work second third, change to smallest size and work last third. If you are folding, repeat process in reverse but do not cast off, graft edge onto inner side of neck opening.

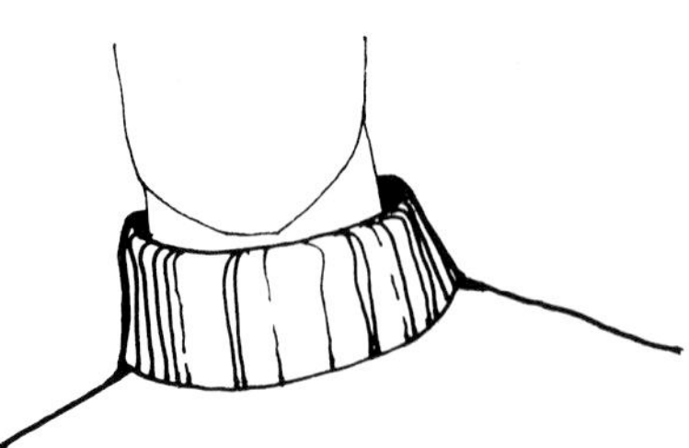

4.25 Polo neck

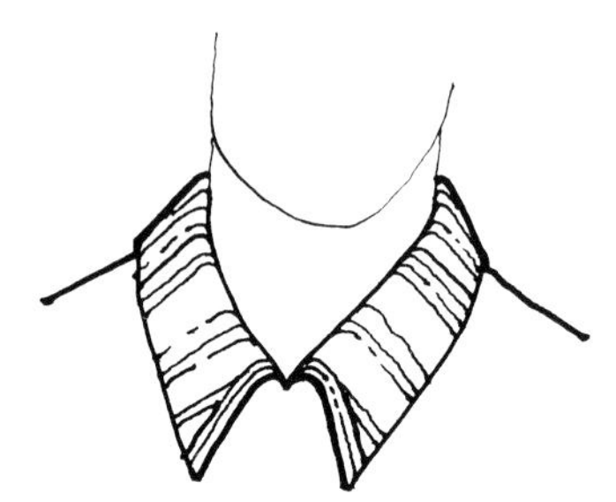

4.29 Chelsea or wing collar

Polo neck

This is knitted onto a round neck opening and folded over. For a tight collar, knit all the length on the same needles used for basic welts. For a looser effect knit the first half on main needles then change to next size larger for second half of length, which is folded outwards. Always cast off loosely either with a larger needle or using the suspended technique (see p. 65).

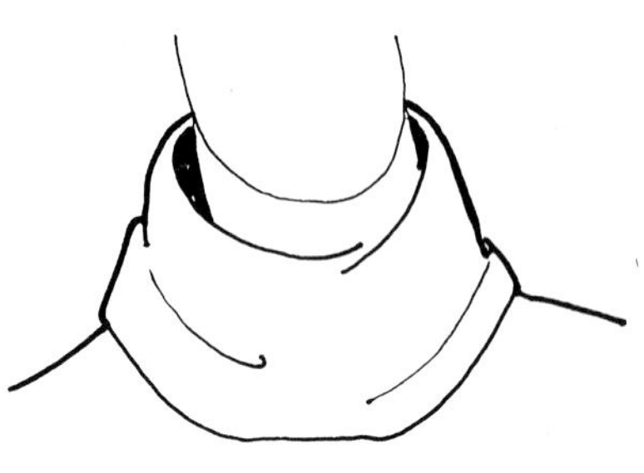

4.26 Cowl neck

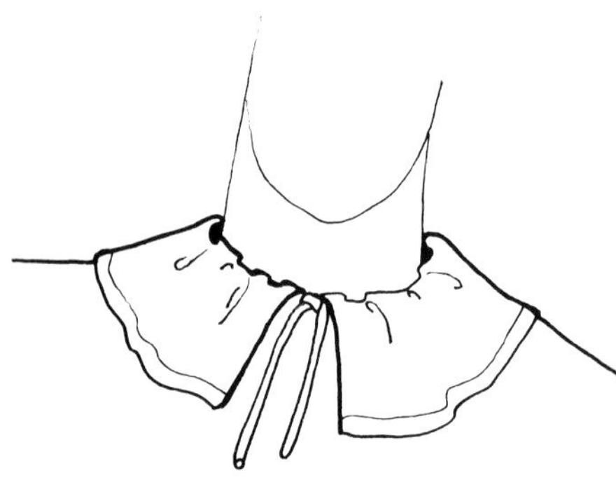

4.30 Ruffle collar

Cowl neck

This is knitted onto a scooped neck, an enlarged round neck opening, and either picked up and knitted, or knitted 'sideways' and stitched onto the opening with a seam.

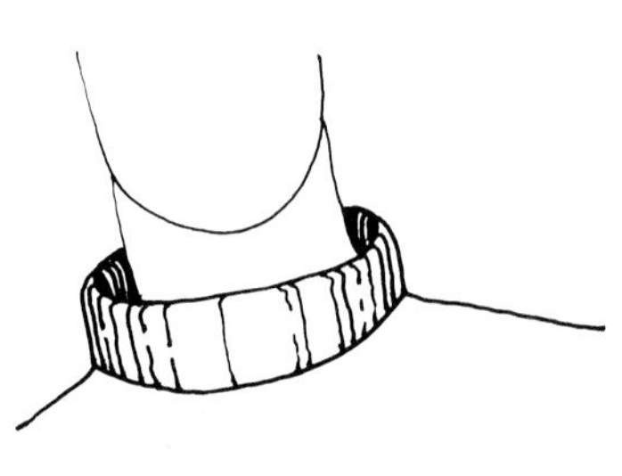

4.27 Standing collar

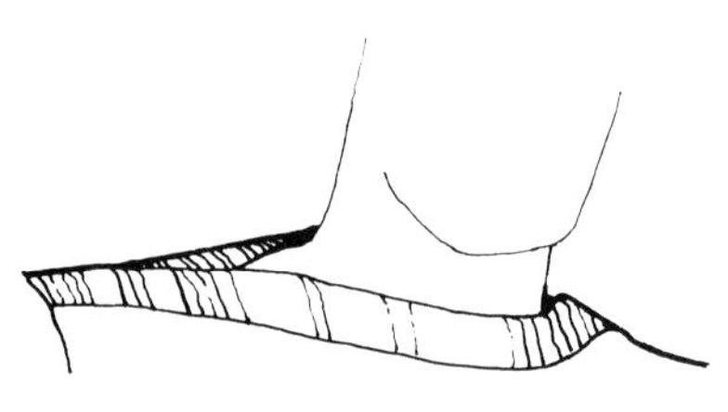

4.31 Boat neck

Standing collar

This is knitted onto a round neck opening, usually folded over and stitched down, in a dense stitch that is able to stand up alone.

Straight collar
This may be fitted onto a round neck opening or have an additional front placket-style shirt opening. It is only possible to pick up and knit this collar with two needles on a shirt neck opening – otherwise four needles are needed, or else it is stitched on, edge to edge, by oversewing. No shaping is necessary in knitting it, if it is knitted in a rib.

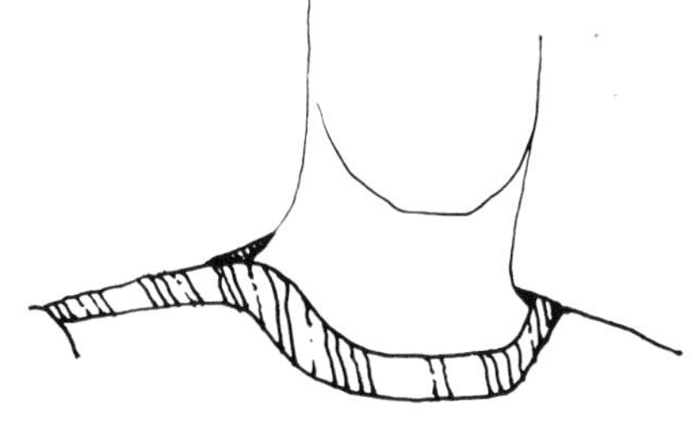

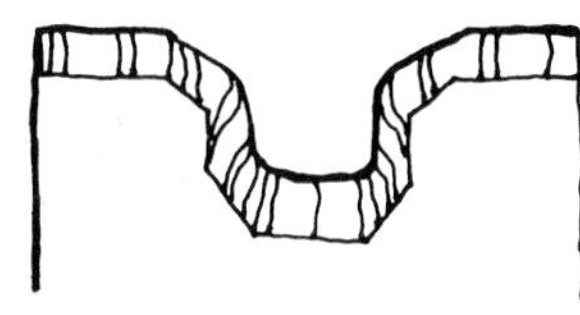

4.32 Envelope neck

Chelsea or wing collar
This is similar to a straight collar but the points hang more towards the front. It may be fitted to a round neck for the wing version or to a V neck when it is known as a Chelsea collar. To get the collar corners to point down they must be shaped at the edges by working regular increases, on alternate rows for a slight slope and every row for a more pronounced slope.

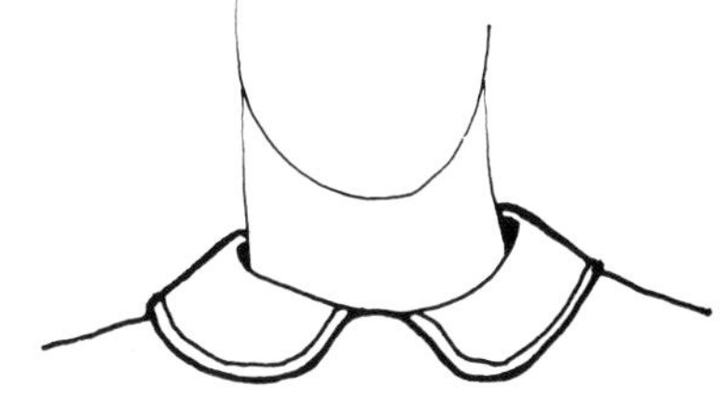

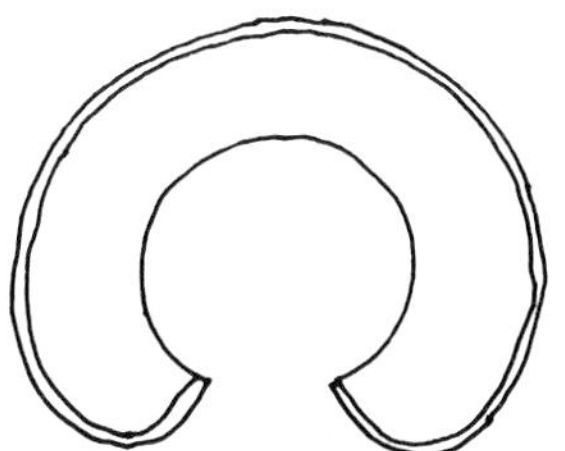

4.33 Peter Pan collar

Ruffle collar
This is normally fitted onto a round neck opening and usually knitted lengthwise using a shaped edge stitch pattern. The more the edging is shaped relative to its shorter edge, the more the collar will ruffle. (See edgings, p. 91.)

Peter Pan collar
This is best knitted in a bias or lengthwise-shaped edging stitch to ensure a flat fit onto the round neck opening of the garment. (See edgings, p. 91.)

Envelope neck
A variation of the boat neck where the front neck is shaped in a wide shallow curve. A welt is then picked up and knitted right across the front. The back is left unshaped. The neck is finished as for the boat neck. This style is especially useful for small babies who hate having things pulled over their heads.

Boat neck
The front and back are knitted alike without shaping and with an edge welt or hem. They can then be stitched up, edge to edge, to form the shoulder seams. For young children this neck opening is often left unstitched with the welts overlapped at the sleeve crown, and a button and loop used to fasten them at the neck.

Sailor collar
This is fitted onto a V neck and worked in stocking stitch with hemmed edges, often in a contrasting colour. A gusset may be fitted inside the apex of the V. It is advisable to plan the shape with a paper cut-out to get a good fit.

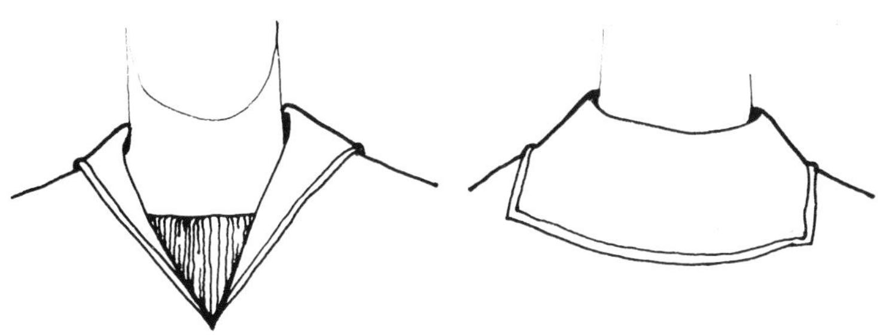

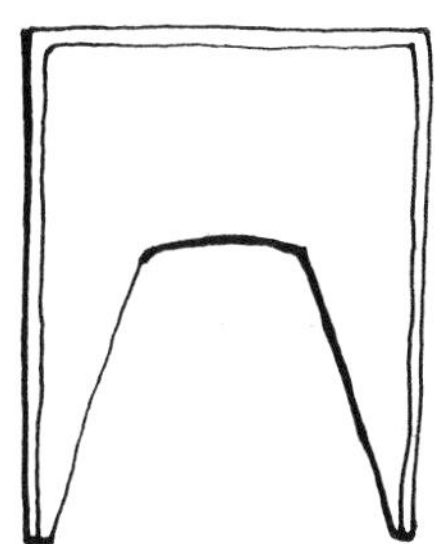

4.34 Sailor collar

HOODS

There are various ways of knitting hoods, all of which can be adapted to form bonnets, and need to be sewn into an ordinary round neck opening. To measure for a hood, rather than using a tape measure (as this often leads to an over-loose fit) pin a section of the knitting together and fit on the head. If this is impossible use a tape and measure from the top of one shoulder seam over the head and down to the other – then deduct 3-5cm to allow for the stretch of the knitting. You can use this method to assess the fit of the hood of an existing garment and deduct in the same way if it is made of cloth.

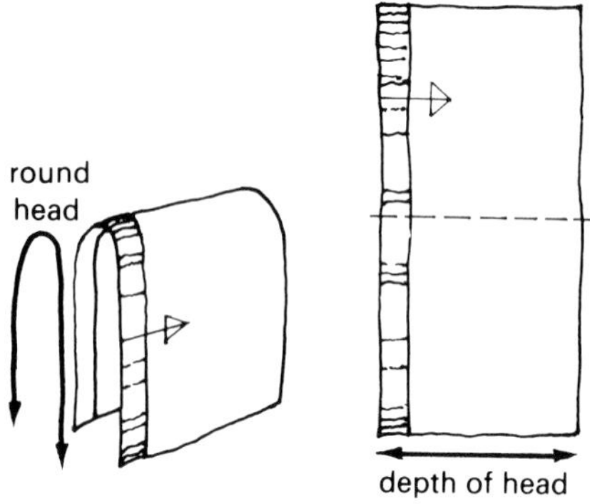

4.35 Simple hood with seam at back of head

Folded and stitched up the back which gives a pointed top

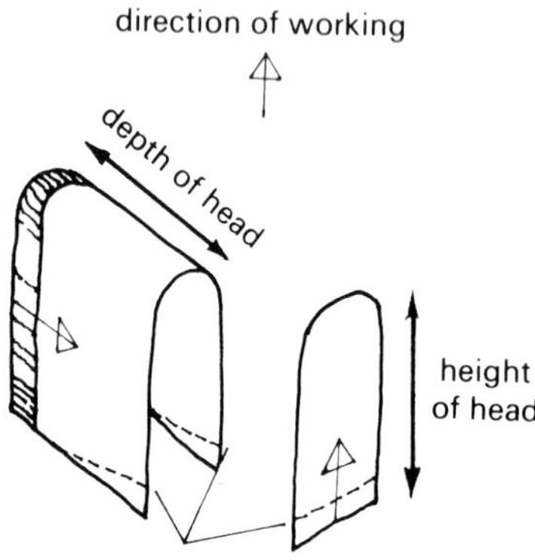

4.36 Hood with back gusset – to avoid a point on top

A gusset is knitted for back of head and stitched into place. Optional – can be shaped so it is shorter at back

Two ways of working the same idea (Figs. 4.37 and 4.38); the first is knitted from front edge, the second from neck edge, with a picked-up welt.

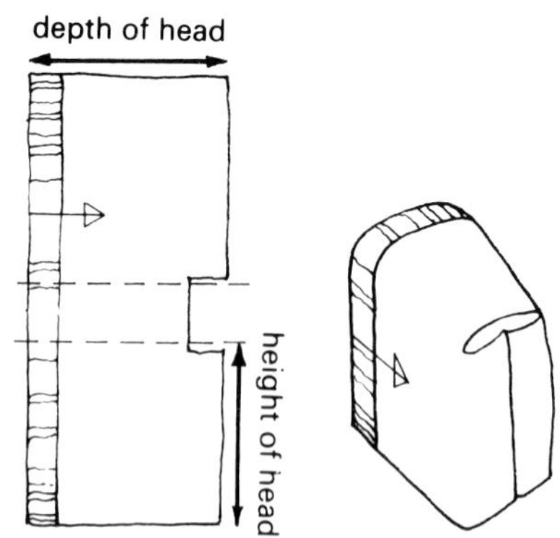

4.37 Hood with extended side panels – again to avoid a point

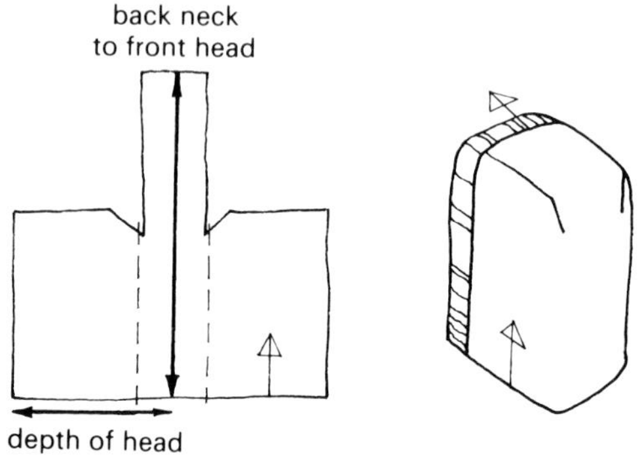

4.38 Hood with extended top panel

BUTTONHOLES AND LOOPS

There are three main types of buttonhole: eyelet, horizontal and vertical. If you have already got the buttons always try a sample buttonhole to be sure of a sensible fit.

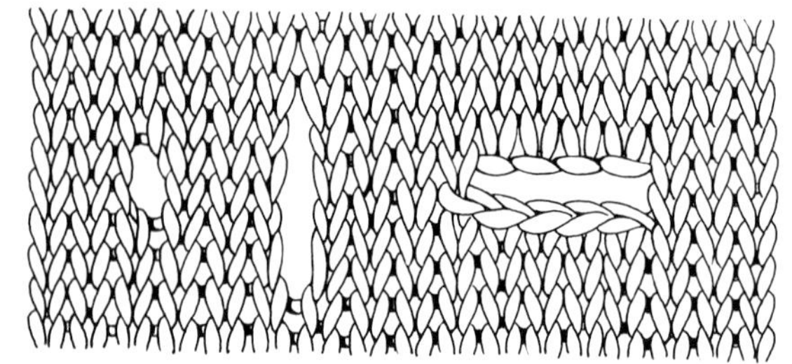

4.39 Working a buttonhole loop

Eyelet or layette buttonhole

Simple version:

row 1: RS work to beg of hole, yon k2tog, work in patt to end row

row 2: work all st, including yon as a st

Stronger version:

row 1: RS work to beg of hole, yon, work in patt to end row

row 2: work to buttonhole, slip over from previous row, yon, work in patt to end row

row 3: work to st before buttonhole, slip, k overs, psso, then k tog next st with over loops by inserting needle first into st then under loops, work in patt to end row

Horizontal buttonhole

row 1: work in patt to beg buttonhole, cast off chosen no. of st + 1, work in patt to end row

row 2: work in patt to buttonhole, cast on with cable method prev cast off st – less one, pick up and knit st from both loops of first cast off st. Work in patt to end row.

A neat method of making a horizontal buttonhole in rib: do not cast off the stitches for buttonhole but knit them with a strand of contrast yarn and leave a long loop of main yarn behind. When you are ready carefully pull out the contrasting strand and put lower stitches onto a safety pin. Use the loop of main yarn to cast off tightly these stitches invisibly (see p. 65), then reinforce the upper stitches by passing the yarn through them several times, taking a vertical stitch at each end of the buttonhole.

Vertical buttonhole

With RS facing, work across to beginning of hole; turn work; continue on these stitches to form one side of hole, finishing with a RS row. Break yarn, leaving a longish length. Join ball of yarn at base of hole and work second side to match the first. Next row: continue on all st. Use the loose end of yarn to reinforce the hole by re-working the stitches that form its edges.

Loops

These can be made either by crocheting a short length of chain or else by using the dressmaker's method below. Whichever you choose it is a good idea to reinforce with a few stitches the edge of

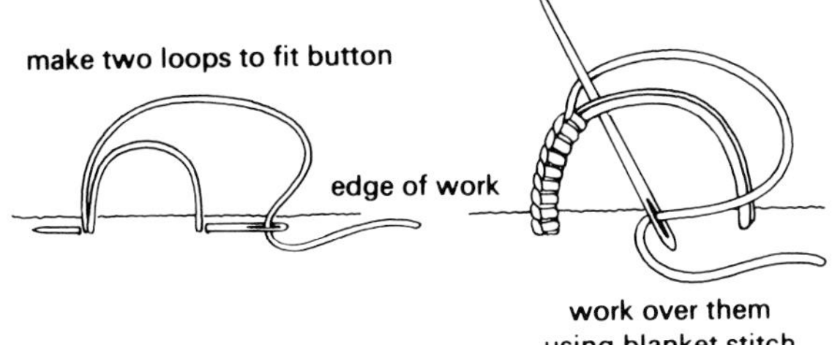

4.40 Finished look of eyelet horizontal and vertical button hole

knitting that is to take the loop. This can be done for the dressmaker's loop by using a strand of wool and a tapestry needle; fasten on and make a loop big enough to take the button or toggle, stitch back to the fasten-on and make a second loop. Again stitch back to fasten-on. Using blanket stitch work round to cover the entire loop, finish off.

PRESSING AND COLD BLOCKING

Both techniques are used to stabilise knitted fabric by the application of water – in the form of steam during pressing or as a mist of cold water in cold blocking. The inept use of an iron on knitting causes a lot of problems, such as excessive flattening, shine or distortion of shape. So the use of cold blocking can avoid all of these and is the only method advisable on 'hair' yarns such as mohair, angora, alpaca and cashmere, and also on glitter yarns. If you follow the instructions below, however, you will be able to press other yarns safely.

Cold blocking

The work needs to be 'blocked' or pinned out first with rust-proof pins. It is important that it is not stretched as you do this. Use a table covered with a large piece of cardboard and a blanket (both to protect the table and to provide a surface that can be safely pinned into) or a carpeted floor. The work has to be left for 24 hours so choose somewhere safe.

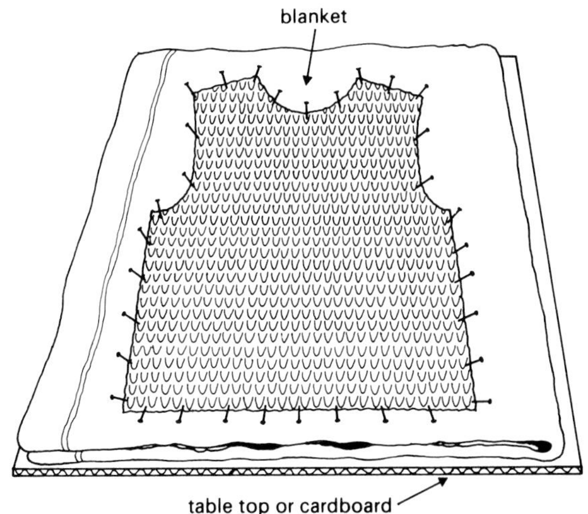

4.41 Cold blocking: pin work onto padded surface with rust proof pins

Uncurl the work with the right side facing and carefully pin round every 2 or 3cm being careful not to stretch it. Check the size at this point with your original measurements as small adjustments are possible. If there are two pieces that match, such as sleeves, lay them one on top of the other with the bottom one wrong side up. This will ensure that they stay the same and are not distorted differently during the process. Beaded pins are easier to find afterwards. When the work has been carefully laid out use a fine mist sprayer to dampen the knitting evenly all over. Leave undisturbed for at least 24 hours and make sure it is completely dry before it is lifted.

Pressing or steaming

Most people advise pinning out the work first – see cold blocking for details. I prefer to use a steam iron rather than a dry iron with damp cloth as I can see exactly what I am doing. Set the iron to steam and then 'hover' it all over the fabric slowly and evenly – do not be tempted to give it a 'good press' or you will end up with work that is lifeless, if not actually scorched. If you have to use a dry iron and damp cloth, hold the iron so that it barely touches the cloth and do not iron to and fro. Whichever method, leave the work for several minutes to dry before lifting it. Moving it while it is hot and damp will cause distortion.

Seams should be steamed in a similar way. Once the fabric has been 'blocked' it is not necessary to pin it out again to press the seams. Just use the hover technique over the seam, on the wrong side of the work. I advise stitching up the shoulders and sewing in the sleeves along an open armhole so that the partly-sewn garment can be pressed. Only then stitch up the sleeve and side seams all in one go. If you do this it is easy to get to the important shoulder seam and sleeve crown. These are the most noticeable seams in any garment; if they are well finished it gives a more professional look to the work.

Pressing tension samples

For commercial patterns these are usually measured before any pressing – unless otherwise stated. But for your own designs it is worth measuring before and after steaming – with the method described above. The point of pressing the sample is to get an accurate guide from which to calculate the size and pattern of the whole garment. If the tension does change with pressing, then it is important to find this out before calculating the pattern. Failure to do this could mean that the garment turns out as much as 5cm longer or wider than you intended.

SEAMING

There are three basic types of seam possible – each suitable for different parts of a garment.

Backstitch seam

Used for cast-off edges such as shoulders. Work with right sides of fabric together, one stitch from edge, using backstitch and sewing into each stitch in turn.

Flat seam

Worked with wrong sides facing onto a seam selvedge (see p. 64). Oversew alternately into the head stitches on each selvedge.

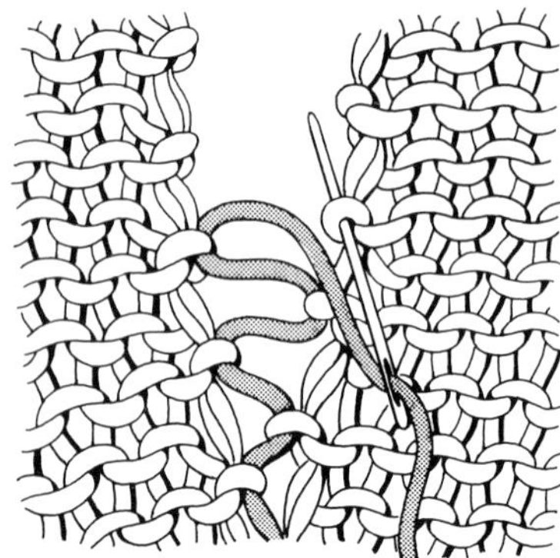

4.42 Flat seams

Vertical grafted seam

Take a stitch behind bar, between edge and first stitch, on each side in turn. Pull up sufficiently for stitches to be invisible – but not so tightly that it causes bunching or gathering.

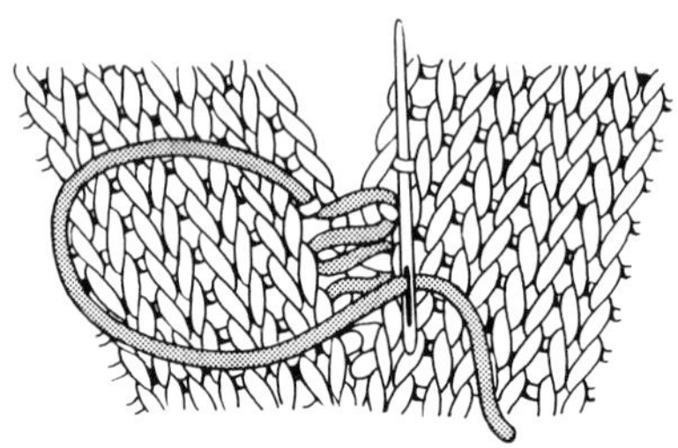

4.43 Vertical grafted seam

Horizontal grafting

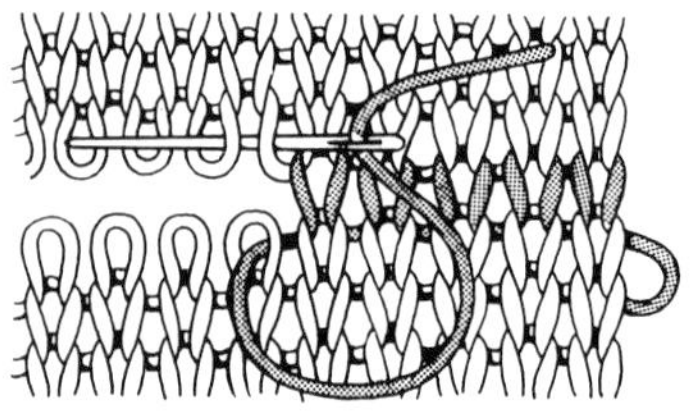

4.44 Methods of horizontal grafting

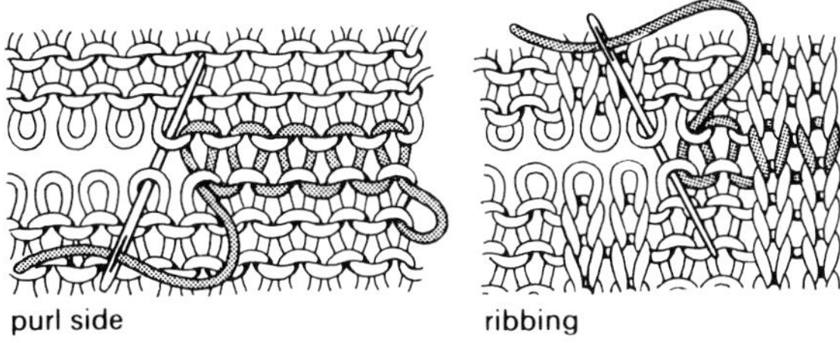

4.44 contd.

CORDS AND TASSELS

Cords can be made with crocheted chains or twisted strands of yarn. To make a twisted cord, measure out 3 to 8 strands (the more, the thicker the cord will be) at least 3 times as long as the length of cord you need. Make sure they are lying evenly and knot them together at each end. If you have a helper, thread a knitting needle through each end – if not, hang one end on a convenient hook or door knob.

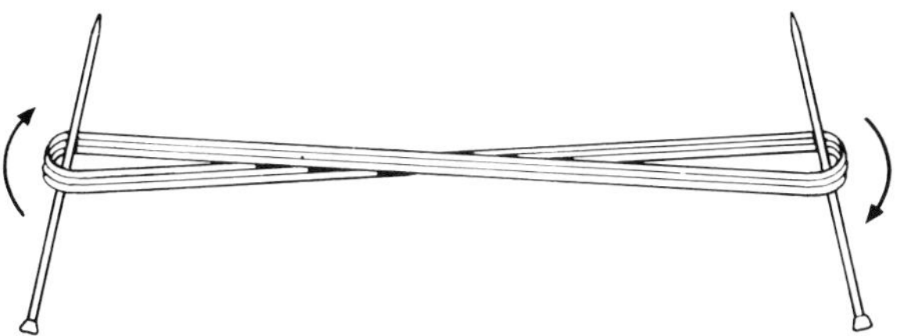

4.45 Making a cord by twisting strands clockwise

Twist the strands clockwise yourself (and your helper can do the same), keeping the cord under slight tension. Keep twisting until the cord begins to snarl up on itself if you release the tension slightly – the more you twist, the better the cord will be. The next bit is tricky, you have to fold the cord in half without snarling it up. I find it best to tread on the middle, keeping the cord under tension all the time, then with a flick of the wrist shake the cord free and it will twist up into a tight even cord. Make a knot a few cm from either end, then untwist the strands at the ends to make a kind of tassel.

Tassel making: I prefer to make tassels using folded card (as wide as the tassel will be long) to wind the yarn round – a bit like making a pompom. The more yarn you use the fatter the tassel will be - and do not forget there is twice as much yarn as you can see on one side of the card.

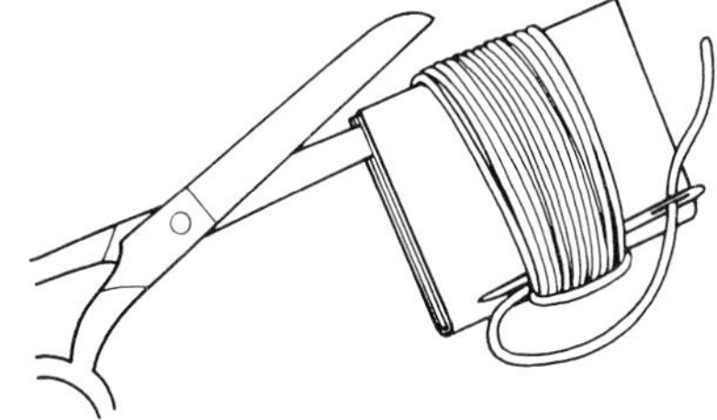

4.46 Tassel yarn is wound round folded card

When you have wound enough, use a tapestry needle and a long strand of yarn to tie a tight knot round all the strands at the fold of the card. Then take a few stitches through the bundle to stop the strands from pulling out. Cut through the bundle between the edges of the card, away from the knot. Then make a waist for the tassel by binding the yarn on the needle round a couple of times and again stitching through the tassel to prevent the binding from moving.

4.47 Bind to make a waist and stitch to hold strands

Lastly stitch up to the top of the tassel and use the remaining strand of yarn to fasten the tassel securely to your garment. Take some scissors and give the tassel a final trim.

5 Stitch dictionary

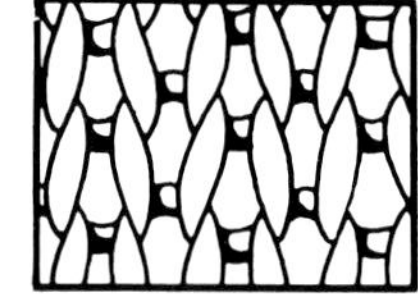

Introduction

This chapter is a resource that I hope will inspire you to try out ideas and gain confidence in your own ability to design. It contains a selection of stitch patterns – each with a rough tension guide – that can be used to knit either the basic patterns given in Chapter 2, or your own ideas.

The stitch patterns are arranged according to the knitting techniques used to produce them – for example, lace patterns, using increases and decreases that create holes and slants to the work. Most of the examples in the chapter have been knitted using 4mm (no. 8) needles and double-knit yarns so a rough comparison of tension and scale is possible. The instructions for each stitch pattern are given alongside either in the form of a row-by-row explanation, or a grid for reverse stocking stitch and jacquard patterns. All the abbreviations needed to understand the patterns are given on pp. 96–97.

CONTENTS

How to use the Stitch Dictionary

When you have chosen a stitch pattern to try you will need to test it by knitting a square using the exact yarn you want for the garment and appropriate needles. As with all knitting, tension is crucial and so it is better to spend time before you start work on the actual garment. Good advance planning always pays off.

If you are using the stitch patterns for one of the basic patterns in Chapter 2 you need to get your sample to match the tensions given. If it is either pattern A or B you will be using a double-knit quality of yarn, starting your sample with 4mm (no. 8) needles, and aiming for a stitch tension of 24 stitches to 10cm (4 in.). With your chosen yarn and needles cast on a multiple of the number of stitches needed for the stitch pattern that equals or is greater than 24 stitches – to make measuring easier. Knit in pattern until your sample measures at least 10cm (4 in.) and cast off.

To check the number of stitches, carefully uncurl the edges of the sample (you can pin it down onto a blanket or ironing board to hold it still). Hold the measure to the knitting and use the point of a needle to help you to identify individual stitches as you count them.

If the tension is exact over the number of stitches needed for the pattern go ahead and work the garment – the number of rows is not nearly so critical but should be within one or two of the given total, particularly for the raglan pattern B (Chapter 2).

If you do not get the right tension you will have to try the sample again with a different needle size. As a rough guide, one needle size = one or two stitches over a 10cm (4 in.) square. Do keep trying until you get it right.

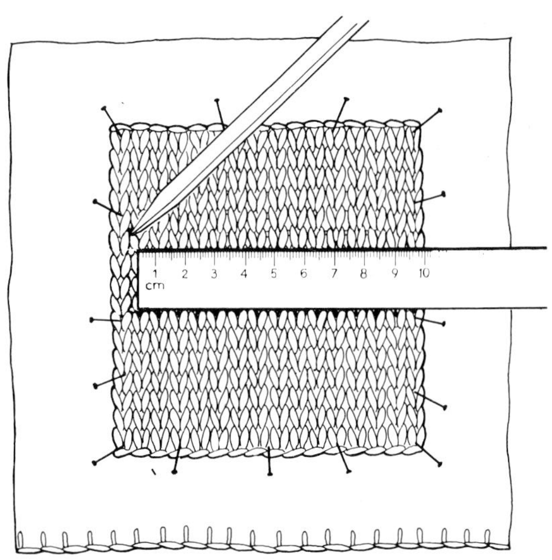

Check tension of your sample over 10 cm by careful counting

Working from grids

For a reverse stocking stitch pattern – on all odd-numbered rows read the grid chart from right to left and work blank squares as k stitches and dots as purl stitches. On all even-numbered rows, work in reverse, that is: blank squares as purl stitches and dots as k stitches.

For a jacquard or Fair Isle pattern – work in stocking stitch, starting on a k row and reading grid chart from right to left, next row work in purl and read from left to right. Continue in this way. (It is possible to create a reversed image or motif by working the grid from the opposite side – which can sometimes be useful.)

Guernsey Marriage Lines

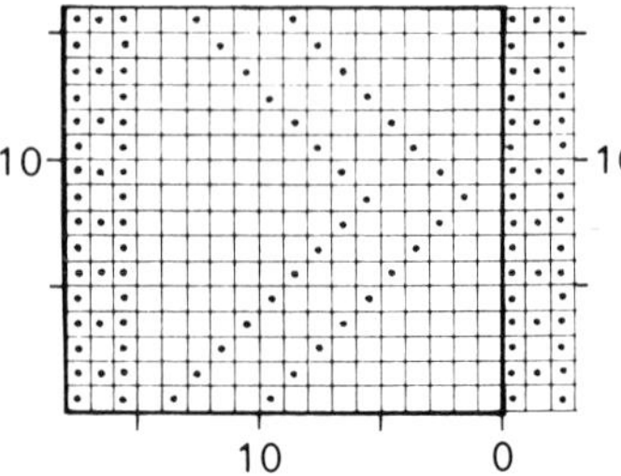

Marriage Lines grid
– multiple of 18 st × 16 rows

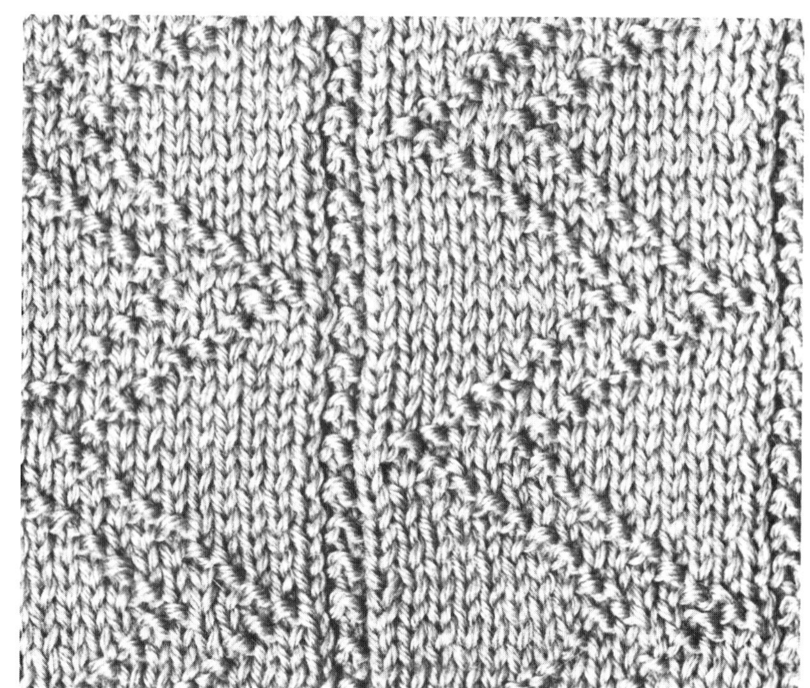

Guernsey Marriage Lines
double-knit on 4mm needles
10cm square = 24 st × 30 rows
suitable for Chapter 2 patterns
A and B

Guernsey Flags and Rigging

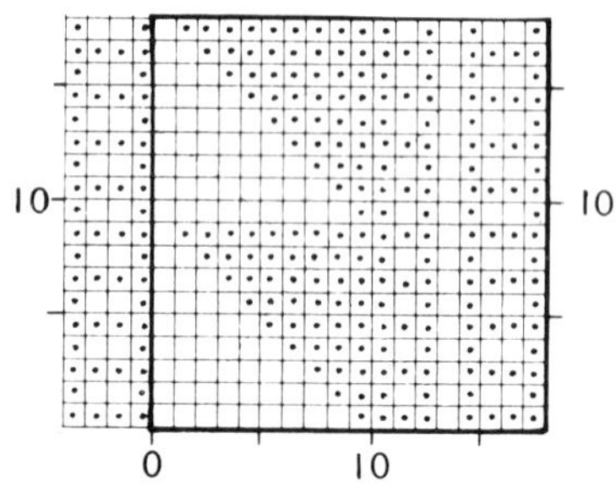

Flags and Rigging grid
– multiple of 18 st × 18 rows

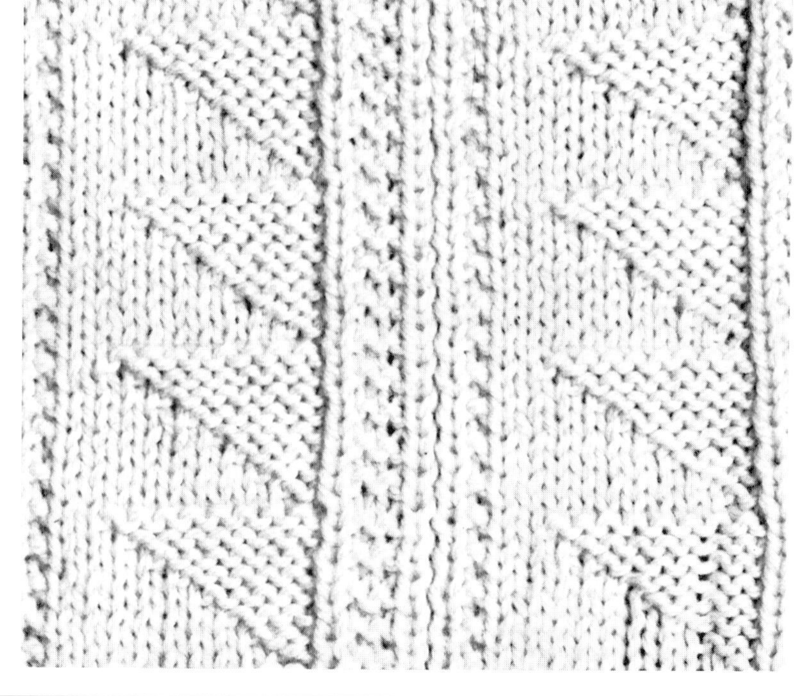

Guernsey Flags and Rigging
double knit on 4mm needles
10cm square = 24 st × 30 rows
suitable for Chapter 2 patterns
A and B

Castellations

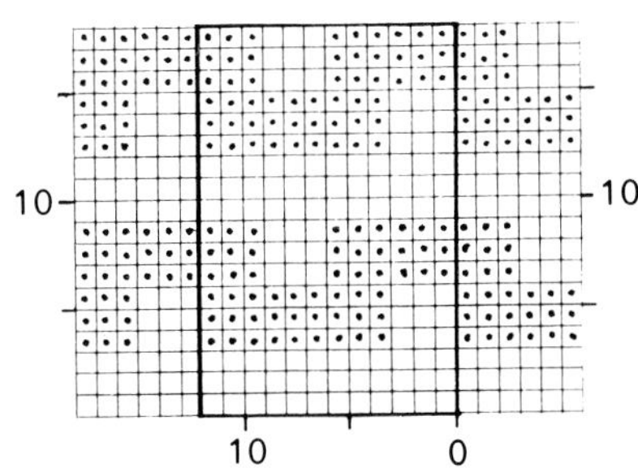

Castellations grid
– multiple of 18 st × 18 rows

Castellations
double-knit on 4mm needles
10cm square = 24 st × 30 rows
suitable for Chapter 2
patterns A and B

Multiple of 12 + 3

1	k row
2	p row
3	k row
4	k3 *p3 k9, rep from * to end row
5 & 6	k the k st and p the p st
7	p3 *k3 p9, rep from * to end row
8 & 9	k the k st and p the p st
10	p row
11	k row
12	p row
13	*p9 k3, rep from * to last 3 st, p3
14 & 15	k the k st and p the p st
16	*k9 p3, rep from * to last 3 st, k3
17 & 18	k the k st and p the p st

Rep these 18 rows

Pyramids

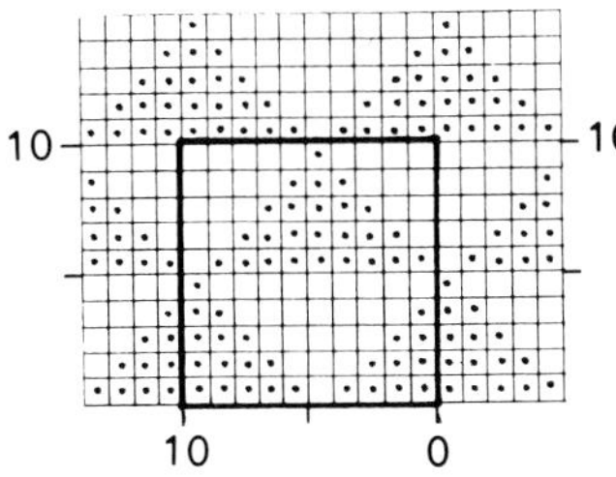

Pyramids grid with
10 st × 10 row repeat

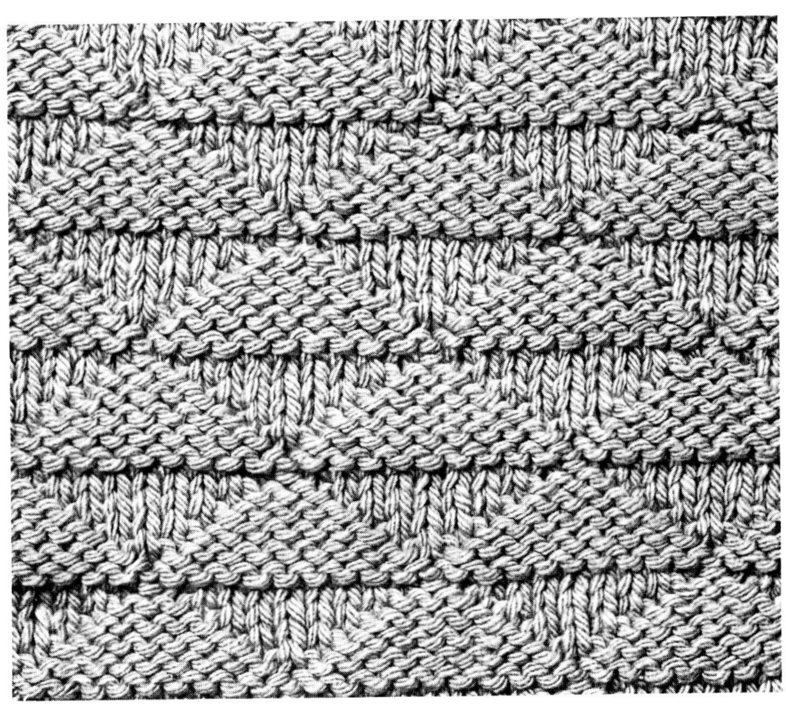

Pyramids (see also jacquard version in colour)
double-knit on 4mm needles
10cm square = 23 st × 28 rows
suitable for Chapter 2 pattern A

Draught Board

Multiple of 6 + 1

1 & 2 k row

3 *p1 k5, rep from * to last st, p1

4 and remaining even no. rows: k the k st and p the p st

5 as row 3

7 *p1 k2 MB k2 rep from * to last st, p1

9 as row 3

Rep these 10 rows

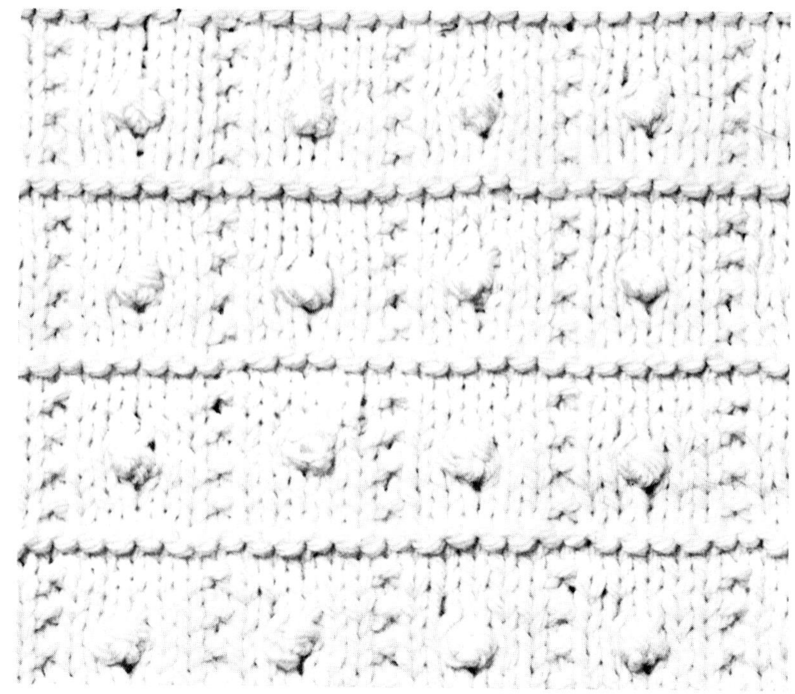

Draught Board
double-knit on 4mm needles
10cm square = 23 st × 28 rows
suitable for Chapter 2 pattern A

Lozenge Quilt

Multiple of 12 + 1

1 k1 *k11 MB, rep from * to last rep, end k1

2 k1 *p11 k1, rep from * to end

3 k1 *p1 k9 p1 k1, rep from * to end

4 and foll. even-numbered rows (unless specified): k the k st and p the p st

5 *k2 p1 k7 p1 k1, rep from * to last st, k1

7 *k3 p1 k5 p1 k2, rep from * to last st, k1

9 *k4 p1 k3 p1 k3, rep from * to last st, k1

11 *k5 p1 k1 p1 k4, rep from * to last st, k1

13 *k6 MB k5, rep from * to last st, k1

14 *p6 k1 p5, rep from * to last st, p1

15 as 11

17 as 9

19 as 7

21 as 5

23 as 3

Rep these 24 rows

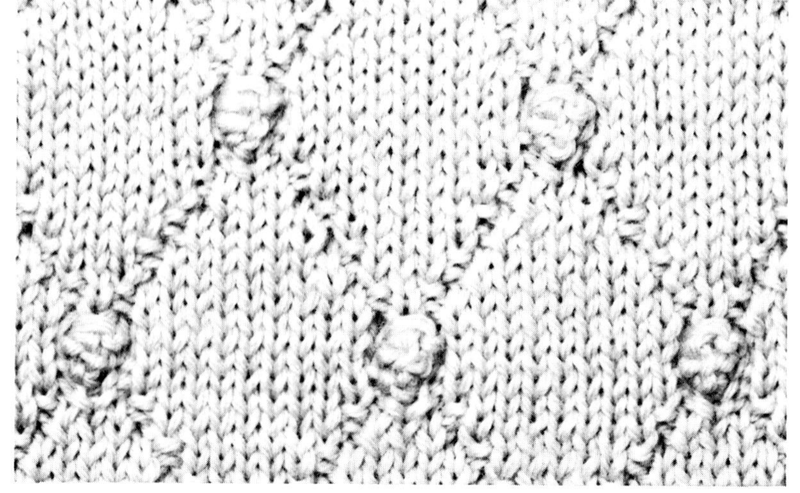

Lozenge Quilt
double-knit on 4mm needles
10cm square = 24 st × 32 rows
suitable for Chapter 2 pattern A

Strings of Beads

Multiple of 6 + 2

Foundation rows:

1 *p2 k1, rep from * to last 2 st, p2

2 k the k st and p the p st

Pattern:

1 *p2 k3 times into next st (k into back, front and back of st), p2 k1 rep from * to last 2 st, p2

2 and all even rows: k the k st and p the p st

3 *p2 k3 p2 k1, rep from * to last 2 st, p2

5 *p2 sl 1, k2tog, psso p2 k1 rep from * to last 2 st, p2

7 *p2 k1 p2 k 3 times as row 1 p2, rep from * to last 2 st, p2

9 *p2 k1 p2 k3, rep from * to last 2 st, p2

11 *p2 k1 p2 sl 1, k2tog psso, rep from * to last 2 st, p2

Rep these 12 rows

Count st only on rows 6 or 12

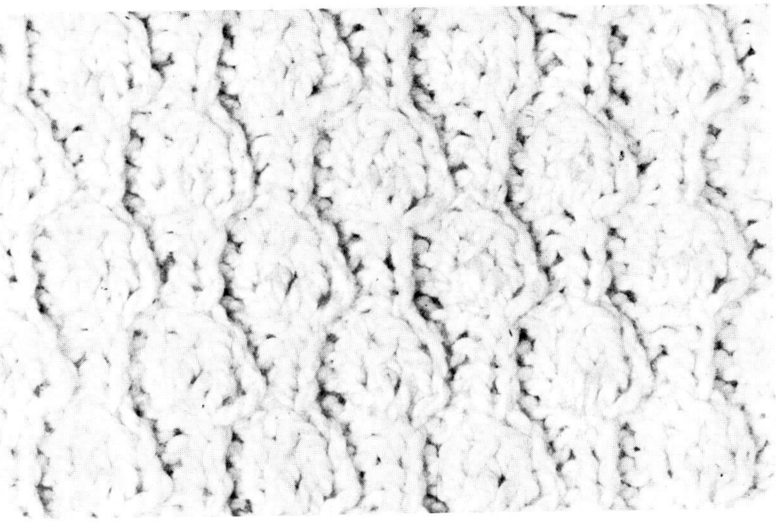

Strings of Beads
double-knit on 4mm needles
10cm square = 24 st × 30 rows
suitable for Chapter 2 patterns A and B

RIBS

Basket Weave

Multiple of 18 + 10

1 k11 *p2 k2 p2, k12, rep from * to last 17 st; p2 k2 p2, k11

2 p1 *k8 (p2 k2) twice, p2, rep from * to last 9 st, k8 p1

3 k the k st and p the p st

4 p11 *k2 p2 k2, p12, rep from * to last 17 st, k2 p2 k2, p11

5–8 rep these 4 rows

9 k row

10 (p2 k2) twice, p12 *k2 p2 k2, p12, rep from * to last 8 st, (k2 p2) twice

11 (k2 p2) twice, k2 *p8 (k2 p2) twice, k2, rep from * to end

12 k the k st and p the p st

13 (k2 p2) twice, k12 *p2 k2 p2, k12, rep from * to last 8 st, (p2 k2) twice

14–17 rep these last 4 rows

18 p row

Rep these 18 rows

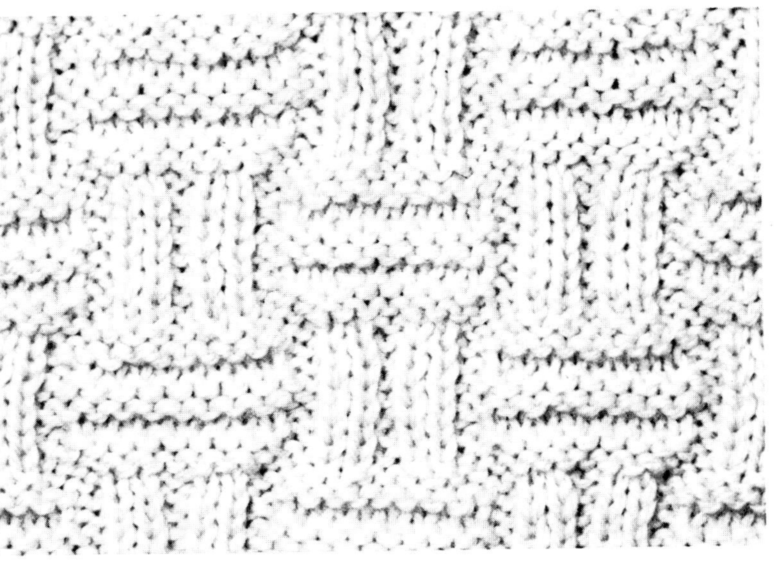

Basket Weave
double-knit on 4mm needles
10cm square = 27 st × 36 rows

Hour Glass

Multiple of 14 + 1

Row	Instructions
1 RS	k1 *yon k2, p3 p3tog p3, k2 yon, k1, rep from * to end
2	p4 *k7, p7, rep from * to last 11 st, k7 p4
3	k2 *yon k2, p2 p3tog p2, k2 yon, k3, rep from * to last 13 st, yon k2, p2 p3tog p2, k2 yon, k2
4	p5 *k5, p9, rep from * to last 10 st, k5 p5
5	k3 *yon k2, p1 p3tog p1, k2 yon, k5, rep from * to last 12 st, yon k2, p1 p3tog p1, k2 yon, k3
6	p6 *k3, p11, rep from * to last 9 st, k3 p6
7	k4 *yon k2, p3tog, k2 yon, k7, rep from * to last 11 st, yon k2, p3tog, k2 yon, k4
8	p7 *k1, p13, rep from * to last 8 st, k1, p7
9	p2tog *p3, k2 yon, k1, yon k2, p3 p3tog, rep from * to last 13 st, p3, k2 yon, k1, yon k2, p3 p2tog
10	k4 *p7 k7, rep from * to last 11 st, p7 k4
11	p2tog *p2, k2 yon, k3, yon k2, p2 p3tog, rep from * to last 13 st, p2, k2 yon, k3, yon k2, p2 p2tog
12	k3 *p9, k5, rep from * to last 12 st, p9 k3
13	p2tog *p1, k2 yon, k5, yon k2, p1 p3tog, rep from * to last 13 st, p1, k2 yon, k5, yon k2, p1 p2tog
14	k2 *p11, k3; rep from * to last 13 st, p11, k2
15	p2tog *k2 yon, k7, yon k2, p3tog, rep from * to last 13 st, k2 yon, k7, yon k2, p2tog
16	k1 *p13 k1, rep from * to last st, k1

Rep these 16 rows

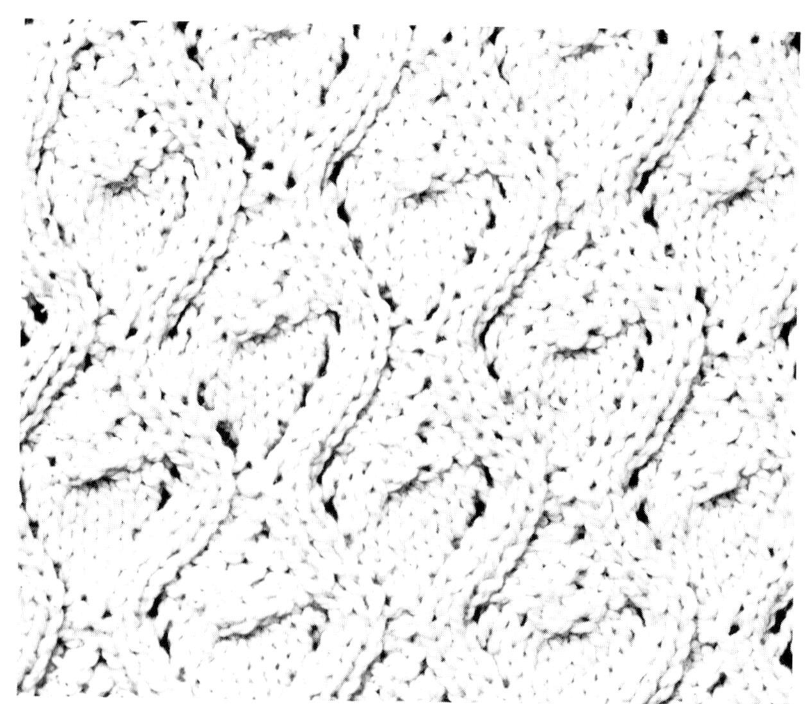

Hour Glass
double-knit on 4mm needles
10cm square = 25 st × 32 rows
suitable for Chapter 2 pattern A

Sheaves

Multiple of 16 + 12

1 k3 p6 *(k2 p2) twice k2 p6, rep from * to last 3 st, k3

2 and all even rows: k the k st and p the p st

3, 5 & 7 as row 1

9 k3 p2 k2 p2 *[sl 10 st onto CN, wind yarn 3 times anti-clockwise round these st, and then work on the CN 10 st: k2 p6 k2] p2 k2 p2, rep from * to last 3 st, k3

11, 15 & 17 k3 *(p2 k2) twice, p6 k2, rep from * to last 9 st, p2 k2 p2, k3

19 k1 *rep from [to], p2 k2 p2, rep from * to last 11 st, [to] k1

Rep these 20 rows

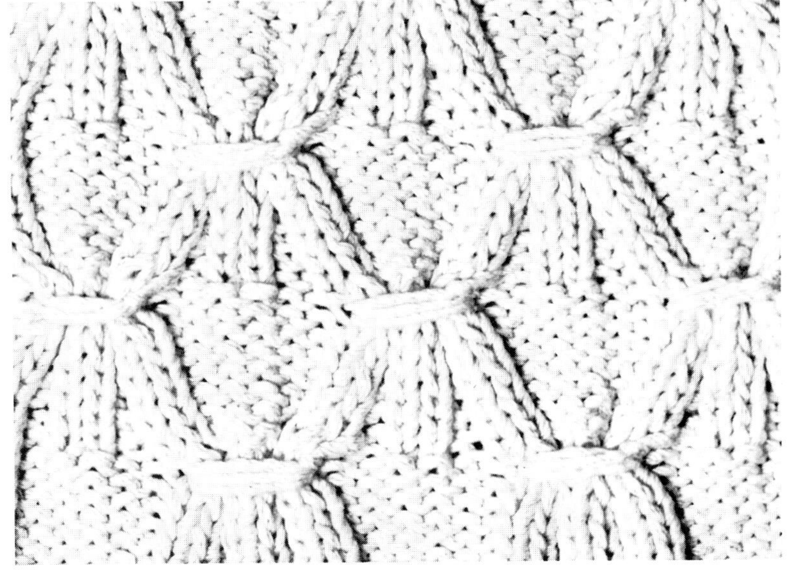

Sheaves
Aran on 4mm needles
10cm square = 24 st × 30 rows
suitable for Chapter 2 patterns A and B

INTERRUPTED OVERALL CABLE

Chalice Cable

Multiple of 32

1	p2 k2 p2, k4, p2 k2 p2, p2 k2 p2, k4, p2 k2 p2
2	k the k st and p the p st
3	as row 1 to end row
4	as row 2 on first 16 st k16
5	as row 1 on first 16 st k16
6	as row 2 on first 16 st k16
7	p2 T6b T6f p2 k16
8	as row 2 k16
9	as row 1 to end row
10	as row 2 to end row
11	as row 1 to end row
12	k16 as row 2 on next 16 st
13	k16 as row 1 on next 16 st
14	k16 as row 2 on next 16 st
15	k16 p2 T6b T6f p2
16	k16 as row 2

Rep these 16 rows

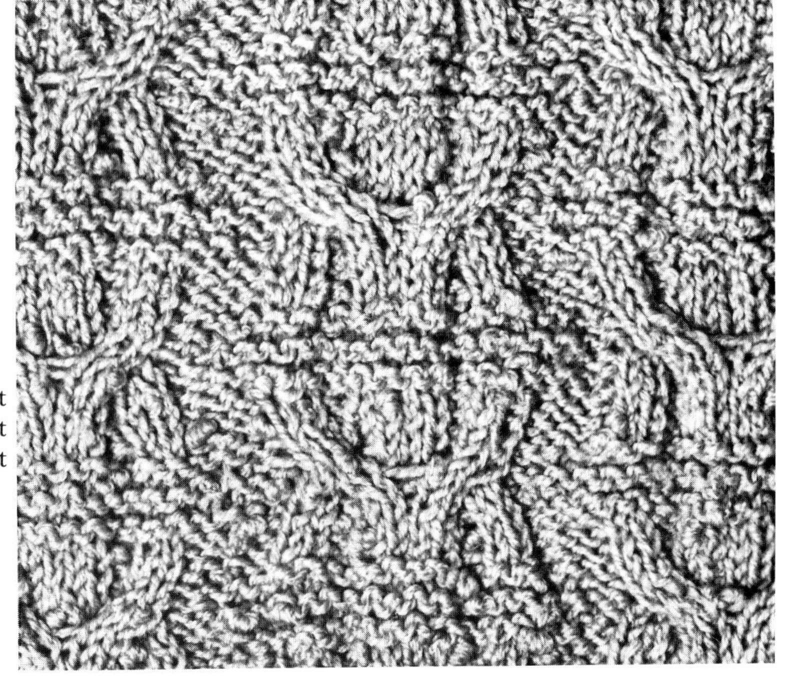

Chalice Cable
double-knit on 4mm needles
10cm square = 28 st × 36 rows

Ridge and Cable

Multiple of 20 + 4

Row	Instructions
1	k2 *p2 k6 p2, k10, rep from * to last 2 st, k2
2	p2 *k2 p6 k2, p10, rep from * to last 2 st p2
3	p2 *p2 k6 p2, p10, rep from * to last 2 st, p2
4	k2 *k2 p6 k2, k10, rep from * to last 2 st, k2
5	k2 *p2 C6F p2, k10 rep from * to last 2 st, k2
6	as row 2
7	as row 3
8	as row 4
9 to 24	rep these 8 rows twice more
25	k row
26	p row
27	p row
28	k row
29	k2 *k10, p2 k6 p2, rep from * to last 2 st k2
30	p2 *p10 k2 p6 k2, rep from * to last 2 st, p2
31	p2 *p10, p2 k6 p2, rep from * to lst 2 st, p2
32	k2 *k10, k2 p6 k2 rep from * to last 2 st, k2
33	k2 *k10, p2 C6F p2, rep from * to last 2 st, k2
34	as row 30
35	as row 31
36	as row 32
37 to 52	rep these last 8 rows (from 29) twice more
53 to 56	as rows 25 to 28

Rep these 56 rows

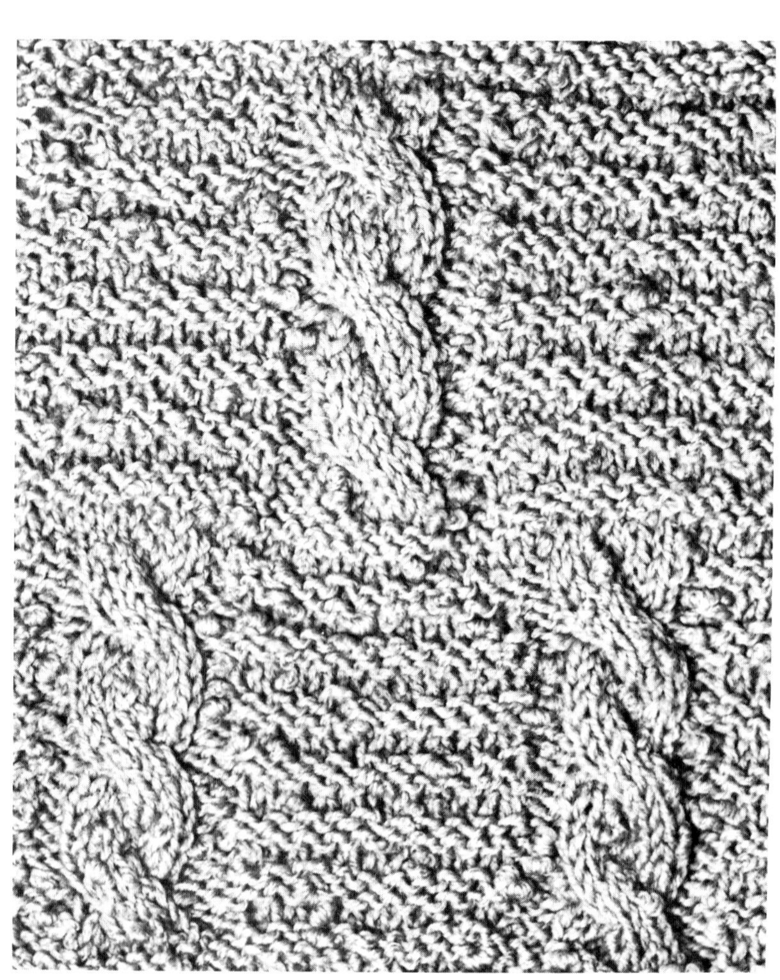

Ridge and Cable
double-knit on 4mm needles
10cm square = 24 st × 38 rows
suitable for Chapter 2 pattern A

Celtic Trellis

Worked over a multiple of 10 + 5 st (minimum 25 st)

Foundation rows:

1 RS:	k3 *p4 k6 rep from * to last 2 st, p2
2 WS:	k2 *p6 k4 rep from * to last 3 st, p3

Pattern:

1	k3 *p4 C6F, rep from * to last 2 st, p2
2	k2 *p6 k4, rep from * to last 2 st, p3
3	*T5F, T5B, rep from * to last 5 st, T5F
4	p3 *k4 p6, rep from * to last 2 st, k2
5	p2 *C6B p4, rep from * to last 3 st, k3
6	as row 4
7	*T5B, T5F, rep from * to last 5 st, T5B
8	as row 2

Rep these 8 rows

Celtic Trellis
double-knit on 4mm needles
17st = 7cm and 34 rows = 10cm

Hearts

Multiple of 14 + 2

1	p5, T3B T3F, p5
2	k5, p2 k2 p2, k5
3	p4, T3B p2 T3F, p4
4	k4 (p2 k4) twice
5	p3, T3B k4 T3F, p3
6	k3 p2, k1 p4 k1, p2 k3
7	p2 (T3B)twice (T3F)twice p2
8	k2 p2, k1 p6 k1, p2 k2
9	p1 (T3B)twice k2 (T3F)twice p1
10	k1 p2, k1 p8 k1, p2 k1
11	p1 k1, T2f T3F, k2, T3B T2b, k1 p1
12	(k1 p1)twice, k1 p6 (k1p1) twice k1
13	p1 k1 p1, T2f T3F, T3B T2b, p1 k1 p1
14	k1 p1 k2, p1 k1 p4 k1 p1, k2 p1 k1
15	p1 T2f T2b p1, C4B, p1 T2f T2b p1
16	k2 C2B, k2 p4 k2, C2F k2

Rep these 16 rows

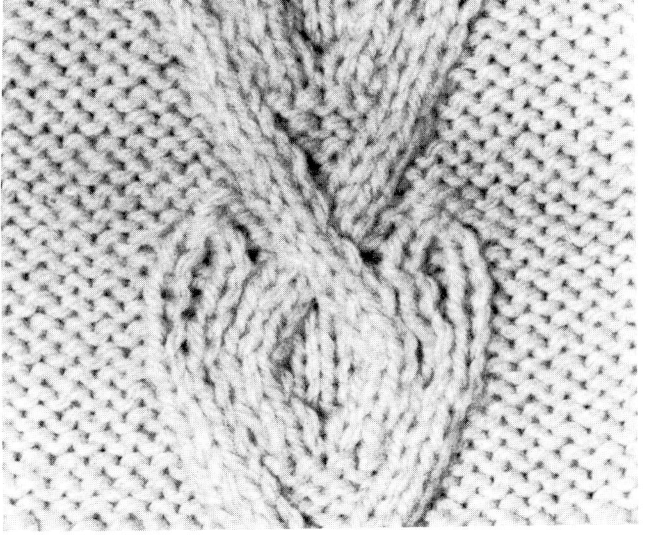

Hearts
double-knit on 4mm needles
16 st = 5.2cm and 32 rows = 10cm

Leaf and Berry Lattice

Multiple of 23+4

1 p12, k1 p1 k1, p12

2 and even-numbered rows k the k st and p the p st

3 p12, sl 2 st onto CN leave to back of work k1, sl p st on LH needle, p this st, k st from CN, p12

5 p11 T2B p1 T2F p11

7 p10 T2B p3 T2F p10

9 p9 T2B p5 T2F p9

11 p8 T2B p3 MB p3 T2F p8

13 p7 T2B p2 MB, p1 k1 p1, MB p2 T2F p7

15 p6 T2B p4 k2tog but sl off only 1 loop, k into rem loop, k2tog tbl, p4 T2F p6

17 p5 T2B p4 k2tog, yon k1 yon, sl1 k1psso p4 C2F p5

19 p4 T2B p4 k2tog k1, yon k1 yon, k1 sl1 k1psso p4 T2F p4

21 p3 T2B p4 k2tog k2, yon k1 yon, k2 sl 1 k1psso p4 T2F p3

23 p2 T2B p4 k2tog k3, yon k1 yon, k3 sl 1 k1psso p4 T2F p2

25 p2 T2F p4, k11, p4 T2B p2

27 p3 T2F p3 pM1Lp, sl 1 k1psso k7 k2tog pM1Ln, p3 T2B p3

29 p4 T2F p3 pM1Lp, sl 1 k1psso k5 k2tog pM1Ln, p3 T2B p4

31 p5 T2F p3 pM1Lp, sl 1 k1psso k3 k2tog pM1Ln, p3 T2B p5

33 p6 T2F p3 pM1Lp, sl 1 k1psso k1 k2tog pM1Ln, p3 T2B p6

35 p7 T2F p3 pM1Lp, sl 1 k2tog psso pM1Ln, p3 T2B p7

37 p8 T2F p7 T2B p8

39 p9 T2F p5 T2B p9

41 p10 T2F p3 T2B p10

43 p11 T2F p1 T2B p11

44 as row 2

Rep these 44 rows

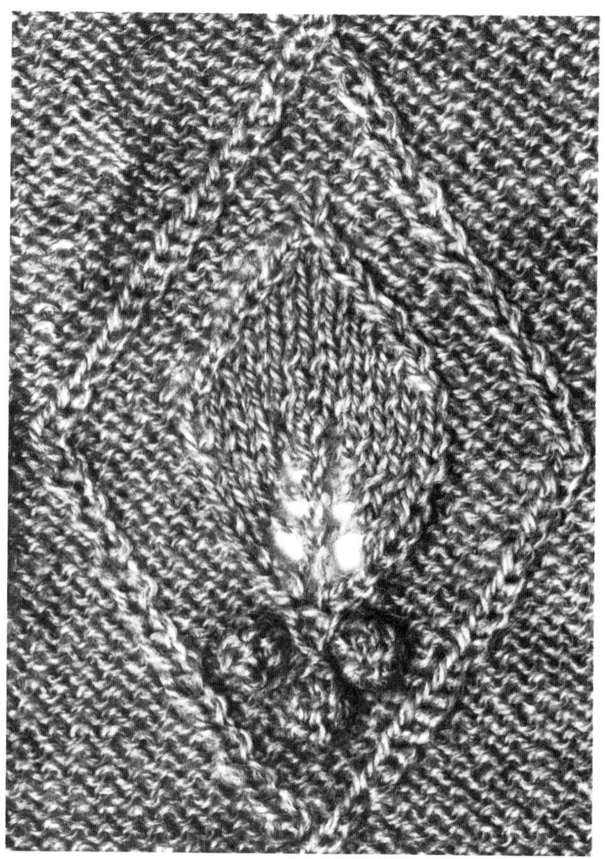

Leaf and Berry Lattice
double-knit on 4mm needles
10cm square = 22 st × 31 rows

(Cables are continued on p. 89)

Twisted Edging

Worked lengthwise over 13 st

1 and all odd-numbered rows (WS): k2, purl to last 2 st, k2

2 sl 1, k3 yon k5 yon k2tog yon k2

4 sl 1, k4 sl 1, k2tog psso k2 (yon k2tog) twice, k1

6 sl 1, k3 sl 1, k1 psso, k2 (yon k2tog) twice, k1

8 sl 1, k2 sl 1, k1 psso, k2 (yon k2tog) twice, k1

10 sl 1, k1 sl 1, k1 psso k2 (yon k2tog) twice, k1

12 k1 sl 1, k1 psso, k2 yon k1 yon k2tog yon k2

14 sl 1 (k3 yon) twice k2tog yon k2

Rep these 14 rows

NB count st on rows, 1, 4, 5, or 14 only

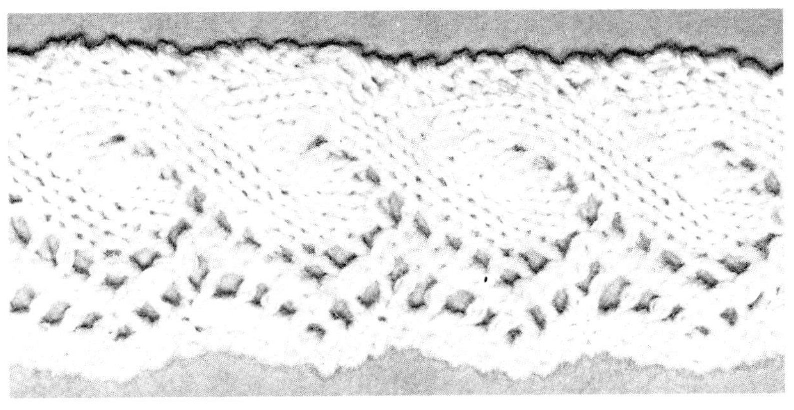

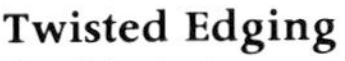

Twisted Edging
double-knit on 4mm needles
(worked lengthwise)
6cm deep and 38 rows = 10cm

Van Dyke Edging

Worked over 12 st

Foundation rows:

1 k2, k3 (yon k2tog) 3 times, k1

2 yon, k row

Pattern:

1 k2, k4 (yon k2tog) 3 times, k1

2 and every foll. 4th row: yon, k to last 2 st, turn work

3 k5 (yon k2tog) 3 times, k1

4 and rem even-numbered rows: k row

5 k2, k6 (yon k2tog) 3 times, k1

7 k7 (yon k2tog)3 times, k1

9 k2, k8 (yon k2tog) 3 times, k1

11 k9 (yon k2tog)3 times, k1

13 k2, k10 (yon k2tog) 3 times, k1

15 k11 (yon k2tog)3 times, k1

16 to 19 k row

20 cast off 9 st, k to last 2 st, turn work (12 st remain)

21 k3 (yon k2tog)3 times, k1

Rep these 22 rows

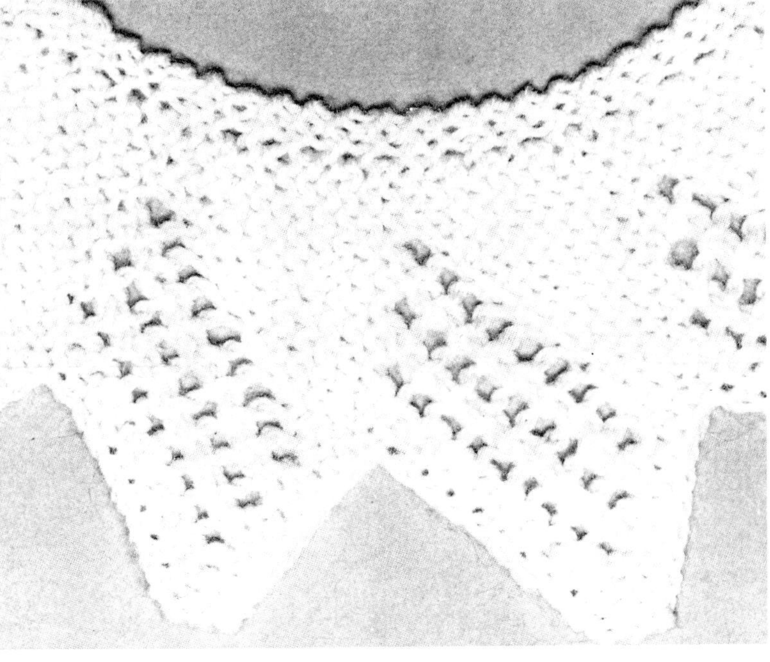

Van Dyke Edging
double-knit on 4mm needles
(worked lengthwise)
10cm to tips and 48 rows =
10cm at straight edge

Flower Rows

Multiple of 13+2
Worked in 4 colours: MC, A for stalk, B and C for alternate bobbles which form flowers

MB =	(B) [(p1 k1)twice p1] all into next st, turn work p5, yb, change to (MC), p5tog, next bobble (C)
1(A)	k row
2(A)	k1 *k5 (k2rn)3 times, k5, rep from * to last st, k1
3(MC)	k1 *sl 1, k1 psso, k3 sl 1 (dropping extra loop) kM1Lp, sl 1 (drop loop) kM1Ln, sl 1 (drop loop) k3 k2tog rep from * to last st k1
4	p1 *p4 (sl 1, kwise, p1) twice, sl 1 kwise, p4, rep from * to last st, p1
5	k1 *sl 1, k1 psso k2 sl 1, k1 kM1Lp sl 1, kM1Ln, k1 sl 1, k2 k2tog, rep from * to last st, k1
6	p1 *p3 (sl 1, kwise, p2) twice, sl 1, kwise, p3, rep from * to last st, p1
7	k1 * k4 kM1Lp k1 kM1Ln k4 k2tog, rep from * to last st, k1
8	p1 *p2 (MB k3) twice MB p2, rep from * to last st, p1
9 & 11	as row 7
10 & 12	p row

Rep these 12 rows

Flower Rows
double-knit on 4mm needles
10cm square = 24 st × 30 rows
suitable for Chapter 2 patterns A and B

Pebble Tuck Stitch

Multiple of 4+3

1	k1 *sl 1, k3, rep from * to last 2 st, sl 1 k1
2	k1 *yf sl 1, yb k3, rep from * to last 2 st, yf sl 1 yb, k1
3	k3 *sl 1, k3, rep from * to end
4	k3 *yf sl 1, yb k3 rep from *to end

Rep these 4 rows

Work as a colour pattern by knitting alternate pairs of rows in contrasting colours. If you use an odd number of colours the pattern appears to repeat diagonally. When worked with an even number of colours it appears vertically striped.

Pebble Tuck Stitch
double-knit on 4mm needles
10cm square = 23 st × 42 rows
suitable for Chapter 2 pattern A

Stars and Mountains

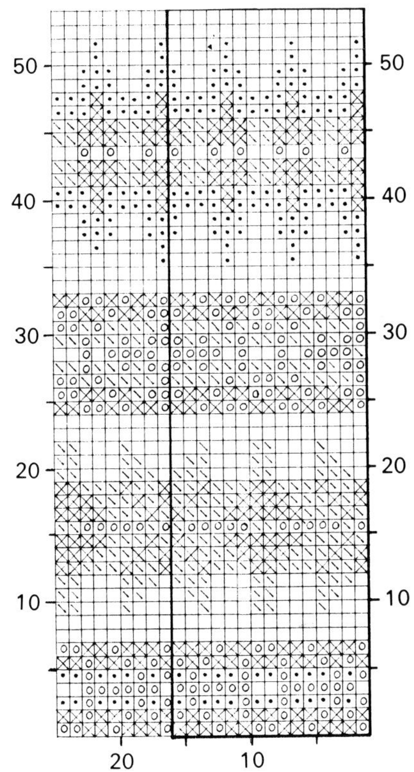

Stars and Mountains grid with 16 st × 54 row repeat (uses MC and four contrast colours)

Stars and Mountains
double-knit on 4mm needles
10cm square = 25 st × 28 rows
suitable for Chapter 2 patterns A and B

Hearts and Flowers

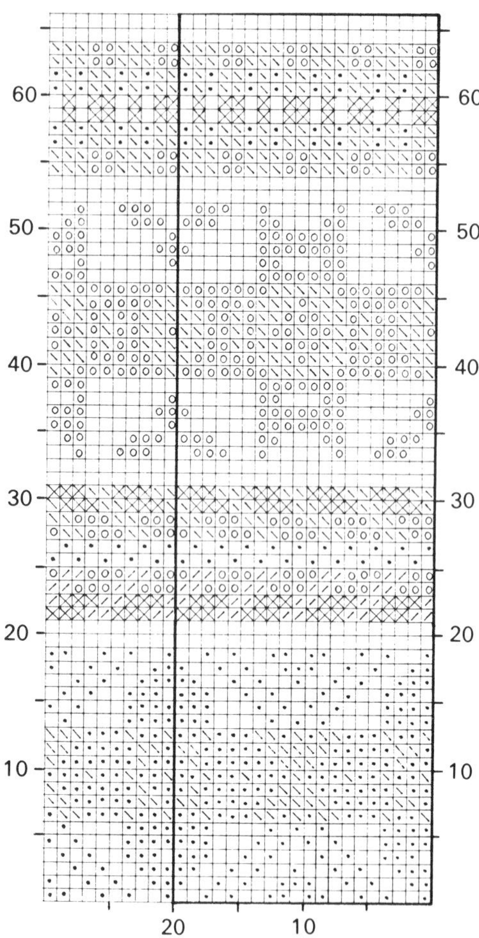

Hearts and Flowers grid with 20 st × 66 row repeat (uses MC and four contrast colours)

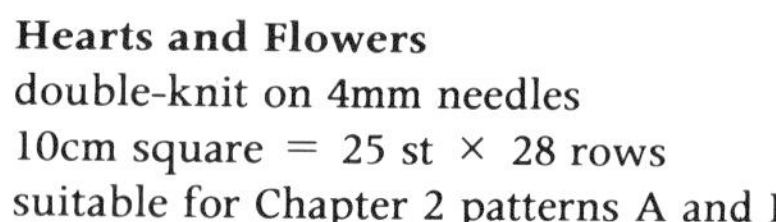

Hearts and Flowers
double-knit on 4mm needles
10cm square = 25 st × 28 rows
suitable for Chapter 2 patterns A and B

Pyramids

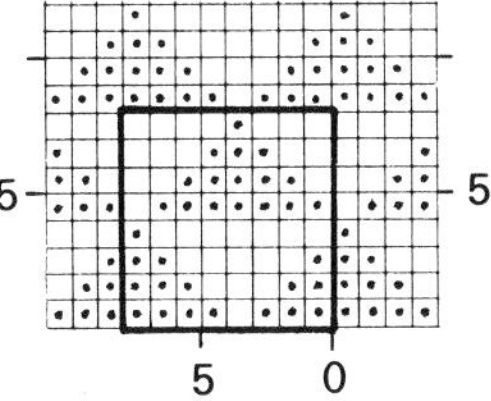

Pyramids grid with
8 st × 8 row repeat

Pyramids (see also reverse stocking stitch version in black and white)
double-knit on 4mm needles
10cm square = 24 st × 28 rows
suitable for Chapter 2 patterns A and B

Sheep

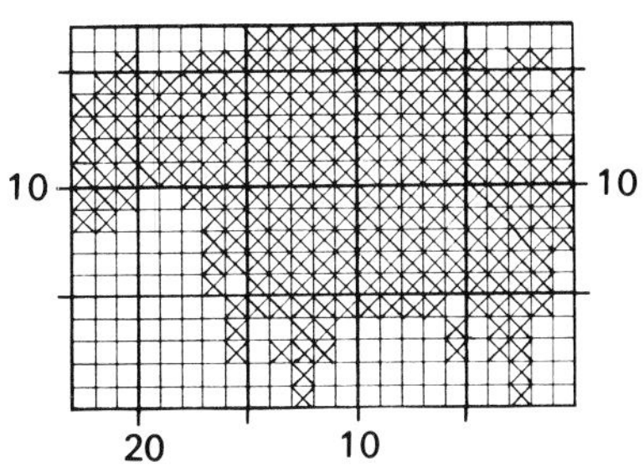

Sheep grid with
23 st × 17 row repeat

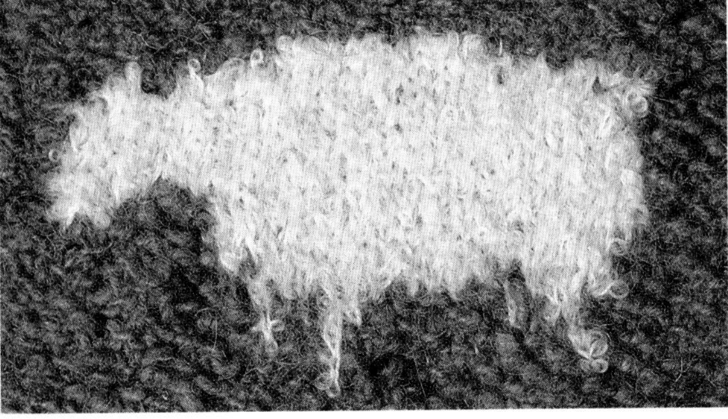

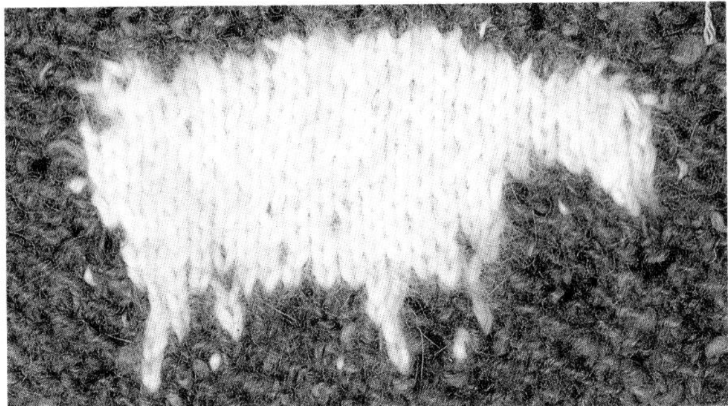

Sheep
double-knit on 4mm needles
10cm square = 25 st × 28 rows
suitable for Chapter 2 patterns A and B

Woven Check

Multiple of 6
Worked in two colours: (A) and (B)

1 *k3(A) k3(B), rep from * to end row
2 *p3(B) p3(A), rep from * to end row
3 *C6B (working k3(B) then k3(A) from CN), rep from * to end row
4 *p3(A) p3(B), rep from * to end row
5 *k3(B) p3(A), rep from * to end row
6 as row 4
7 k3(A) *C6F (working k3(A) then k3(B) from CN), rep from * to last 3st, k3(B)
8 as row 2

Rep these 8 rows

Woven Check
chunky on 6mm needles
10cm square = 30 st × 24 rows

Tuck Stitch Ripple

Multiple of 10 + 1
Worked in two colours A and MC – use two balls of main colour, MC1 and MC2
Foundation row: (A) k row (or cast on with A)

1(MC1) *sl 1 kwise and carry yon above st, p9, rep from * to last st, sl 1 kwise yon
2, 4 & 6 as row 1
3 & 5 *sl 1 kwise yon, k9 rep from * to last st, sl 1 kwise yon
7(A) k1 *p9 (k the sl st and all loops tog), rep from * to end
8(MC2) k5 *sl 1 kwise yon, k9, rep from * to last 6 st, sl 1 kwise yon, k5
9, 11 & 13 as row 8
10 & 12 p5 *sl 1 kwise yon p9, rep from * to last 6 st, sl 1 kwise yon, p5
14(A) k5 *(p the sl st and all loops tog) k9, rep from * to last 6 st, (p the sl st and all the loops tog) k5

Rep these 14 rows

Tuck Stitch Ripple
double-knit on 4mm needles
10cm square = 21 st × 42 rows

Tweed Pattern

Multiple of 5
Worked in three colours: A B C

1(A)	k row
2(B)	*k4 sl 1, rep from * to end
3	*yb, sl 1, p4 rep from * to end
4	as row 2
5(C)	k row
6(A)	k2 *yb sl 2 st, k3, rep from * to last 3 st, yb sl 2 st, k1
7(B)	p row
8(C)	k row
9(A)	k row
10(B)	k2 yb sl 1 *k4 yb sl 1, rep from * to last 2 st, k2
11	p2 yb sl 1 *p4 yb sl 1, rep from * to last 2 st p2
12	as row 10
13(C)	k row
14(A)	*sl 2 st k3, rep from * to end
15(B)	p row
16(C)	k row
17(A)	k row
18(B)	*yb sl 1 k4, rep from * to end
19	*p4 yb sl 1, rep from * to end
20	as row 18
21(C)	k row
22(A)	*k3 yb sl 2 st, rep from * to end
23(B)	p row
24(C)	k row
25(A)	k row
26(B)	k3 *sl 1 k4, rep from * to last 2 st, sl 1, k1
27	p1 *sl 1, yb sl 1, p4, rep from * to last 4 st, sl 1, p3
28	as row 26
29(C)	k row
30(A)	k1 *sl 2 st, k3, rep from * to last 4 st, sl 2 st, k2
31(B)	p row
32(C)	k row

Rep these 32 rows

Tweed Pattern
chunky on 5mm needles
10cm square = 16 st × 24 rows
suitable for Chapter 2 pattern C

Ears of Corn

Multiple of 25 + 4

Row	Instructions
1	k12, p1 k2 p1 k2 p1, k10
2	p10, k1 p2 k1 p2 k1, p12
3	and remaining odd-numbered rows (unless specified): k the k st and p the p st
4 to 9	as rows 1 and 2
10	p10, sl next 7 st onto CN, wind wool 3 times anti-clockwise round st on CN, (k1 p2 k1 p2 k1) on st from CN, p12
12	p8, p2tog kM1Ln, k1 p2 k1 p2 k1, p12
14	p7, p2tog kM1Ln, k2 p2 k1 p2 k1 kM1Lp p2tog, p10
16	p7, T3B k1 p2 k1 p2 k2 kM1Lp p2tog, p9
18	p2 k1 p3, T3B p1 k1 p2 k1 p2 k1 T3F, p9
19	proceed as usual to last 5 st: k2tog pM1Ln p1 k2
20	p2 T3F, p1 k2 p1 T2B, p2 k1 p2 k1 p1 T3F p8
22	p3 T3F k1 sl prev st over, k1 pM1Ln, p1 k1 p3, k1 p2 k1 p2 k2 p5, k1 p2
23	k2 p1 pM1Lp k2tog, proceed as usual to last 7 st: kM1Lp p2tog tbl p1 k4
24	p8, T2B p3 k1 p2 T2F, p1 T3F, p2 T3B p2
26	p7, T2B p4 k1 p3 T2F, p1 T3F T3B p3
28	p7, k1 p5 k1, p4 k1 p2 pM1Lp, sl 1, sl next st onto CN leave to front, k st from LN psso, sl 1 off CN onto RN, k st from LN psso, pM1Ln p4
29	k7, proceed as usual to end row
30	p6, MP k1 MP, p4 k1 p4 T2F, p9
31	proceed as usual but k st over MP
32	p6, MP k1 MP, p3 C2B p5 k1, p9
34	p6, MP k1 MP, p3 k1 p5, MP k1 MP, p8
36, 38	as row 34
40	p7, MP p3, MP k1 MP, p4 MP k1 MP, k8
42	p11, MP k1 MP, p4, MP k1 MP, p8
44	p11, MP k1 MP, p5 MP p9
46	p11 MP k1 MP p15
48	as row 46
50	p12, MP, p16
51	p to end row

Allow chosen amount of stocking stitch before rep these rows

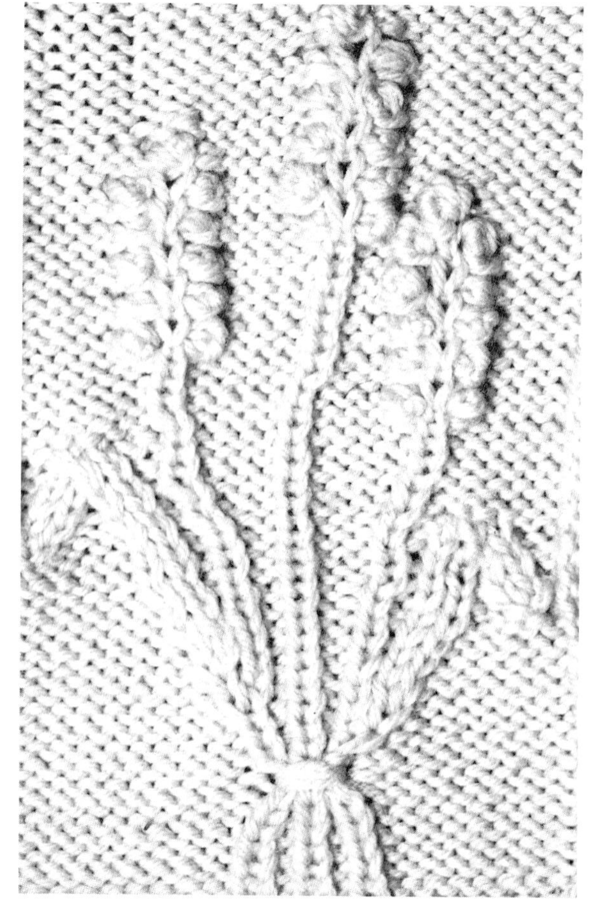

Ears of Corn
double-knit on 4mm needles
10cm square = 23 st × 32 rows
suitable for Chapter 2 pattern A

Medallions and Ribbons

Multiple of 15 + 10

Row	Instructions
1 WS	k10 *p1 k3 p1, k10, rep from * to end
2 & 3	k the k st and p the p st
4	p10 *T2b p1 T2f p10, rep from * to end
5	as row 2
6	p10 *p1 T3f p1, p10, rep from * to end
7	k10 *k1, p1 k1 p1, k1 k10, rep from * to end
8	p10 *T2f p1 T2b p10, rep from * to end

9 and remaining odd-numbered rows (unless specified): as row 2

Row	Instructions
10	p9 *T2f p3 T2b p8, rep from * to last st, p1
12	as row 2
14	p9* T2b p3 T2f p8
16	as row 4
18	as row 6
19	as row 7
20	as row 8
22	as row 2
24	p10 *T2b MB T2f p10, rep from * to end
25	as row 1
26	p10 *p1, MB k1 MB, p1 p10, rep from * to end
27	as row 1
28	p10 *k5 p10, rep from * to end
30	p9 *T3B p1 T3F p8, rep from * to last st, p1
32	p7 *MB, T3B p3 T3F MB p4, rep from * to last 3 st, p3
34	p7 *MB p5 MB p4, rep from * to last 3 st, p3
36	p7 *MB, T3F p3 T3B, MB p4, rep from * to last 3 st, p3
38	p9 *T3F p1, T3B p8, rep from * to last st, p1
40	k10 *p5 k10 rep from * to end
42	as row 28
43	as row 1
44	p10 *p1, MB k1 MB, p1, p10, rep from * to end
45	as row 1
46	p10 *T2b MB T2f p10, rep from * to end
47	as row 1
48	as row 2

Rep these 48 rows

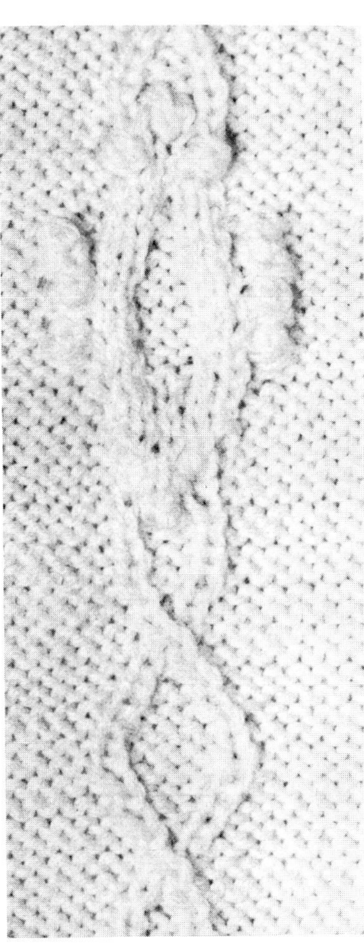

Medallions and Ribbons
4-ply on $3\frac{1}{4}$mm needles
10cm square = 28 st × 30 rows

Braids and Bobbles

Multiple of 11

Row	Instructions
1	p3 T5f p3
2	k3, p2 k1 p2, k3
3	p2 C3B p1 C3F p2
4	k2, p3 k1 p3, k2
5	p1 C3B, k1 MB k1, C3F p1
6	k1 p4 k1 p4 k1
7	C3B k2 p1 k2 C3F
8	p row

Rep these 8 rows

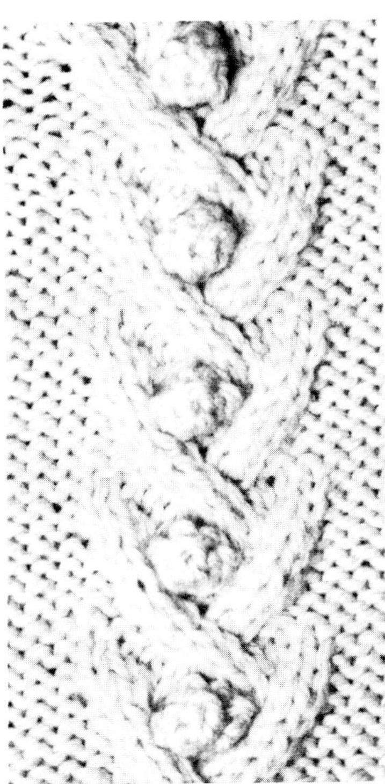

Braids and Bobbles
double-knit on 4mm needles
10 st = 4.5cm and
29 rows = 10cm

Tulip Pattern

Multiple of 18 (minimum 36 st)
Foundation rows:
work 6 rows of stocking stitch starting with a p row

Pattern:

7 k8 *p2 k1 T14F (sl 7 onto CN leave to front, k7 then k7 from CN) k1, rep from * to last 10 st, p2 k8

8 p8 *k2 p16 rep from * to last 10 st, k2 p8

9 p1 *k5 k2tog, yon p2 yon, sl 1, k1 psso, k5 p2, rep from * ending last rep p1 (inst p2)

10 k1 p6 *k4 p6 k2 p6, rep from * to last 11 st, k4 p6 k1

11 p1 *k4 k2tog, yon p4 yon, sl 1, k1 psso, k4 p2, rep from * ending k1 (inst k2)

12 k1 *p5 k6 p5 k2, rep from * ending k1 (inst k2)

13 p1 *k3 k2tog, yon p6 yon, sl 1, k1 psso, k3 p2, rep from * ending p1 (inst p2)

14 k1 *p4 k8 p4 k2, rep from * ending k1 (inst k2)

15 p1 *k2 k2tog, yon p8 yon, sl 1, k1 psso, k2 p2, rep from * ending p1 (inst p2)

16 k1 *p3 k10 p3 k2, rep from * ending k1 (inst k2)

17 p1 *k1 k2tog, yon p10 yon, sl 1, k1 psso, k1 p2, rep from * ending p1 (inst p2)

18 k1 *p2 k12 p2 k2, rep from * ending k1 (inst k2)

19 p1 *k2tog, yon p12 yon, sl 1, k1 psso, k2, rep from * ending p1 (inst p2)

20 k row

21 to 26 stocking stitch

27 p1 *k1, T14F k1 p2, rep from * ending p1 (inst p2)

28 k1 *p16 k2, rep from * ending k1 (inst k2)

29 sl 1 *yon sl 1, k1 psso, k5 p2 k5, k2tog yon p2, rep from * ending p1 (inst p2)

30 k2 *p6 k2 p6 k4, rep from * ending k2 (inst k4)

31 p2 *yon sl 1, k1 psso, k4 p2 k4 k2tog p4, rep from * ending p2 (inst p4)

32 k3 *p5 k2 p5 k6, rep from * ending k3 (inst k6)

33 p3 *yon sl 1, k1 psso, k3 p2 k3, k2tog yon p6, rep from * ending p3 (inst p6)

34 k4 *p4 k2 p4 k8, rep from * ending p3 (inst p6)

35 p4 *yon sl 1, k1 psso, k2 p2 k2, k2tog yon p8, rep from * ending p4 (inst p8)

36 k5 *p3 k2 p3 k10, rep from * ending k5 (inst k10)

37 p5 *yon sl 1, k1 psso, k1 p2 k1, k2tog yon p10, rep from * ending k5 (inst k10)

38 k6 *p2 k2 p2 k12, rep from * ending k6 (inst k12)

39 p6 *yon sl 1, k1 psso, p2 k2tog yon p12, rep from * ending p6 (inst p12)

40 k7 *p1 k2 p1 k14, rep from * ending k7 (inst k14)

Rep these 40 rows

Tulip Pattern
double-knit on 4mm needles
10cm square = 26 st × 31 rows

Chevrons

Multiple of 13 + 3

1 k5 *p6 k7, rep from * ending row k5 (inst k7)
2 p3 *p2tog, k3 yon k3, p2tog, p3, rep from * to end
3 k4 *p7 k5, rep from * ending k4 (inst k5)
4 p2 *p2tog, k3 yon k1 yon k3, p2tog p1, rep from * to last st, p1
5 k3 *p9 k3 rep from * to end
6 p1 p2tog *k3 (yon k3) twice, p3tog, rep from * ending p2tog p1 (inst p3tog)
7 k2 *p2 k1, rep from * ending row k2 (inst k1)
8 p2 *k3, yon k5 yon, k3 p1, rep from * ending p2
9 p row
10 p5 *k5 k2tog p7, rep from * ending p5 (inst p7)

Rep these 10 rows

Do not count st on rows 8 to 10

Chevrons
double-knit on 4mm needles
10cm square = 24 st × 30 rows
suitable for Chapter 2 patterns A and B

Ripples

Multiple of 13

1 *k4 (yon k1) 5 times, yon k4 rep from * to end
2 p row
3 *(k2tog) 3 times, k7 (k2tog) 3 times, rep from * to end
4 k row
5 p row
6 k row
7 *p4 (yon p1) 5 times, yon p4, rep from * to end
8 k row
9 *(p2tog) 3 times, p7 (p2tog) 3 times, rep from * to end
10 p row
11 k row
12 p row

Rep these 12 rows

For additional effect work rows 3 & 4 and 9 & 10 (marked /) in contrast yarn or colour.

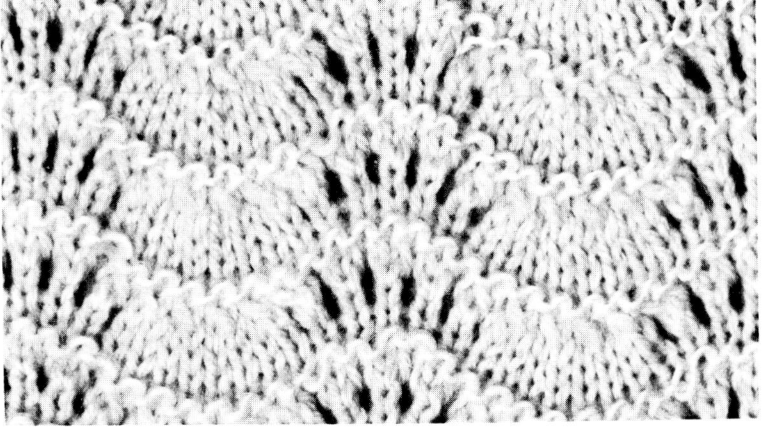

Ripples
double-knit on 4mm needles
10cm square = 22 st × 31 rows

Leaves

Multiple of 16 + 2

Row	Instructions
1	p2 *sl 1, k1 psso, k5 k2tog, p2, k1 yon k1 yon k1, p2, rep from *
2	k2 *p5, k2, p7, k2, rep from * to end
3	p2 *sl 1, k1 psso, k3 k2tog, p2, k2 yon k1 yon k2, p2, rep from *
4	k2 *p7, k2, p5 k2, rep from * to end
5	p2 *sl 1, k1 psso, k1 k2tog, p2, k3 yon k1 yon k3, p2 rep from * to end
6	k2 *p9, k2 p3, k2, rep from * to end
7	p2 *sl 1, k2tog, psso, p2, k9, p2, rep from * to end
8	k2 *p9, k2, kM1Lp k1 kM1Ln, k2, rep from * to end
9	p2 *k1 yon k1 yon k1, p2, sl 1, k1 psso k5 k2tog p2 rep from *
10	k2 *p7, k2, p5, k2, rep from * to end
11	p2 *k2 yon k1 yon k2, p2, sl 1, k1 psso k3 k2tog, p2, rep from *
12	k2 *p5, k2 p7 k2, rep from * to end
13	p2 *k3 yon k1 yon k3, p2, sl 1, k1 psso k1 k2tog, p2 rep from *
14	k2 *p3, k2 p9 k2, rep from * to end
15	p2 *k9, p2, sl 1, k2tog psso, p2, rep from * to end
16	k2 *kM1Lp k1 kM1Ln, k2 p9 k2, rep from * to end

Rep these 16 rows

Leaves
double-knit on 4mm needles
10cm square = 23 st × 32 rows
suitable for Chapter 2 pattern A

Zigzag Ribbons

Multiple of 14 + 11

1	*k2tog k3, yon k1 yon, k3 k2tog tbl p3** rep from * to last 11 st, end rep k2tog tbl
2, 4 6 & 8	*p11 k3, rep from * to last 11 st, p11
3	*k2tog k2, yon k3 yon, k2 k2tog tbl p3** rep from * to last 11 st, end rep k2tog tbl
5	*k2tog k1, yon k5 yon, k1 k2tog tbl p3** rep from * to last 11 st, end rep k2tog tbl
7	*k2tog, yon k7 yon, k2tog tbl p3** rep from * to last 11 st, end rep k2tog tbl
9	yon k2 k2tog tbl p3, rep from * to ** as row 1 to last 4 st, k2tog tbl, k1 k twice into last st
10, 12, 14 & 16	p4 *k3 p11, rep from * to last 7 st, k3 p4
11	yon k2 k2tog tbl p3, rep from * to ** as row 3 to last 4 st, k2tog k1 k twice into last st
13	k1 yon k1 k2tog tbl p3, rep from * to ** as row 5 to last 4 st k2tog tbl yon k2
15	k2 yon k2tog tbl p3, rep from * to ** as row 7 to last 4 st, k2tog tbl yon k2

Rep these 16 rows

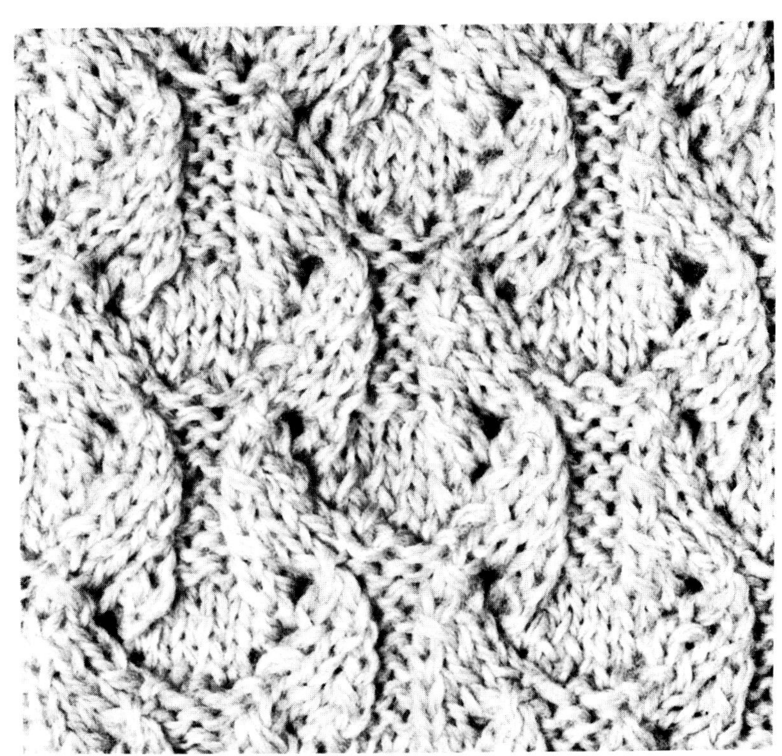

Zigzag Ribbons
double-knit on 4mm needles
10cm square = 28 st × 36 rows

6 Altering, revamping and recycling

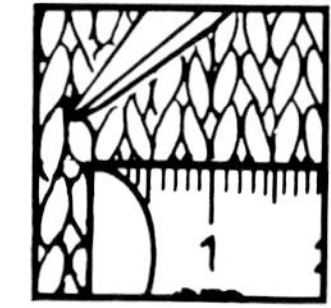

Updating and altering existing garments

If you have any knitted garments that you are bored with but which are not bad enough either to give away or to unravel, why not re-vamp them? The easiest way of doing this is to add decoration in the form of Swiss Darning, embroidery or beadwork.

Swiss Darning

First (by trial and error), find a yarn whose thickness matches as nearly as possible that of the original. Then plan your motif, using graph paper and following the instructions given in Chapter 4.

Embroidery and sewn beadwork

If you want to use traditional embroidery techniques on knitting, you may find it difficult because the fabric stretches. To avoid this problem, try applying a fine iron-on stiffening. This will allow you to use an embroidery frame which makes the whole process easier. It is then possible to use a wide variety of embroidery stitches and sewn-on beads. Crewel and other 'wool work' techniques are particularly effective.

Alteration

You may want to alter the shape of a knitted garment rather than to embellish it. There are two main problems. First: knitted fabric is produced by the continuous looping of a single strand of yarn – cutting into it will cause unravelling or laddering. Second: you will need to match the tension of the original knitting unless you graft the work. If you are altering a garment that you originally knitted, it is a relatively simple matter to adjust the length provided that you have kept a record of tension, needle size, etc. or that you have managed to work this out by trial and error. To adjust the width is more difficult.

Altering length – shortening

The usual way of doing this is to remove a section of the main pattern immediately above the welt. To do this cut the yarn at the side and pull out a strand at the top of the section to be removed. (This is necessary as most welts are worked in rib which cannot be unravelled from the bottom up.) The unwanted section can then be unravelled from the top down, including or excluding the welt. You then pick up the bottom loops of the shortened main pattern and add a new welt by knitting downwards. Alternatively, graft back the original welt.

You can remove wrinkles from the unravelled yarn by following the directions given opposite.

Altering length – increasing

If you want to do this invisibly the yarn and tension will need to match the original garment exactly. If, as is most likely, you have no such yarn, you will need to disguise the process by working in some way that seems part of the original design or makes sense in some other way. For example: remove a section of the main pattern and prepare to knit downwards (as for shortening), re-cycling the unravelled yarn for use as stripes of pattern between stripes of a contrasting extra yarn. For additional length, the yarn from the welt can also be worked in this way and the contrast yarn used for a new welt. The way you choose to work will depend on how much extra length is needed.

Altering width – increasing

The easiest way of doing this is to add an extra panel in a way that seems consistent with the original design. The problem, as with lengthening, is that of matching tension and yarn. Unless you can cannibalise yarn from elsewhere in the garment, you will have to improvise with contrasting yarn. I would advise replacing all or some of the welts with new ones worked in the contrasting yarn. Use the same contrasting yarn to pick up stitches vertically from the section that needs the extra width. Then knit a welted panel to match the new welts.

Altering width – decreasing

If the reduction is small – say, up to 5cm(2in.) round the body – the easiest thing is to unpick the seams and to re-sew them as in dressmaking, with about 1m($\frac{1}{2}$in.) of seam allowance. If the seam is carefully pressed open, it should not be too noticeable. If more has to be removed, you will have problems with bulkiness at the seams unless you cut the knitting. Most modern sewing machines have a 'stretch' stitch or 'over-locking' setting which can be used to prevent unravelling. Sew along the appropriate edge(s) before cutting close to the stitching line. Rejoin the pieces with the seam allowance described above.

Turning a jumper into a cardigan or enlarging a neckline

Use a sewing machine to pre-stitch an edge before cutting to the new shape (as for decreasing width). When changing a jumper to a cardigan, run two lines of parallel stitching for straight edges, adjusting the angles as necessary for shaped edges, before cutting between them. Finish the stitched but raw edges by working a doubled-over welt to encase them. **Either** pick up stitches about 1cm($\frac{1}{2}$cm.) from the edge on the right side of the work (by knitting into the side loops) and work a welt long enough to fold over and sew down on the wrong side; **or** knit a separate welt and sew it neatly down on both right and wrong sides. (This method can be used to turn a round neck opening into a V neck.)

Reducing a neck opening

If this is a matter of correcting a slightly loose opening – but not of changing its shape – then count the number of stitches that have been picked up for the welt. Unravel the welt carefully and pick up slightly fewer stitches (evenly). Matching the tension as nearly as possible, use the old yarn to knit a new welt. If you want to change a large opening into a small one, it will not be possible to do this invisibly, so you will have to make it look like part of the design. For example: you can knit an insertion to fill a V-neck opening and to convert it to a round or polo neck by using the original stitch pattern, tension and yarn – the join line accentuated by contrasting piping. Or else you can work a contrasting insertion that looks like a second sweater worn permanently underneath.

How to remove wrinkles from unravelled yarn

There are two ways of doing this, one of them quicker than the other. The results are equally effective but the steaming method is not suitable for hair or glitter types of yarn.

Wetting method

The unravelled yarn is wound into hanks. Do not attempt to wind all the yarn into one hank: it is best to allow one hank for each original ball used. Tie each hank loosely with a 'figure of eight' tie in four places.

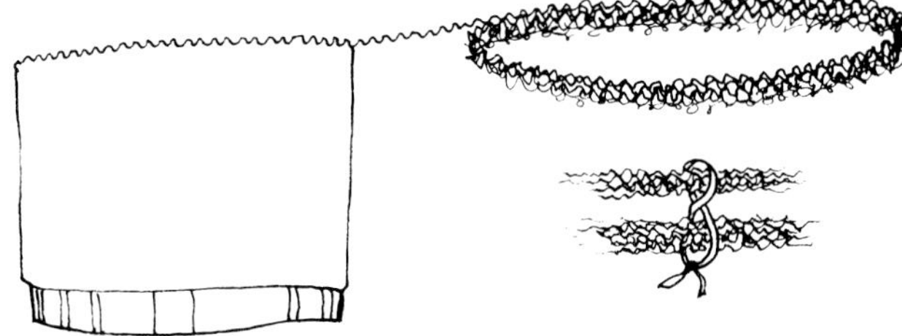

6.1 Once the seams have been unpicked, unravel from the top down and wind into hanks. Tie the hank in at least four places with the same yarn.

This form of tying prevents the strands of yarn from becoming mixed up during wetting and drying.

Rinse the prepared hanks very gently until they are thoroughly wet. Squeeze out the excess water but leave the yarn dripping wet as it is the weight of the water that will straighten the yarn.

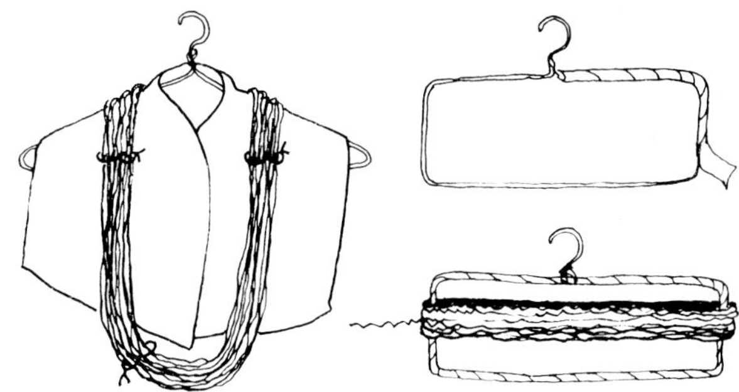

6.2 (Left) Wrap a towel round a coat hanger and drape the wet hank over it. Turn the hank round from time to time as it dries.

6.3 (Right) Bind the hanger with a strip of neutral-coloured cloth. Wind the wet yarn round the hanger to stretch it as it dries.

Suspend the hank over a wire coat hanger, with a small towel (white or pale in colour) or piece of white rag to protect the yarn from the wire. Turn occasionally to prevent the yarn against the wire from becoming marked or kinked. Allow to dry naturally, away from any direct source of heat.

Steaming method

Bend an old wire coat hanger to the shape shown and bind it with strips of white rag. Wind the unravelled yarn onto the hanger fairly tightly. Wind only one original ball at a time, repeating the process for each ball. Secure the end and steam the yarn either over a pan of boiling water or with a steam iron held above the yarn (it must not touch). Allow the yarn to dry thoroughly before winding off into new balls.

Abbreviations

st	stitch(es)
patt	pattern
rep	repeat
no.	number
beg	beginning
LN	left-hand needle
RN	right-hand needle
RS	right side of work
WS	wrong side of work
cm	centimetre(s)
in.	inch(es)
foll	following
alt	alternate
dec	decrease
inc	increase
ret	return
inst	instead of
CN	cable needle
k	knit stitch
p	purl stitch
kwise	refers to a stitch slipped as though to knit it
pwise	refers to a stitch slipped as though to purl it
k2tog	knit 2 stitches together (more stitches can be knitted together in the same way)
p2tog	purl 2 stitches together (more stitches can be purled together in the same way)
k2rn	wind the wool round needle twice when knitting a stitch
tbl	work through back of loop (to twist the stitch)
yon	yarn over needle, to make a loop or stitch
yb	yarn backwards
yf	yarn forwards
sl	slip
psso	pass slipped stitch over
pnso	pass next stitch over
p2sso	pass two slipped stitches over
M1L	make 1 stitch by lifting worked loop on previous row by using
M1Ln	*either* from below next stitch
M1Lp	*or* from below previous stitch; this loop can be worked
kM1L	*either* by knitting the lifted stitch
pM1L	*or* by purling the lifted stitch
MB	make berry: knit into the front and back and front of the next stitch, turn work and knit the stitches, turn work and purl the stitches, turn work and knit the stitches, then pass the 2nd and 3rd stitches over the 1st stitch
MP	make pip: (k1 p1 k1 p1 k1) into the next stitch, lift the 2nd stitch on the right-hand needle over the 1st stitch, then repeat this process with the 3rd, 4th and 5th stitches separately

Cable abbreviations

C2B	knit into back of 2nd stitch on left-hand needle, then knit first stitch, slip both stitches off left-hand needle together
C2F	knit into front of 2nd stitch on left-hand needle, then knit first stitch, slip both stitches off left-hand needle together
C4B	slip 2 stitches onto cable needle and hold at back, knit 2 stitches from left-hand needle, then knit 2 stitches from cable needle
C4F	slip 2 stitches onto cable needle and hold at front, knit 2 stitches from left-hand needle, then knit 2 stitches from cable needle
C6B	slip 3 stitches onto cable needle and hold at back, knit 3 stitches from left-hand needle, then knit 3 stitches from cable needle
C6F	slip 3 stitches onto cable needle and hold at front, knit 3 stitches from left-hand needle, then knit 3 stitches from cable needle
T2b	purl 2nd stitch on left-hand needle through back of loop, knit 1st stitch in the usual way, slip both stitches off together
T2f	knit 2nd stitch on left-hand needle, purl 1st stitch and slip both stitches off together
T2F	slip 1 stitch onto cable needle and hold at front, purl next stitch from left-hand needle, then knit 1 stitch from cable needle

T2B slip 1 stitch onto cable needle and hold at back, knit 1 stitch from left-hand needle, then purl 1 stitch from cable needle

T3f slip 1 stitch onto cable needle and hold at front, knit 1 stitch through back of loop, purl 1 stitch from left-hand needle, then knit 1 stitch from cable needle through back of loop

T3b slip 2 stitches onto cable needle and hold at back, knit 1 stitch from left-hand needle, then purl 1 stitch and knit 1 stitch from cable needle through back of loop

T3F slip 2 stitches onto cable needle and hold at front, purl 1 stitch from left-hand needle, then knit 2 stitches from cable needle

T3B slip 1 stitch onto cable needle and hold at back, knit 2 stitches from left-hand needle, then purl 1 stitch from cable needle

T5f slip 2 stitches onto cable needle and hold at front, knit 2 stitches and purl 1 stitch from left-hand needle, then knit 2 stitches from cable needle

T5b slip 3 stitches onto cable needle and hold at back, knit 2 stitches from left-hand needle, then purl 1 stitch and knit 2 stitches from cable needle

T5F slip 3 stitches onto cable needle and hold at front, purl 2 stitches from left-hand needle, then knit 3 stitches from cable needle

T5B slip 2 stitches onto cable needle and hold at back, knit 3 stitches from left-hand needle, then purl 2 stitches from cable needle

T6f slip 2 stitches onto cable needle and hold at front, knit 2 stitches and purl 2 stitches from left-hand needle, then knit 2 stitches from cable needle

T6b slip 4 stitches onto cable needle and hold at back, knit 2 stitches from left-hand needle, then purl 2 stitches and knit 2 stitches from cable needle

Acknowledgements

I would like to thank the yarn manufacturers listed below for their generous provision of classic yarns for sample squares and garments illustrated in this book.

This is not a standard knitting pattern book and although the exact yarn type and shade numbers are given it may be that they are not available when you buy this book. I have tried, with advice from the spinners, to use popular yarns throughout. If you do want to knit as exactly as possible any of the garments illustrated you should get advice from your local stockist about equivalent qualities and, most importantly, knit a square to check your tension before starting on the whole garment.

I wish you happy and creative knitting.

Spinners' addresses

Emu Ltd
Leeds Rd
Greengates
Bradford
W. Yorks BD10 9TE

Emu Yarns
tel. 0274 614 031

Hayfield Textiles Ltd
Hayfield Mills
Glusburn
nr Keighley
W. Yorks BD20 8QP

Hayfield Yarns
tel. 0535 33333

Patons & Baldwins Ltd
PO Box 22
Darlington
Co Durham DL1 1YQ

Patons & Baldwins
tel. 0325 381 010

French Wools
Station House
81–3 Fulham High Street
London SW6 3JW

Pingouin
tel. 071 371 5772

Flanshaw Lane
Alverthorpe
Wakefield
W. Yorks WF2 9ND

Sirdar Yarns
tel. 0924 371501

Twilleys of Stamford Ltd
Roman Mill
Stamford
Lincs PE9 1BG

Twilleys Yarns
tel. 0780 52661

Carter & Parker Ltd
Gordon Mills
Netherfield Rd
Guiseley
W. Yorks LS20 9PD

Wendy Wools
tel. 0943 72264

Index